"Mark Rooker has written a brilliant, much needed book for America today. No civil society can exist without laws, and only laws based on God's authority can endure and ensure equal justice for all. The Ten Commandments are the foundation for all such laws. Read this book and teach it to your children. It will be an inestimable investment in your life and your progeny's future."

Jim DeMint
U.S. Senator from South Carolina and author of the *New York Times* best seller, *Saving Freedom: We Can Stop America's Slide into Socialism.*

"Mark Rooker has produced a book that is beautifully written and intellectually exhilarating. Since the Ten Commandments are central to biblical ethics and biblical ethics is central to Christian ethics, what Rooker has written should be required reading for anyone doing Christian ethics or engaging present culture on moral issues."

Daniel R. Heimbach
Professor of Christian Ethics
Southeastern Baptist Theological Seminary
Research Institute Fellow, SBC Ethics & Religious Liberty Commission
Editor, B&H Christian Ethics Series
Chairman, ETS Christian Ethics Planning Unit

"I heartily recommend Mark Rooker's *The Ten Commandments*. It has the right balance between carefully exegeting the biblical text and including relevant questions that arise from our contemporary scene. Each commandment is treated with fairness and with an eye to its contemporary application. In a day when the Church seems to be so short on teaching biblical ethics, here is just the solution pastors, lay leaders, and concerned laity need to reestablish our ethical and moral roots."

Walter C. Kaiser, Jr.
President Emeritus, Gordon-Conwell Theological Seminary

"Dr. Rooker has given us another important study on the Ten Commandments. In a day when moral absolutes are being challenged, it will be refreshing to have such a scholarly guide through God's 'Ten Words.' Read it with profit."

Jerry Vines
Pastor emeritus, First Baptist Church, Jacksonville, Florida

THE TEN COMMANDMENTS

OTHER BOOKS IN THIS SERIES:

THE TEN COMMANDMENTS

ETHICS FOR THE TWENTY-FIRST CENTURY

MARK F. ROOKER

SERIES EDITOR: E. RAY CLENDENEN

ACADEMIC

NASHVILLE, TENNESSEE

The Ten Commandments:
Ethics for the Twenty-first Century

ISBN: 978-0-8054-4716-3

Published by B&H Publishing Group
Nashville, Tennessee

Dewey Decimal Classification: 222.16
Subject Heading: TEN COMMANDMENTS\CHRISTIAN ETHICS

Printed in the United States of America

1 2 3 4 5 6 7 8 9 10 11 12 • 17 16 15 14 13 12 11 10
SB

Dedication

In memory of John Rooker,
my great-great-great-grandfather,
Revolutionary War veteran, and
pastor of Flint Hill Baptist Church
of Fort Mill, South Carolina, 1792–1840

In celebration of the birth of
Samantha Lauren Rooker,
my first grandchild

TABLE OF CONTENTS

LIST OF ABBREVIATIONS

AB	Anchor Bible
ABD	*Anchor Bible Dictionary*
ACCS	Ancient Christian Commentary on Scripture
ANET	*Ancient Near Eastern Texts Relating to the Old Testament*
BBR	*Bulletin for Biblical Research*
BDB	Brown, F., S. R. Driver, and C. A. Briggs. *A Hebrew and English Lexicon of the Old Testament*
BECNT	Baker Exegetical Commentary on the New Testament
BN	*Biblische Notizen*
BR	*Bible Review*
BSac	*Bibliotheca sacra*
BZ	*Biblische Zeitschrift*
BZAW	Beihefte zur Zeischrift für die alttestamentliche Wissenschaft
CBQ	*Catholic Biblical Quarterly*
CT	*Christianity Today*
DJG	*Dictionary of Jesus and the Gospels*
DLNT	*Dictionary of the Later New Testament and Its Developments*
DNTB	*Dictionary of New Testament Background*
DOTP	*Dictionary of Old Testament Pentateuch*
DPL	*Dictionary of Paul and His Letters*
DSS	*Dead Sea Scrolls*
EDBT	*Evangelical Dictionary of Biblical Theology*
EDT (1984)	*Evangelical Dictionary of Theology* (1984)
EDT (2001)	*Evangelical Dictionary of Theology* (2001)
EJ	*Encyclopedia Judaica*, 2nd ed.
EncMiqr	*Encyclopedia Miqra'it* [Hb.]
ET	*Evangelische Theologie*
GKC	*Gesenius' Hebrew Grammar*, ed. E. Kautzsch, tr. A. E. Cowley
HALOT	Koehler, L., W. Baumgartner, and J. J. Stamm, *The Hebrew and Aramaic Lexicon of the Old Testament*, trans. and ed. M. E. J. Richardson
HAT	Handbuch zum Alten Testament
Hb.	Hebrew
IBHS	*An Introduction to Biblical Hebrew Syntax*, B. H. Waltke and M. O'Connor
Int	*Interpretation*
JBL	*Journal of Biblical Literature*

JETS	*Journal of the Evangelical Theological Society*
JSB	Jewish Study Bible
JSNTSup	Journal for the Study of the New Testament: Supplement Series
LEH	Lust, J., E. Eynikel, and K. Haupsie, *Greek-English Lexicon of the Septuagint*
LSJ	Liddell, H. G., R. Scott, H. S. Jones, *A Greek-English Lexicon.* 9th ed. with revised supplement
LXX	Septuagint
MT	Masoretic Text
NAC	New American Commentary
NDBT	*New Dictionary of Biblical Theology*
NICOT	New International Commentary on the Old Testament
NIDOTTE	*New International Dictionary of Old Testament Theology and Exegesis*
NTS	*New Testament Studies*
OTL	Old Testament Library
Payne Smith	*Thesaurus syriacus*
SBLDS	Society of Biblical Literature Dissertation Series
SJT	*Scottish Journal of Theology*
SwJT	*Southwestern Journal of Theology*
TB	Theologische Bücherei: Neudrucke und Berichte aus dem 20. jahrhundert
TDOT	*Theological Dictionary of the Old Testament*
TLOT	*Theological Lexicon of the Old Testament*
TynBul	*Tyndale Bulletin*
VE	*Vox evangelica*
VT	*Vetus Testamentum*
WBC	Word Biblical Commentary
WTJ	*Westminster Theological Journal*
ZAW	*Zeitschrift für die alttestamentliche Wissenschaft*

SERIES PREFACE

We live in an exciting era of evangelical scholarship. Many fine educational institutions committed to the inerrancy of Scripture are training men and women to serve Christ in the church and to advance the gospel in the world. Many church leaders and professors are skillfully and fearlessly applying God's Word to critical issues, asking new questions, and developing new tools to answer those questions from Scripture. They are producing valuable new resources to thoroughly equip current and future generations of Christ's servants.

The Bible is an amazing source of truth and an amazing tool when wielded by God's Spirit for God's glory and our good. It is a bottomless well of living water, a treasure-house of endless proportions. Like an ancient tell, exciting discoveries can be made on the surface, but even more exciting are those to be found by digging. The books in this series, NAC Studies in Bible and Theology, often take a biblical difficulty as their point of entry, remembering B. F. Westcott's point that "unless all past experience is worthless, the difficulties of the Bible are the most fruitful guides to its divine depths."

This new series is to be a medium through which the work of evangelical scholars can effectively reach the church. It will include detailed exegetical-theological studies of key pericopes such as the Sermon on the Mount and also fresh examinations of topics in biblical theology and systematic theology. It is intended to supplement the New American Commentary, whose exegetical and theological discussions so many have found helpful. These resources are aimed primarily at church leaders and those who are preparing for such leadership. We trust that individual Christians will find them to be an encouragement to greater progress and joy in the faith. More important, our prayer is that they will help the church proclaim Christ more accurately and effectively and that they will bring praise and glory to our great God.

It is a tremendous privilege to be partners in God's grace with the fine scholars writing for this new series as well as with those who will be helped by it. When Christ returns, may He find us "standing firm in one spirit, with one mind, working side by side for the faith of the gospel" (Phil 1:27).

E. Ray Clendenen
B&H Publishing Group

AUTHOR'S PREFACE

It was the first time I as a young boy had ever gone to the big city of Dallas, Texas, to a movie theater. My older brother Andy and his friends were going to watch the new movie, *The Ten Commandments* by Cecil B. DeMille. My parents said Andy could go but only if he would take his younger brother. He protested somewhat but, urged on by his friends, reluctantly agreed. It was the first movie I have a memory of seeing. That early experience left an indelible and unshakable impression on my psyche. I am grateful now that in the providence of God He has allowed me to return to explore the depths of His Word in contemplating the meaning of the Ten Commandments for Western culture and especially for the church today.

At the end of the process of working on this volume, many deserve recognition and thanks. As the bulk of this work was completed during my sabbatical leave from Southeastern Baptist Theological Seminary for the academic year 2006–7, I am especially indebted to President Daniel Akin, the administration, and the board of trustees for a generous sabbatical policy, which allows faculty to dedicate time to serious academic research.

My special thanks goes to Dr. E. Ray Clendenen of the B&H Publishing Group, who is serving as editor of the NAC Studies in Bible and Theology series. I have appreciated Ray's leadership in overseeing this series as well as his encouragement in seeing the project through ahead of schedule. I have had the opportunity and pleasure to work with Ray on several projects now and deeply appreciate his kindness and patience, but even more so his skill and ability in overseeing this work.

The reader of this volume will clearly see that the Ten Commandments are founded on the creation account of Gen 1–2. As a result, God's design for the family plays a vital role in the contents of the Ten Commandments. With this in mind it is only fitting that I convey the importance and contribution of my immediate family in my personal life. I would like to thank all of them for their tolerance of my idiosyncrasies as well as putting up with my numerous poor attempts at humor. When I think of what my family has meant to me, I can think of no blessing, apart from the gift of salvation that I have in Christ, that more indicates God has smiled upon me. I would like to express my gratitude to my wife Carole, to my oldest son Nathaniel and his wife Hanni, as well as to my sons Jonathan and Joshua. I also celebrate the birth of my granddaughter Samantha, who has already brought great joy to my life.

Mark F. Rooker
Wake Forest, North Carolina

INTRODUCTION

The Influence of the Ten Commandments

Although written more than 3,500 years ago, the Ten Commandments remain among the most controversial topics at the beginning of the twenty-first century. While some, including Ted Turner, have suggested that their usefulness has come to an end,[1] the Ten Commandments have stood the test of time and will continue as long as civilization exists. The influence of the Ten Commandments on the Western world is beyond doubt. No other document has had such a great influence on Western culture.

The two greatest rulers of medieval Europe, Charlemagne of the Franks (c. AD 742–814) and Alfred the Great of England (AD 849–99), both established legal systems based on biblical laws that included the Ten Commandments. The Laws of Alfred (c. AD 890) began with a recitation of the Ten Commandments along with excerpts from other portions of the Mosaic Law.[2]

The influence of the Ten Commandments has also been clearly felt in the United States, where lawmakers recognized their indebtedness to the system of laws found in the Ten Commandments. In 1636, the General Court of Massachusetts argued that the laws of the colony be "agreeable to the Word of God," reflecting the sentiment of the founders that all law had its source in God.[3] Later John Adams wrote, "As much as I love, esteem and admire the Greeks, I believe the Hebrews have done more to enlighten and civilize the world. Moses did more than all of their legislators and philosophers."[4] The influence of the

---

[1] See J. Vines, *Basic Bible Sermons on the Ten Commandments* (Nashville: Broadman Press, 1992), 12.

[2] J. Eidsmoe, "Operation Josiah: Rediscovering the Biblical Roots of the American Constitutional Republic," in *The Christian and American Law: Christianity's Impact on America's Founding Documents and Future Direction,* ed. H. Wayne House (Grand Rapids: Kregel Publications, 1998), 87–88.

[3] L. Walker, "The Abiding Value of Biblical Law," in House, *The Christian and American Law,* 215.

[4] See Z. Haraszti, *John Adams and the Prophets of Progress* (Cambridge: Harvard University Press, 1952), 246.

Ten Commandments is evident from their prominence at the ultimate location for legal argument in the United States, the Supreme Court in Washington, D.C., where they are the focus of the images that surround the building. Newt Gingrich has called this "the most striking religious imagery . . . that of Moses with the Ten Commandments."[5] They are displayed also at the center of the sculpture over the east portico of the building, inside the courtroom, as well as being engraved over the chair of the chief justice and on the bronze doors of the court.[6]

The significance of the Ten Commandments and their influence on American culture can be observed from the *White Plains (NY) Reporter*, dated September 19, 1929:

> No man in more than two thousand years has been able to improve upon the Ten Commandments as the rule of life. To no other origin than to Divine Revelation can they be ascribed. Man constantly improves upon his own handiwork. There never will be a need for an Eleventh Commandment. The Ten contain all there is to guide human conduct in the proper channels.[7]

In more recent American history (January 1983), Federal Judge John C. Knox, whose jurisdiction included New York City, stated in a public address that the laws of this republic were founded on the Ten Commandments.[8] As Harvard Law School Professor Alan M. Dershowitz recently said: "The Ten Commandments are clearly a precursor to all Western Law, including American Law."[9]

The Ten Commandments have thus left an indelible stamp on the laws and values of the West as a unique legal constitution. They have become the foundation for both Jewish and Christian morals and ethics[10] and are regarded as such in most introductory books on reli-

---

[5] N. Gingrich, *Rediscovering God in America* (Nashville: Thomas Nelson, 2006), 87.

[6] Ibid.

[7] J. Lewis, *The Ten Commandments* (New York: Freethought Press Association, 1946), xiv.

[8] Ibid., xiii.

[9] *Ten Commandments,* Mindwork Media Group for the History Channel. A & E Television Networks 2006. See also R. Rushdoony, *The Institutes of Biblical Law* (Nutley, NJ: The Craig Press, 1973), 1–2.

[10] C. Dohmen, *Exodus 19–40* (Freiburg: Herder, 2004), 132.

gion.[11] Martin Luther made the Ten Commandments the basis of his Christian catechism when he stated:

> Thus we have in the Ten Commandments a summary of divine instructions, telling us what we have to do to make our whole life pleasing to God and showing us the true source and fountain from and in which all good works must spring and proceed; so that no work or anything can be good and pleasing to God, however great and costly in the eyes of the world, unless it is in keeping with the Ten Commandments.[12]

The Ten Commandments are foundational for ethics and religious instruction. Or as Josh McDowell has stated, "The Ten Commandments . . . represent the most famous codification of absolute truth in the history of humanity."[13]

The high point of miraculous events in the Old Testament would be the revelation of God on Mount Sinai before all Israel. The main element in that biblical account is the declaration of the Ten Commandments (Deut 4:32–33).[14] The Ten Commandments are God's good gift to Israel, just delivered from bondage in Egypt. Faithfulness to these laws was the means whereby the nation would become a "kingdom of priests and a holy nation" (Exod 19:6).

The Significance of the Ten Commandments in the Old Testament

The Ten Commandments are literally the "Ten Words" (*ăśeret haddĕbārîm*) in Hebrew. The use of the term *dābār*, "word," in this phrase distinguishes these laws from the rest of the commandments (*miṣwâ*), statutes (*ḥōq*), and regulations (*mišpāṭ*) in the Old Testament. We find explicit reference to the expression "Ten Words" in Exod 34:28; Deut 4:13; 10:4. The Greek translation of "Ten Words" is *deka logoi,* from which we get the English word "Decalogue."[15]

---

[11] R. Freund, "The Decalogue in Early Judaism and Christianity," in *The Function of Scripture in Early Jewish and Christian Tradition,* JSNTSup 154, ed. C. Evans and J. A. Sanders (Sheffield: Sheffield Academic Press, 1988), 124–41.

[12] Lewis, *The Ten Commandments,* xiv; see Dohmen, *Exodus 19–40,* 132.

[13] J. McDowell and B. Hostetler, *Right from Wrong* (Dallas: Word Publishing, 1994), 91.

[14] S. Albeck, "The Ten Commandments and the Essence of Religious Faith," in *The Ten Commandments in History and Tradition,* ed. B. Z. Segal (Jerusalem: Magnes, 1990), 261.

[15] There may be an allusion to the Decalogue in Exod 18 by the ten occurrences of the root דבר, which occurs another ten times in the narrative of the revelation at Mount Sinai (Exod

The Ten Commandments should be viewed as fundamental to all the laws of the Bible. They may be compared to the Constitution of the United States, and the laws that follow (Exod 21:1–23:19) as somewhat analogous to sections of federal law dealing with particular matters.[16]

The Ten Commandments in Old Testament Narrative Literature

In their divine call to their strategic ministries, Moses and Joshua were instructed to live in accordance with the law (Exod 19:3–6; Josh 1:7–8; cf. 23:6). This pattern was continued throughout biblical history from the time of Joshua to the exile (see 1 Kgs 15:1–5 as an example). At the dedication of the temple, Solomon reaffirmed the primacy of the commandments and the covenant made at Sinai (1 Kgs 8:9). When Hezekiah was commended for doing right in the eyes of the Lord, it was because he kept the commandments (2 Kgs 18:6; 23:1–3).[17]

The Ten Commandments in Prophetic Literature

A growing majority of Old Testament scholars affirm that the Old Testament prophetic literature shows traces of the Ten Commandments.[18] The prophets appear to presuppose knowledge of the Decalogue in Israel as illustrated by a listing of many of the Ten Commandments in Hos 4:2. Hosea, perhaps the first writing prophet, was strongly dependent on the Decalogue. This is clear not only with regard to mention of several of the Ten Commandments in Hos 4:2. The Decalogue appears to inform the entire message of the prophet (see Hos 3:1; 8:6; 13:4; 14:4). Almost all the basic words of the Decalogue belong in Hosea's vocabulary.[19] The Decalogue was thus clearly in

19:1–20:1). See U. Cassuto, *A Commentary on the Book of Exodus,* trans. I. Abrahams (Jerusalem: Magnes, 1974), 251. For the use of the number ten in postbiblical Jewish tradition, see Rabbi D. Wax, ed., *The Ten Commandments* (Lakewood, NJ: Taryag Legacy Foundation, 2005), 36.

[16] D. Stuart, *Exodus,* NAC (Nashville: B&H, 2006), 441.

[17] D. J. Wiseman, "Law and Order in Old Testament Times," *VE* 8 (1973): 6, 8, 12–14, 19.

[18] M. Weiss, "The Decalogue in Prophetic Literature," in *The Ten Commandments in History and Tradition,* ed. B. Z. Segal (Jerusalem: Magnes, 1990), 67.

[19] See A. Jepsen, "Beiträge zur Auslegung und Geschichte des Dekalogs," *ZAW* 79 (1967): 300.

existence and authoritative for the nation in the eighth century BC (see also Jer 7:9), the time of Hosea's ministry.[20] Moreover, the quotations of the Decalogue in Pss 50:18–19; 81:10 also point to an early existence of the Decalogue in northern Israel, according to Moshe Weinfeld.[21]

The Ten Commandments in Poetic Literature

Psalms 50 and 81 may refer to renewal ceremonies conducted on the Festival of Shavuot, the Festival of the Giving of the Torah. It was customary at the festival to dramatize the revelatory event at Mount Sinai and to make a renewed oath celebrating the reception of the law.[22]

The Talmud (*b. Meg.* 31a) and *Jub.* 6:17–22 mention continued observance of the Festival of Shavuot, in the third month of the Jewish year.[23]

The Special Role of the Ten Commandments

The placement of the tablets of the Ten Commandments inside the most holy article of the tabernacle/temple furniture, the ark of the covenant, indicates how special they were. The ark was made for the Ten Commandments. Storing the tablets inside the ark is analogous to the ancient Near Eastern custom of depositing important documents beneath statues of gods.[24] An illustration of this practice occurred during the reigns of Hittite King Shuppiluliumas (c. 1375–35 BC) and King Mattiwaza of Mittani in Upper Mesopotamia. After entering into a covenant agreement, each of these parties deposited a copy of the covenant agreement before the shrine of the deity in his god's temple.[25]

---

[20] The relationship between Jer 7:9 and the Decalogue is somewhat chiastic as Jeremiah lists the violations in the following order—stealing, murder, adultery, false witness, and idolatry. We also find the order of the commandments listed in a different order in Jesus' reply to the rich ruler in Luke 18:20.

[21] M. Weinfeld, *Deuteronomy 1–11,* AB (New York: Doubleday, 1991), 242.

[22] M. Weinfeld, "The Uniqueness of the Decalogue and Its Place in Jewish Tradition," in Segal, *The Ten Commandments in History and Tradition,* 35.

[23] M. Greenberg, "The Tradition Critically Examined," in Segal, *The Ten Commandments in History and Tradition,* 114; Weinfeld, "The Uniqueness of the Decalogue and Its Place in Jewish Tradition," 38–39.

[24] M. Greenberg, "The Tradition Critically Examined," 89.

[25] See N. Sarna, *Exodus,* JPS Torah Commentary (Philadelphia, New York: Jewish Publication Society, 1991), 108.

The Ten Commandments express the eternal will of God. This is known by the conviction of the human conscience but more explicitly by the ancient pagan law codes discovered in the Near East.[26] Many of these law codes contain statutes similar to the Ten Commandments, which indicate their recognition of basic intrinsic moral values. Indeed, the laws in the Decalogue are not entirely new to Israel. The Bible presupposes a moral code long before the theophany on Mount Sinai. This is indicated in earlier biblical events such as the slaying of Abel by his brother Cain (Gen 4), as well as the judgments of the flood (Gen 6–9) and the destruction of Sodom and Gomorrah (Gen 19). The expression of God's will in the Decalogue is commensurate with His nature.

We see in the Ten Commandments something of what God is like. These commandments are imperatives, and they appear throughout the Pentateuch, except the tenth commandment ("Thou shalt not covet").[27] Deliberate violation of one of the first six commandments carried a mandatory death penalty because such violation invited the Lord's wrath and thereby threatened the foundations of Israelite society. All offenses in Old Testament law with a mandatory death penalty can be related to the Ten Commandments. The prohibition on coveting was by its nature not open to judicial penalty.[28]

Exodus 20 and Deuteronomy 5: The Two Versions of the Ten Commandments

Between the two versions of the Ten Commandments in the Pentateuch (Exod 20:2–17; Deut 5:6–21) at least 20 differences have been noted.[29] The reason for these differences (while not as significant as one might initially assume) may largely be explained simply be-

[26] The first two of the Ten Commandments have no parallels in the ancient Near East; thus in this work we begin to refer to possible literary parallels to other ancient laws with the third commandment.

[27] The Ten Words are the principles of the law and its foundation; the rest of the directives from God are judgments, laws, and statutes. See A. Ehrlich, *Miqrâ kî-Peshutô* (New York: KTAV, 1968), 171 [in Hb.].

[28] C. J. H. Wright, *An Eye for an Eye: The Place of Old Testament Ethics Today* (Downers Grove, IL: InterVarsity, 1983), 153.

[29] T. Elssner, "Das dekalogische Namensmissbrauch-Verbot (Ex 20,7/Dtn 5,11)," *BN* 114/115 (2002): 61.

cause of the different settings of the two covenant statements—one emphasizes establishment of the law on Mount Sinai (Exodus), and the other emphasizes observance of the already established law on the plains of Moab (Deuteronomy).[30] As Douglas Stuart has noted: "The differences are just what one would expect between an original covenant formulation and its renewal formulation a generation later."[31] The differences may best be reflected in the Deuteronomy additions in commandments four and five, where we find the expression "just as the LORD commanded you" (Deut 5:12,16).[32] This expression harkens back to the giving of the Decalogue on Mount Sinai in Exod 20 and reinforces the position that Deuteronomy means "second statement of the law." The stress on the reference to the Lord's command here and not in Exod 20 is because of the different situation. In Deut 5 Moses announces the Decalogue to the Israelites, so the emphasis is on the expressed reference to what the Lord had spoken; in Exod 20 the narrator communicates what God had spoken earlier on Mount Sinai.[33] Scholars of all persuasions are in general agreement that Exod 20 is earlier than Deut 5.[34]

As the Ten Commandments in Exod 20 and Deut 5 have a different historical time frame as well as geographical location, they also have a differently nuanced purpose. This is seen particularly in the Sabbath commandment. In Exod 20, the Sabbath is grounded on the commemoration of the creation. God made everything in six days and rested on the seventh. The fourth commandment thus instructs God's people to do their work in six days and rest on the seventh. In Deut 5, however, God's people are to "observe" (*šāmar*) the Sabbath so that their servants could rest (Deut 5:14) and to remember that they were

---

[30] "Deuteronomy" means "the second statement of the law." See R. Youngblood, "Counting the Ten Commandments," *BR* 10,5 (1994): 32.

[31] Stuart, *Exodus*, 457n45.

[32] The phrase is characteristic of Deuteronomy (Deut 20:17; see also Deut 4:23; 6:17; 13:5[6]; 28:45 for examples of conceptually similar phrases.

[33] Dohmen, *Exodus 19–40*, 100. Many scholars such as Walter Eichrodt take passages such as Exod 20 at face value and contend that the Decalogue should be attributed to Moses; W. Eichrodt, "The Law and the Gospel," *Int* 11 (1957): 28.

[34] C. Levin, "Der Dekalog Am Sinai," *VT* 35, 2 (1985): 165–91, esp. 165, 168, 172–74; E. Nielsen, *Deuteronomium*, HAT (Tübingen: J. C. B. Mohr, 1995), 72. See also *Miqráot Gedolot*, 5 vols. (Jerusalem: Eshkol, 1976), 1:85 [in Hb.]; M. Carasik, מקראות גדולות. *The Commentators' Bible: The JPS Miqráot Gedolot. Exodus* (Philadelphia: Jewish Publication Society, 2005), 160.

slaves to the Egyptians for 400 years (Gen 15:13; Deut 5:15). This different purpose is reflected in the difference of the two main verbs of the Sabbath law. In Deut 5 the main verb is *šāmar* ("observe") instead of the root *zākar* ("remember") in Exod 20. While *šāmar* functions as a technical term, *zākar* is used to preserve the historical memory of creation.[35] In this work we will follow the presentation of the Ten Commandments in Exod 20, the initial giving of them, but point out any differences in Deut 5.

The Significance of the Ten Commandments in Judaism

The Ten Commandments were highly esteemed in the practice of early Judaism. Recitation of the Decalogue evidently was originally part of the daily temple service (*m. Tam.* 5.1). This is particularly evident in the Second Temple period, in which we discover that the liturgical practice of reciting the Ten Commandments preceded the citation of the Shema (Deut 6:4). The Nash papyrus, as well as the LXX of Deut 6:4, offers external evidence of the combination of the Ten Commandments with the Shema, apparently reflecting an established Jewish practice. That the Decalogue was joined to the Shema is also evidenced by *tepillîn*, black leather boxes containing scriptural verses that were found at Qumran.[36] The ancient order of biblical passages in the *tepillîn* correspond to the liturgy in the Second Temple, as described in the Mishnah.[37]

A replica of the two tablets of the Decalogue has long been used as a symbol decorating many Jewish synagogues.[38] Whoever enters a

---

[35] Weinfeld, "The Uniqueness of the Decalogue and its Place in Jewish Tradition," 7.

[36] In nineteenth-century Sephardic prayer books, the Shema is cited along with the Ten Commandments.

[37] Greenberg, "The Tradition Critically Examined,"117; R. Collins, "Ten Commandments," *ABD* 6:386; E. Urbach, "The Role of the Ten Commandments in Jewish Worship," in Segal, *The Ten Commandments in History and Tradition,* 163. But in order to avoid the suspicion that Judaism valued the Decalogue more highly than the remaining portions of the law, the recitation of the Ten Commandments was at one time struck from the synagogue service. The practice was revived, however, both in Babylonia and Palestine (Urbach, "The Role of the Ten Commandments in Jewish Worship," 182; U. Leupold, "The Decalogue in Rabbinic Judaism and Early Christianity," in *Ambulatio Fidei: Essays in Honour of Otto W. Heick,* ed. E. Schultz [Waterloo, Ontario: Waterloo Lutheran University, 1965], 7).

[38] E. Melammed, "Observe and Remember," in Segal, *The Ten Commandments in History and Tradition,* 214.

synagogue today will almost certainly see the two tablets of the law above the ark. On them, in an abbreviated form, you will find the Ten Commandments. They have become the principal symbol of Judaism.[39]

The Ten Commandments have been viewed within Judaism as the essence of the Torah. Many have noted that all 613 laws of the Torah correspond to the 613 letters of the Ten Commandments in Exod 20, hence the Decalogue appears to represent the embodiment of all laws and statutes of the Pentateuch.[40] Since the first century BC, the Ten Commandments have been regarded as a summary of biblical law or as headings for all its categories.[41]

The Significance of the Ten Commandments in Christianity

The New Testament church accepted the Decalogue as the substance of Christian ethics at an early date. Early attestation of its importance is clear not only from the numerous citations of the Ten Commandments in the New Testament (Matt 5; 19; Mark 10; Luke 18:20; Rom 13:9; Jas 2:11) but also from the apostle Paul stating emphatically that the tenth commandment convinced him he was a sinner (Rom 7:7–8). Under the teaching of the tenth commandment, sin stirred up a world of iniquity in his heart. The New Testament nowhere rescinds the ethics of the Ten Commandments.

According to the *Epistle of Barnabas* (14:1–5), the tablets of stone of the Decalogue were not given to the Jews (they were broken) but

---

[39] G. Sarfatti, "The Tablets of the Law as a Symbol of Judaism," in Segal, *The Ten Commandments in History and Tradition*, 383.

[40] Dohmen, *Exodus*, 135; Greenberg, "The Tradition Critically Examined," 119. The numerical value of the term for "law" (תּוֹרָה) is 611. According to tradition, the number of laws is 613. Subtracting the first two of the Ten Commandments, which were spoken directly by God, would give the equivalent of 611 laws transmitted by Moses. See Wax, *The Ten Commandments*, 66, 90.

[41] See Philo, *Decal.*, 157–58, 165; Greenberg, "The Tradition Critically Examined," 117; G. Vermes, "The Decalogue and the Minim," in *In Memoriam Paul Kahle*, ed. M. Black and G. Fohrer (Berlin: Verlag, 1968), 233; See also Philo, *Decal.*, 154; E. Urbach, *The Sages: Their Concepts and Beliefs*, trans. I. Abrahams (Jerusalem: Magnes, 1975), 360–64; and J. Tigay, *Deuteronomy*, JPS Torah Commentary (Philadelphia: Jewish Publication Society, 1996), 63, 355. Philo's *De decalogo* is the earliest attempt to determine the impact of the Ten Commandments on the history of Jewish thought (Y. Amir, "The Decalogue According to Philo," in Segal, *The Ten Commandments in History and Tradition*, 121).

to the Christians. Irenaeus takes the Decalogue as the original law written on the hearts and souls of the patriarchs.[42] The prayers from the *Apostolic Constitutions* and the *Letter of Pliny to Trajan* show that even in the second century some Christians viewed the precepts of the Decalogue as central to community life.[43]

Saint Augustine was one of the first fathers to regard the Decalogue as an adequate statement of the law of Christ. A survey of more than 25 catechisms of the fifteenth century discloses that the Decalogue reigned supreme as the moral teaching of the church.[44] It forms the ethical and moral basis for all relationships, whether human or divine, since morality is that which represents "conformity to the character and will of God."[45] As these commandments mirror the character of God, they shine the floodlight on our transgressions and sins (see 1 Tim 1:8–11). As contemporary author John Holbert has stated: "These Ten Commandments are hardly all we need to know about the rule of God in our lives, but they are a wonderful starting point for us to discover, or to rediscover, just what it is God wants from us, as well as just what it is that God has done for us"[46]

The Enumeration of the Ten Commandments

Division of Verses

A distinctive feature of the Ten Commandments, in both the Exodus and Deuteronomy versions, is the employment of two different sets of accents or cantillation signs. The only other passage in the Old Testament that has a set of two cantillation signs is Gen 35:22.

Later Masoretic scribes introduced what has been called the *rebîaʿ* system of accents. The *rebîaʿ* accent is a disjunctive accent that has a diamond shape and is placed over the accented syllable. In this

---

[42] Leupold, "The Decalogue in Rabbinic Judaism and Early Christianity," 8.

[43] See K. Burton, "The Decalogue as Essential Torah in Second Temple Judaism," *Journal of the Adventist Theological Society* 9,1–2 (1998): 317.

[44] M. Butler, "Must We Teach Morality According to the Decalogue?" *Worship* 37,5 (1963): 294.

[45] W. Kaiser Jr., *Toward Old Testament Ethics* (Grand Rapids: Zondervan, 1983), 85.

[46] J. Holbert, *The Ten Commandments* (Nashville: Abingdon Press, 2002), 138.

system, all verses in which the Lord speaks in the first person constitute a separate commandment.[47] This system of accentuation divides
the text into "words," in contrast with the lower accentuation which
divides the text according to verses *(pesûqîm)*. The lower cantillation
is believed to have originated in Israel, while the upper system came
from Babylonia.[48]

Later Jewish communities would use one system for public reading
and the other for private reading.[49] On the Feast of Shavuot (Weeks),
one chanted the commandments in a versification that represents the
way Israel heard the Ten Commandments at Mount Sinai—some long
utterances along with some short utterances. On the Sabbath Torah
reading portion in Exod 18:1–20:23, one chanted the commandments
according to the normalizing cantillation that breaks the passage into
verses of usual length.[50]

Related to this Masoretic distinction, Masoretic scribes divided the
Hebrew text into "paragraphs" *(Parashot)*. They displayed by the use
of paragraphs different methods of dividing up the Decalogue. The
first paragraph begins with "I am the LORD your God" and ends with
"of those who love Me and keep My commands" (Exod 20:6; Deut
5:10). The second paragraph begins with "Do not misuse the name of
the LORD your God" (Exod 20:7; Deut 5:11). But we find a different
paragraph division with regard to the laws on coveting. In the Deuteronomy version the tenth commandment is divided into two paragraphs: "Do not desire your neighbor's wife" is the first paragraph,
and the rest of the verse, "or covet your neighbor's house, his field,
his male or female slave, his ox or donkey, or anything that belongs to
your neighbor," functions as the second paragraph (Deut 5:21).

Division of Tablets

The Old Testament records that the Ten Commandments were written on two tablets of stone. The texts do not tell us, however, which
commandments were written on which stone. Various views about the

---

[47] M. Breuer, "Division by Verses or Commandments," in Segal, *The Ten Commandments in History and Tradition*, 310.

[48] Ibid., 323.

[49] W. Propp, *Exodus 19–40*, AB (New York: Doubleday, 2006), 166.

[50] Greenberg, "The Tradition Critically Examined," 97.

arranging of these commandments on the stones have been suggested.[51] The most-debated issue is the placement of the fifth commandment. Was the fifth commandment on the first tablet or the second?

Many argue that the two-tablet tradition demands we see the parental law as belonging to the first Decalogue table. The parents are viewed in the Decalogue as representatives of God and not merely as neighbors.[52] In what might be the oldest comment on the Decalogue (Lev 19), the parental law could be viewed as belonging to the first table because it is listed ahead of the fourth commandment, on observing the Sabbath law (Lev 19:3). The first table was believed to contain the commandments more directly related to one's relationship to God. In Lev 19:3, the meaning of the parental law has been intensified by the use of the verb *yr'* ("fear") rather than *kbd* ("honor"): "Each of you is to respect (lit. fear; *yr'*) his mother and father." This verb is normally reserved as an expression of a person's response to God.

Many scholars who believe that the parental law is the last on the first tablet understand that the promise in the fifth commandment, "that you may have a long life in the land that the LORD your God is giving you," refers to the entire first table of the law. This is the position of many who see the parental law as the last on the first tablet. Similarly, the Jewish philosopher Philo believed there were five commandments on each tablet and that the fifth commandment had a special connection to the laws concerning one's relationship to God:

> Thus one set of enactments begins with God the Father and Maker of all, and ends with parents who copy His nature by begetting particular persons. Parents stand by their nature on the border-line between the mortal and the immortal . . . because the act of generation assimilates them to God, the Generator of the All. Like all human beings they come to an end; but on the other hand, their ability to create life endows them with a touch of the Divine.[53]

The division of the tablets in Jewish art is normally that of five laws on each tablet, with the first tablet concluding with the parental law.

---

[51] The two-tablet tradition is mentioned most frequent in Deuteronomy (4:13; 9:10–11,15,17; 10:1).

[52] H. Kremers, "Die Stellung des Elterngebotes im Dekalog," *ET* 21 (1961): 155–56.

[53] See Y. Amir, "The Decalogue According to Philo," 156–57. Abarbanel also believed that the parental law was among the five divine commandments on the first tablet (G. Blidstein, *Honor Thy Father and Mother: Filial Responsibility in Jewish Law and Ethics* [New York: KTAV, 1976], 22).

In Christian art, on the other hand, the two tablets are divided some-times after the Sabbath commandment and sometimes after the fifth commandment.[54]

Another position on the occurrence and enumeration of the Ten Commandments on two tablets comes by way of analogy from the ancient Near East, where two copies of a covenant agreement were produced, one for each party. One was for the vassal and the other for the suzerain.[55] Based on this analogy, each partner, in this case God and the people, had a copy. In this unique situation, though, both copies were kept in one place, the ark of the covenant, the meeting place of God with His people (Exod 25:16; see *y. Sheq.* 6.1). The only other information in the Bible about the writing on the two tablets is that they were written on both sides (Exod 32:15).[56] The division of the Decalogue into two tablets is not mentioned in Exod 20 but is found in Exod 34 and Deut 5. Nowhere in the Bible is there indication of how the commandments were to be divided. What we do know is that there were ten "words."[57]

The Traditional Divisions of the Ten Commandments

The Ten Commandments begin with "I am the Lord" and end with reference to one's neighbor, showing the twofold concern of relation-ship with God and relationship to one's fellow man. But the fact that the second half of the Decalogue occurs in conjunction with the first half, which focuses on one's relationship to God, gives these com-mandments elevated importance. The phrase "YHWH (your God)" appears in each of the first five commandments, whereas in the sec-ond pentad the Tetragrammaton (Yahweh; Lord) does not occur at all. The Deuteronomy version of the Decalogue enhances the unity and uniformity of the second five even further by making them virtually

---

[54] Dohmen, *Exodus,* 135.

[55] Youngblood, "Counting the Ten Commandments," 34.

[56] See A. Phillips, *Ancient Israel's Criminal Law: A New Approach to the Decalogue* (Oxford: Basil Blackwell, 1970), 7; E. Merrill, Deuteronomy, NAC (Nashville: B&H, 1994), 143.

[57] B. Childs, *The Book of Exodus: A Critical-Theological Commentary* (Louisville: Westminster John Knox, 1974), 395.

one sentence.[58] The Jewish sages distinguished between the first five commandments, which were addressed to the Israelites alone and therefore use the Tetragrammaton, and the last five commandments, which were addressed to the nations and therefore do not mention God's name (see *Pesiq. R, 21*).[59]

In Jewish tradition, Exod 20:2 constitutes the first "word," and it is not a commandment but a declaration that the Lord God delivered the Israelites from Egyptian bondage.[60] Exodus 20:3–6 thus constitutes the first commandment which prohibits worship of other gods and includes the related notion of prohibiting idolatry.[61] The issue of Masoretic accentuation as well as the Masoretic paragraph division is important for the Jewish tradition with regard to the first and second commandments. These scribal notations support the understanding that the law prohibiting worship of other gods and the law prohibiting idolatry should be read as a single law.[62] According to this interpretation, the expression, "You must not bow down to them or worship them," in Exod 20:5 would refer not to the singular idol (Exod 20:4) but to the plural "other gods" in Exod 20:3.[63]

Saint Augustine and Martin Luther represent the Catholic tradition regarding the division of the Ten Commandments. Similar to the Jewish tradition, they affirmed that Exod 20:3–6 constitutes one commandment and come up with ten words by dividing the tenth commandment on coveting into two commandments.[64]

---

[58] Weinfeld, *Deuteronomy 1–11*, 313.

[59] M. Weinfeld, "The Uniqueness of the Decalogue and Its Place in Jewish Tradition," 34.

[60] Most critical scholars take this declaration as a general introductory remark to the Ten Commandments. D. Christensen, *Deuteronomy 1:1–21:9*, rev. WBC (Nashville: Thomas Nelson, 2001), 106. For evidence within Jewish tradition that "I am the LORD your God" was not considered the first commandment, see Wax, *The Ten Commandments*, 66–67.

[61] Even if the first and second commandments are combined as one, it is still pragmatic to discuss the concepts of each separately given their individually extreme importance to the history of Israel.

[62] Furthermore, many Jewish scholars maintain that the Masoretic accent system in Judg 6:8–10; Ps 81:10–11 supports the traditional Jewish position concerning the first and second commandments. This rendering is problematic and open to other interpretations, however. Note the punctuation in *Tanakh* for Exod 20:3–6 (Greenberg, "The Tradition Critically Examined," 99).

[63] Kremers, "Die Stellung des Elterngebotes im Dekalog," 157. Similarly, the reference to God's jealousy in the second commandment would apply to the first commandment as well, and this was the reason it was placed only after the second commandment. See Tigay, *Deuteronomy*, 65.

[64] In Deut 5, the Masoretes divided the commandment prohibiting coveting into two

The traditional Protestant view divides verses 3–6 into two commandments, the first and second. Brevard Childs argues that this is the most natural division, as the second commandment served a function distinct from the first, which prohibited worship of other gods.[65] The second commandment addresses the mode of worship, while the first commandment should be viewed as describing the object of worship.[66] This distinction may be supported by what appears to be a reference to two commandments in 1 Kgs 14:9. This division has early attestation among such significant interpreters as Josephus, Philo, R. Ishamael (*Sifre Numbers* [112]), and Origen. In this work we will follow the traditional Protestant enumeration.[67]

The Ten Commandments in Their Ancient Near Eastern Background

Communication by writing first appeared toward the end of the fourth millennium BC in the ancient Near East. A few hundred years after the invention of writing, the earliest recognizable legal records appear. The Near East is thus home to the world's oldest known system of law, clearly predating the earliest legal records of any other civilization. The laws of ancient Near Eastern cultures represent a special genre of literature, which has remarkably close parallels among the neighbors of ancient Israel. The basic features of these archaic laws were passed down virtually unchanged for 3,000 years.

The most famous law code is Codex Hammurabi from Babylonia of the eighteenth century BC.[68] Many of the legal collections such as Hammurabi's code were compiled by the king to report to the gods the king's success in carrying out his duties as absolute monarch. The

---

commandments by insertion of the paragraph marker. Youngblood contends, however, that the tenth commandment on coveting appears to be a single commandment according to the apostle Paul (Rom 7:7; 13:9). Youngblood, "Counting the Ten Commandments," 50.

[65] Childs, *The Book of Exodus*, 407.

[66] Kaiser, *Toward Old Testament Ethics*, 85–86.

[67] Christensen likewise maintains that the Protestant view is the clearest. Christensen, *Deuteronomy 1:1–21:9*, 106. Mordecai Breuer, however, emphatically states that the Protestant position is the only system that cannot possibly be supported by the Masoretic accent system (Breuer, "Division by Verses or Commandments," 312–13).

[68] R. Westbrook, ed., *A History of Ancient Near Eastern Law*, 2 vols. (Leiden; Boston: Brill, 2003), 1:1; id., "The Laws of Biblical Israel," in *The Hebrew Bible: New Insights and Scholarship* (New York: New York University Press, 2008), 100.

legal cases were designed to show the gods what a just administration the king had established. Thus, the laws did not have their source in the gods but were a propaganda tool by the king. The gods did not instruct the people or the king as to how they ought to run society or to conduct their lives. For Israel on the other hand, God was the source of law, and the king was under the law (Deut 17:14–20). The goal of the law in ancient Israel was to produce an understanding of what God was like and thereby provide moral and ethical guidelines for individual and national conduct.[69]

Biblical Law Is Unique

In Mesopotamia, offenses were ultimately viewed in relation to how they led to the detriment of society. In Mesopotamian law, the injuring of a nobleman would commonly entail a far heavier penalty than the infliction of an identical injury to a commoner or slave. In Israel, by contrast, equality before the law for all social groups, including aliens and immigrants, is made explicit in Exod 12:49; Lev 19:34; and Num 15:16.[70] In Israel, all offenses were ultimately offenses against God.[71] Biblical law interweaves the spiritual, cultic, moral, and legal spheres without differentiation as life is treated holistically before God. Thus all infractions are religious transgressions. This understanding of the law, as well as the understanding that the law was directly given by God, was unique in the ancient world.[72]

The new ideas expressed in the first half of the Ten Commandments constituted a radical revolution in the religious conceptions of the ancient Near East. Unique is the presentation of the Ten Commandments as absolute prohibitions, which lifts them above any circumstance and every accident of detail. On the other hand, in the second half of the Decalogue, no reasons are given for compliance

---

[69] J. Walton, "Cultural Background of the Old Testament," in *Foundations for Biblical Interpretation*, ed. D. S. Dockery, K. A. Mathews, and R. B. Sloan (Nashville: B&H, 1994), 261.

[70] C. J. H. Wright, *An Eye for an Eye: The Place of Old Testament Ethics Today* (Downers Grove, IL: InterVarsity, 1983), 166.

[71] See J. Walton, *Ancient Israelite Literature in Its Cultural Context* (Grand Rapids: Zondervan, 1989), 80; B. Arnold and B. Beyer, eds., *Readings from the Ancient Near East* (Grand Rapids: Baker Academic, 2002), 104.

[72] H. Ringgren, "מִצְוָה *miṣwâ*," *TDOT* 8:509; N. Sarna, *Exploring Exodus: The Origins of Biblical Israel* (New York: Schocken Books, 1996), 144.

as these laws are recognized as foundational for all societies; without such laws no society would exist.[73]

One area in which the biblical laws possibly are indebted to the ancient Near Eastern law codes may be found in the structure of these other ancient codes. Many believe that the structure of the Ten Commandments, as well as other law codes, follows the general structure of ancient Near Eastern treaties, particularly the Hittite treaty of the second millennium BC. This connection has the air of authenticity, as the format of the Ten Commandments would follow the patterns of universally recognized legal instruments in order that they would be intelligible to the Israelites.[74] The elements of the suzerain-vassal treaty form may be observed in Exodus from the following outline:

1. Preamble: identity of the king (Exod 20:2)
2. Historical prologue (Exod 20:1–2)
3. Stipulations (Exod 20–31)
4. Ceremonial meal (Exod 24:9–11)
5. Deposition (Exod 25:16)
6. Blessings and curses (Lev 26)

Execution of Justice

As a means to execute justice, a measure-for-measure principle was established early in ancient Near Eastern law. For example, if a man killed another man's son, the victim's father could kill the son of the man who had killed his son. Similarly, if a man's daughter was raped, he might be allowed to rape the rapist's wife.[75] This practice is at odds with biblical criminal law, which does not give the right to punish anyone but the culprit in both civil and criminal cases (Ezek 18:4,20).

The punishment of imprisonment for a fixed period of time was not customary in Israel or the rest of the ancient Near East, but jails have

---

[73] Cassuto, *A Commentary on the Book of Exodus*, 237, 239.

[74] Sarna, *Exodus*, 102; W. Kaiser Jr., "Exodus," in *The Expositor's Bible Commentary*, vol. 2, ed. F. Gaebelein (Grand Rapids: Zondervan, 1990), 420.

[75] See J. Finkelstein, "מִשְׁפָּט, מִשְׁפָּט, הַמִּשְׁפָּט במזרח הקדמון," *EncMiqr* 5:613 [in Hb.]. These forms of substitutionary punishment were outlawed in Israel (Deut 24:16).

been found that were used to hold certain political prisoners.[76] While
the absence of imprisonment as a punishment may seem odd to a modern Westerner, it must be admitted that time spent in jail has not often
led to rehabilitation of the criminal in many if not most cases.

Ethical Laws in Ancient Near Eastern Law Codes

In contrast with the first four laws of the Decalogue, the ethical
commands of the interpersonal commandments (commandments
5–10) are mirrored in ancient Near Eastern texts. These ancient texts
are from the time of Moses and earlier. One example is the "Declaration of Innocence" from the *Book of the Dead*, an Egyptian text from
the New Kingdom (c. sixteenth century BC). In chapter 25 of this
document we find the confession of a recently deceased individual
who stated that he did not violate specific laws. An unfavorable confession would not allow such a person to enter the next world. What
is remarkable about these laws is their similarity to the Ten Commandments. Similarly, in Mesopotamian magical texts known as the
Shurpu series, sins such as bearing false witness, disrespect for parents, theft, adultery, and murder are all mentioned.[77] According to
Jacob Finkelstein, the principles of righteousness and uprightness are
givens and existed in the world at the beginning of creation.[78] Pagan
law codes represent a certain level of morality as they in no way com-
mend murder, theft, and adultery as ideal modes of behavior.[79]

On the other hand, gods of the ancient Near East outside of Israel
were not obliged to be ethical, moral, or even fair. These gods were
guilty of theft, adultery, murder, and coveting. They revealed nothing
about themselves or their expectations from their worshippers.[80]

As we now turn to the context of the Ten Commandments themselves (Exod 20:1–17), we reach the climax of the book of Exodus

[76] Ibid., 608.

[77] See Greenberg, "The Tradition Critically Examined," 110–11; Sarna, *Exodus,* 102.

[78] Finkelstein, "משפט המשפט במזרח חקדמון," 5:610.

[79] J. Barr, "Biblical Law and the Question of Natural Theology," in *The Law in the Bible and
in Its Environment,* ed. Timo Veijola, The Finnish Exegetical Society in Helsinki (Göttingen:
Vadenhoeck & Ruprecht, 1990), 4.

[80] C. H. Gordan, "The Commandments," CT 8 (1964): 3–6; Walton, "Cultural Background
of the Old Testament," 272.

and the central portion of the Pentateuch. All that came before the Ten Commandments in the Pentateuch was a preparation for them, and all that follows is a supplement or result of them.[81]

The Context of the Ten Commandments

In Exod 20, the Ten Commandments begin with the statement, "I am the LORD your God,[82] who brought you out of the land of Egypt" (Exod 20:2).[83] As Exod 20:2 makes clear, this declaration is given within the context and framework of grace.[84] The liberation of Israel from bondage to Pharaoh gave the Lord the sovereign right to establish rules for His people that should in turn characterize their behavior. "The indicative of God's grace comes before and is the foundation and authority for the imperative of the law and responsive obedience. . . . The very meaning of the law is grounded in the gospel of God's saving in history (Deut 6:20–25)."[85]

It was right that the Lord is called the God of Israel because He was the one who brought Israel out of Egypt. Israel in turn was obligated to receive His divinity and sovereignty over them. The statement "I am the Lord" hints further that here the promise was fulfilled that was given to Moses at the time he was sent to Israel (see Exod 6:7; cf. Gen 15:7; 31:13).[86] This deliverance was a presupposition throughout all the demands of the law. The demands of God follow the gift of God

---

[81] See Cassuto, *A Commentary on the Book of Exodus,* 235.

[82] Self-presentations, in the form of a nominal sentence with the personal pronoun as subject, are common in the openings of royal inscriptions in the ancient Near East (Weinfeld, *Deuteronomy 1–11,* 285). This self-presentation is introduced with the phrase אֱלֹהִים וַיְדַבֵּר "Then God spoke," which occurs elsewhere only in Gen 8:15 and Exod 6:2.

[83] The following phrase "house of slavery" occurs in Exod 13:3,14; Deut 5:6; 6:12; 7:8; 8:14; 13:5,10; Josh 24:17; 1 Kgs 6:8; Jer 34:13; Mic 6:4. Throughout the second millennium BC, Egypt captured or bought large numbers of slaves from neighboring lands (Tigay, *Deuteronomy,* 64). Ninety-one times we are told, "Yahweh brought Israel out of Egypt." It is impossible to overstate the significance of this affirmation for Israel's history in the biblical period.

[84] W. Eichrodt, "The Law and the Gospel," *Int* 11 (1957): 33; Jepsen, "Beiträge zur Auslegung und Geschichte des Dekalogs," 291; W. Dumbrell, "The Prospect of Unconditionality in the Sinaitic Covenant," in *Israel's Apostasy and Restoration: Essays in Honor of Roland K. Harrison,* ed. A. Gileadi (Grand Rapids: Baker, 1988), 148.

[85] C. Wright, *The Mission of God* (Downers Grove, IL: InterVarsity, 2006), 59. See E. Nielsen, *Deuteronomium,* HAT (Tübingen: J. C. B. Mohr, 1995), 77.

[86] A. Hakam, *The Book of Exodus* (Jerusalem: Mossad Harav Kook, 1991), 275 [in Hb.].

and the gift of God should be ever present in the mind to motivate obedience to God's commands.[87]

The Order of the Commandments

The commandments give every indication of being arranged in a hierarchical order. The obligations of man before God precede matters between men. Even within the first five commandments there is a hierarchy: the obligation to correctly worship God precedes the duty to honor His name, and both of these injunctions precede honoring His holy day. Each of these injunctions contains the phrase "the Lord your God."[88] There is also a hierarchical order among the five ethical commandments: the value of life, the marriage bond, the right to private possession, reliability of public testimony, and the prohibition of guilty desires. This final commandment aims at preventing murder, adultery, stealing, and false witness.[89] It is rightly seen that the parental law is pivotal as one moves from obligations to God to obligations to fellow human beings and society. The transitional nature of the fifth commandment explains why there is debate whether this commandment should be read with the previous four and why some traditions believe it was listed with the previous four on the first tablet of the Decalogue. However, violation of any of the first six commandments brought the death penalty. The medieval commentator Nahmanides explained the interconnection of the Ten Commandments in the following way:

> Here, then, are the Ten Commandments: five dealing with the honor of the Creator, and five for the benefit of humanity. For, as we observed, honoring one's father is part of honoring God. Only for the second, third, and fifth commandments does the text explain their consequences. But no reward or punishment is mentioned for the others. For the last five are simply for the welfare of humanity; observing them is its own reward. But idolatry is a sin so severe that its consequences needed to be spelled out. It seems to me that "I . . . am an impassioned God" (v. 5) corresponds to "You shall have no other gods besides Me" (v. 3), while "showing kindness" (v. 6) corresponds to "I

---

[87] Holbert, *The Ten Commandments*, 14.

[88] References to the Israelites as "My people" and the Lord as Israel's "[your] God" are at the core of Israel's special covenant relationship with God (see Exod 6:7; Lev 26:12).

[89] Greenberg, "The Tradition Critically Examined," 114. What we find in the Ten Commandments are prohibitions without reference to punishment. Later in biblical law the consequences for violating these commandments are spelled out.

the LORD am your God" (v. 2). For one is punished for violating a prohibition and rewarded for fulfilling a positive commandment.[90]

Thus the religious demands precede the interpersonal demands because there must be a sense of accountability before God to guarantee the observance of socio-moral demands with regard to our fellow man. Social concern stems from and must be rooted in the religious conscience. Hence a profession of belief in God and the observance of religious ritual are undermined, if not negated, if they are not accompanied by proper treatment of one's fellow man.[91]

The Opening Prologue

The opening prologue (Exod 20:2) serves as a preface to the whole law and should not be viewed as uniquely linked to the first commandment only.[92] Thus the prologue makes clear that all the commands that follow are integrally connected to God's act of self-revelation.

The prologue also connects the Exodus narrative to the preceding chapters. In the way that God introduces himself in Exod 20:2, the entire history from Exod 3 (cf. 19:4) is recalled (see 6:2,6; 12:12). Thus Exod 3 is at pains to point out that the call of Moses in this new work continues and is in harmony with the patriarchal promises. Exodus 1:17 and 2:23–25 had already shown the transition indicating that God's later work is based on promises He made to the patriarchs. Indeed, since Exod 6:4 referred to the exodus as a fulfillment of the patriarchal covenants, the promise of Exod 19:5, in the immediate context of the Ten Commandments, would seem to point in this same direction.[93] It is now in the period of the exodus that the significance of the divine name *Yahweh*, which was first mentioned early in the Genesis narrative, will come to light.[94] The promises to the patriarchs in Genesis are linked to the creation of the nation of Israel in Exodus. In Exod 19 Israel's call cannot be detached from the details of God's revelation of His name to Moses in Exod 3:13–15.[95] "The first half of

---

[90] Carasik, מקראות גדולות. *The Commentators' Bible*, 163.
[91] Sarna, *Exploring Exodus*, 144.
[92] It serves also as an introduction to the whole Decalogue.
[93] Dumbrell, *Covenant and Creation*, 80–81.
[94] J. A. Motyer, *The Revelation of the Divine Name* (London: Tyndale, 1949), 25.
[95] For the first time since Exod 3:1–4:17, the Lord speaks in a special place.

Exodus is all about rescue from forced service to a pagan nation, and the second half is all about proper service for the one true God by keeping his covenant."[96]

Service of Pharaoh will now be replaced by the service of Yahweh, as Israel had declared itself ready to live according to His will (Exod 19:7–8). God brought His people to Sinai and through Moses instituted a covenant with them. Exodus 19:3b–8 reveals the nature of this Mosaic covenant. After the people agreed and underwent a period of preparation, they met God on the mountain as He appeared in a glorious theophany (Exod 19:9–25). Now God declared to the people His covenant, first through the Ten Commandments (Exod 20:1–17) and then by more specific regulations (Exod 21:1–23:33). After hearing all the stipulations of the covenant, the people restated their commitment to their Deliverer, "We will do everything that the LORD has commanded" (Exod 24:3; cf. Exod 19:8). The covenant was then formally ratified through animal sacrifice (Exod 24:4–8).

The history of Israel from this moment on will be nothing more than a commentary on the degree of fidelity Israel exhibits to this covenant. While God's commitment to His people will be invariable and unshakable, Israel's ability to receive blessing from the Lord is directly proportional to the degree of her covenant faithfulness in observing the Mosaic law. Thus the arrival of the Israelites on Mount Sinai forges the climactic stage of Israel's national and spiritual identity. From this point on, Israel will be inextricably bound to the Lord by a covenant relationship.[97] The Ten Commandments thereby become the code by which Israel is "a priestly kingdom and a holy nation" (19:6).

Thus the introduction formula points forward to a new stage in the relationship between God and his people. The formula identifies the authority of God to make known to His people how He has graciously acted on Israel's behalf and how He desires for them to live before Him.[98]

---

[96] Stuart, *Exodus*, 438.
[97] Sarna, *Exodus*, 102.
[98] Childs, *Exodus*, 401.

The Addressees of the Ten Commandments

The prologue to the Ten Commandments opens with the statement, "I am the LORD your God who brought you out of the land of Egypt" (Exod 20:2). The Ten Commandments are addressed to the nation of Israel as indicated by the independent personal pronoun "you," which is grammatically in the second-person masculine singular. This does not indicate that only individual males were being addressed. Rather, all the people of Israel are addressed with "you."

The "you" addressed in this commandment must include both males and females since both are specified in the list of those covered by the fourth commandment ("your son or your daughter, your male or female slave").[99] All biblical laws are addressed to males and females alike.[100]

The Ten Commandments were given directly to every individual Israelite without any intermediaries such as priests, kings, or other leaders who could impose the Torah on the people. God spoke to each individual and commanded each one. In the words of *Leqaḥ Tov*: "Why were the Ten Commandments proclaimed in the singular? To tell you that every Israelite has to feel that the Torah was given to him and that he personally has to observe it."[101]

---

[99] Hakam, *Exodus*, 284–85; Wax, *The Ten Commandments*, 72, 97.

[100] C. Keil and F. Delitzsch, *Commentary on the Old Testament, the Pentateuch*, vol. 2, trans. J. Martin (Grand Rapids: Eerdmans, 1973), 124.

[101] S. Albeck, "The Ten Commandments and the Essence of Religious Faith," 287–88.

Chapter 1

THE FIRST COMMANDMENT

Do not have other gods besides Me.

Introduction

The ancient Near Eastern world was steeped in the belief and worship of many gods. God revealed Himself to Moses and the children of Israel in the midst of this pagan, polytheistic culture. In pagan thought, no one god was ultimate, and gods were believed to be finite and not absolute. No one god was believed to possess unlimited wisdom or power. Rather, they were considered to be more like superhumans than sovereign deities. They had impulses and desires and committed evil acts.[1]

The characteristic mark of pagan thought was the belief in the existence of a primordial realm above the gods that had control over activities of the gods. The gods were dependent on this realm from which they emerged. It was believed the gods were merely personal embodiments of seminal forces, all on a par with one another and all rooted in the primordial realm.[2] The gods were thus believed to have origins; many of them were believed to have come into being through procreation. The same ancient Near Eastern mythological literature that addresses the creation of the world also speaks of the creation of the gods.[3] All aspects and forces of the natural world were believed to be associated with some deity, as nature was nothing but the manifestation of the divine. In many ways pagan worship was the worship of the forces of nature.[4]

---

[1] See E. R. Clendenen, "Religious Background of the Old Testament," in *Foundations for Biblical Interpretation,* ed. D. Dockery, K. Mathews, and R. Sloan (Nashville: B&H, 1994), 275; and Y. Kaufmann, *The Religion of Israel: From Its Beginnings to the Babylonian Exile,* trans. and abridged by M. Greenberg (New York: Schocken Books, 1960), 39.

[2] Kaufmann, *The Religion of Israel,* 21–23.

[3] Y. Kaufmann, "דָּת יִשְׂרָאֵל," *EncMiqr* 2:727 [in Hb.].

[4] J. Walton, *Ancient Near Eastern Thought and the Old Testament* (Grand Rapids: Baker Academic, 2006), 91, 97, 103; H. Frankfort, J. Wilson, T. Jacobsen, and W. Irwin, *The Intellectual Adventure of Ancient Man* (Chicago: The University of Chicago Press, 1946), 366–67; and T. Jacobsen, *The Treasures of Darkness* (New Haven: Yale University Press, 1976), 73.

The notion that gods were subject to the primordial realm led to the belief that gods could be influenced by magic and ritual. Rituals were performed to manipulate the gods to act in one's favor. Pagan worshippers would try to please or placate a god by providing a sacrifice of food or drink. If the god was satisfied with the offering, it was believed, he would be appeased and perhaps act to benefit the devotee. In a world that adhered to pagan beliefs, man sought to control the gods for his own advantage.

The Meaning of the First Commandment

In the first commandment we find a prohibition against the worship and service of any other god than Yahweh, the true God and Lord of Israel. The Hebrew formula *lōʾ yihyeh (lĕ)* ("do not have")[5] means to keep or refrain from having a relationship with. The positive (nonnegated) statement *yihyeh (lĕ)* was a comma idiom for the establishment of a marriage. The positive statement later became the formulaic expression for the unique covenant relationship between God and Israel,[6] as the terminology for marriage became the classical terminology for Israel's covenant relationship with God.[7] The most intimate of all relationships on the human plane became the analogy for God's intimate relationship with His people. This commandment implies that there may be no third parties in a person's relationship with God, just as there may be no intruding third parties in a marriage. Indeed, the expression of not pursuing *ʾĕlōhîm ʾăḥērîm* ("other gods") is reminiscent of a wife pursuing *ʾîš ʾaḥēr* ("another man," Deut 24:2). As Jeffrey Tigay has noted:

---

[5] The verb is in the singular, which may indicate the prohibition addresses forming an association with even "one god." U. Cassuto, *A Commentary on the Book of Exodus*, trans. I. Abrahams (Jerusalem: Magnes, 1974), 241. This notion is perhaps reinforced by the fact the Aramaic targum does not read "other gods" in Exod 20:3, but אלה אחרן, "another god."

[6] The formula is used for the marriage relationship in Lev 21:3; Num 30:7; Deut 24:2,4; Judg 14:20; 15:2; Ruth 1:13; Ezek 16:8; Hos 3:3, and for the covenant between God and Israel in Gen 17:7; Exod 6:7; Lev 11:45; 20:26; 22:33; 25:38; 26:12; Num 15:41; Deut 26:17–18; 27:9; 29:12; 2 Sam 7:24; Jer 7:23; 11:4; 13:11; 24:7; 30:22; Ezek 11:20; 14:11; 36:28; 37:23; Hos 1:9[8]. In Jer 31:32 God refers to His relationship with Israel by the phrase, (וְאָנֹכִי בָּעַלְתִּי בָם) "I had married them." See C. Dohmen, *Exodus 19–40* (Freiburg: Herder, 2004), 106.

[7] The technical Hebrew term for covenant (בְּרִית) is also used to apply to the marriage bond (Prov 2:17; Ezek 16:8; Mal 2:14).

> In practical terms the commandment means that Israelites may have no rela-
> tionship of any kind with other gods; they may not build altars, sanctuaries,
> or images to them, make offerings to them, consult them, prophesy or take
> oaths in their names, or even mention their names.[8]

The Lord (Yahweh) will brook no rival in His universe because the
Lord is the God who brought the people out of the house of bondage.[9]

Exclusive Monotheism

The prescription for the first commandment is for God's people not
to have any other gods ʿal pānā(a)y ("besides Me"). This last phrase has
been the subject of much discussion. Suggested renderings include:
(1) "next to me," (2) "except me," (3) "over me, to my disadvantage,"
(4) "in front of me," (5) "opposite me, before my face," and (6) "in
defiance of me."[10] Illustrations from biblical usage can be garnered
for each of these meanings. The object of the preposition (translated
"Me") is the Hebrew word pānîm, "face." This word occurs more than
2,100 times in the Old Testament and is often used metaphorically, as
here, referring to the person as a whole.[11] The rendering "besides Me"
is harmonious with the early versions of the LXX, Syriac, Vulgate, and
Aramaic targums.[12] The use of the personal pronoun places a stress
on the personal nature of the command (see Exod 20:2). Men may be
able to evade the eyes of other men, but they will not be able to escape
the notice of God as they pay homage to other gods.

The Bible and Monotheism

Many critical scholars maintain that what we find here in the prohibition to worship other gods is a tacit acknowledgement that the
Israelites believed other gods existed, but now they are called on to

---

[8] J. Tigay, *Deuteronomy*, JPS Torah Commentary (Philadelphia: Jewish Publication Society, 1996), 64.

[9] See J. C. Holbert, *The Ten Commandments* (Nashville: Abingdon, 2002), 19.

[10] *HALOT*, 2:944. Waltke and O'Connor prefer the rendering "over against me" (*IBHS*, 218).

[11] A. S. van der Woude, "פָּנִים pānîm," *TLOT* 2:995.

[12] The LXX does, however, translate the phrase more literally in Deut 5. There, the LXX translates the phrase πρὸ προσώπου μου, "before my face." Childs affirms that "besides Me" is still the best rendering. B. Childs, *The Book of Exodus: A Critical-Theological Commentary* (Louisville: Westminster John Knox, 1974), 402–3.

worship Yahweh as the only God.[13] Yet the Bible is clear that there is but one God (see Isa 40:12–31; 43:8–13; 45:5–6; 46:5–13). "Today, recognize and keep in mind that the LORD is God in heaven above and on earth below; there is no other" (Deut 4:39); "I am the first and the last. There is no God but Me" (Isa 44:6). As one reads Pss 95–99, psalms that enthusiastically speak of the one God who reigns as king and judge over all the earth, there is no room for polytheistic thoughts.[14] There are no other gods in reality. The belief in other gods, however, was ingrained in ancient Near Eastern society, and the Israelites were tempted to adopt pagan concepts and views. The gods were something only in the sense that the people of God had to contend with the idea of them. The temptation to acknowledge and show allegiance to something other than the true God is real in the human experience. As Yehezekel Kaufmann says: "In reality there are no other gods. Belief in the existence of other gods was real and ingrained in the polytheistic world of Israel's day though in fact other gods did not exist. A believer would not have a relationship with another god, real or imagined."[15] The first commandment does not affirm that other gods exist even though it refers to them. They are merely constructs of the human imagination or belong to the created order.[16] This law addresses the beliefs of people from a culture inundated with the polytheistic view of the world; it does not affirm that other gods actually exist.

The First Commandment in the Old Testament

The teaching of the first commandment permeates the Holy Scriptures, both Old Testament and New Testament. The prohibition

[13] See W. Keszler, "Die Literarische, Historische und Theologische Problematik des Dekalogs," VT 7 (1957): 9; and more recently M. Heiser, "Monotheism, Polytheism, Monolatry, or Henotheism?" BBR 18,1 (2008): 1–30, esp. 25, 27.

[14] I. Hinneman, "אַחְדּוּת הָאֱלֹהִים," EncMiqr 1:204 [in Hb.].

[15] The Religion of Israel, 149–51. See Rabbi D. Wax, ed., The Ten Commandments (Lakewood, NJ: Taryag Legacy Foundation, 2005), 71–72.

[16] A. S. Hartom and M. D. Cassuto, "Exodus" and "Leviticus" in Torah, Prophets, Writings (Tel Aviv: Yavneh, 1977), 71 [in Hb.]; I. Hinneman, "אַחְדּוּת הָאֱלֹהִים," 1:204. See also Rashi and Ibn Ezra in Miqráot Gedolot, 5 vols. (Jerusalem: Eshkol, 1976), 1:83–84 [in Hb.]; M. Carasik, מקראות גדולות. The Commentators' Bible: The JPS Miqra'ot Gedolot. Exodus (Philadelphia: Jewish Publication Society, 2005), 157; C. Wright, The Mission of God (Downers Grove, IL: InterVarsity, 2006), 82, 153, 161–62.

regarding worship of other gods is seen in Exod 22:20[19], which forbids sacrificing to another god; Exod 23:13, which bars mention of the names of other gods; Exod 34:14, which forbids bowing down to another god; and Deut 11:16, which forbids serving or worshipping other gods. The violation of the first commandment in the making of the golden calf was such a gross transgression of God's law that Moses smashed the tablets that contained all the Ten Commandments (Deut 9:17). But the worship of illicit gods did not stop in this early stage of Israel's history. [17]

Worship of Foreign Gods in Israel's Early History

The history of Israel was plagued by the sin of worshipping other gods. From the time of entering Canaan, the Israelites came under the influence of Canaanite religion and worshipped gods and goddesses such as Baal, Asherah, and Ashtoreth. The worship of Baal appears to have been widespread in the time of Judges (Judg 2:11; 3:7; 6:25, 29–30), when "everyone did whatever he wanted" (Judg 17:6; 21:25), as well as in the time of Samuel (1 Sam 7:3–4). Near the end of Solomon's reign, altars were built that were dedicated to the pagan gods Chemosh and Milcom (Molech) (1 Kgs 11:5–7). This practice was in sharp contrast with what Solomon articulated in his prayer at the dedication of the temple. On that occasion Solomon prayed that all nations would recognize Israel's God as the only God (1 Kgs 8:60). In response to Solomon's prayer, God promised that as long as the nation did not worship and serve other gods, the people could remain in the land and worship at the temple in Jerusalem (1 Kgs 9:6–8).

Worship of Foreign Gods in the Divided Kingdom

The downward trend of the worship of foreign gods did not retreat during the time of the divided kingdom (931–586 BC). In the northern kingdom of Israel, the worship of Baal gained such prominence that King Ahab built an altar to Baal and worshipped him in public (1 Kgs 16:31–32). Ahab's wife, Queen Jezebel, was supported

---

[17] Indeed, even before Israel's history began, the patriarch Abraham (Josh 24:2), his relatives (Gen 31:19), and his descendants (Gen 35:2) worshipped other gods.

by an entourage of 450 prophets of Baal and 400 prophets of Asherah (1 Kgs 18:19). The worship of Baal in the southern kingdom of Judah appears to have been introduced or at least enhanced by Jezebel's daughter, Queen Athaliah (2 Kgs 11:18).

The most atrocious promoter of the worship of other gods had to be King Manasseh, the son of Hezekiah. During Manasseh's reign the temple in Jerusalem became a virtual pantheon for foreign deities (2 Kgs 21). The atrocities taking place then in the nation's most holy site appear to be the basis for Ezekiel's visions (Ezek 8:1–11:25; 16:17; 20; 23). The worship of foreign gods during Manasseh's reign is specifically cited as the cause for the Babylonian exile (2 Kgs 23:26; Jer 11:9–10; 15:3–4).

Worship of Foreign Gods in the Prophetic Literature

The prophet Hosea criticized the worship of Baal in the northern kingdom (Hos 1:1–3:5; 11:2; 13:1) while Jeremiah in particular was critical of those who had chosen to pay homage to Baal in the southern kingdom (Jer 2:4–8; 9:12–16; 11:13,17; 12:16; 19:5; 23:13,27; 32:29). In addition, Sakkuth was worshipped in the northern kingdom (Amos 5:26) while Tammuz was worshipped by the Judeans (Ezek 8:14).[18] In the end both northern and southern kingdoms were defeated because their following after other gods was breaking the covenant in the most fundamental way.[19]

The First Commandment in the New Testament

The Old Testament perspective that there is only one God to be worshipped is also prevalent in the New Testament. This is seen most explicitly in the temptation of Christ. When Satan offered Jesus the kingdoms of the world if He would bow down to him, Jesus quoted Deut 6:13: "Worship the Lord your God, and serve only Him" (Matt 4:10). The New Testament is clearly monotheistic (Acts 17:22–31). God is one (Rom 3:30; 1 Cor 8:6; Gal 3:20; 1 Tim 2:5; Jas 2:19). The New Testament teaches that the worship of another god or a part of

---

[18] G. Bacon and S. Sperling, "Idolatry," *EJ* 9:710–11.
[19] Wright, *The Mission of God*, 381.

God's creation leads to perversion and separation from God (Rom 1:18–25). When Jesus was asked what was the greatest commandment, He began by pronouncing the Shema, "Listen, Israel! The Lord our God, the Lord is One" (Mark 12:29; cf. Deut 6:4).

God in Three Persons

The New Testament provides us clearer revelation of the nature of this one God. The Trinity is the designation for the one God revealed in Scripture as Father, Son, and Holy Spirit. This means that within the one essence of the Godhead there are three "persons" who are not three gods, or three modes of God, but equally and coeternally God.[20] God is one who exists in three distinct and coequal persons.[21] The Father is God, and the Son (John 1:1; 10:30; 14:9; Col 2:9) and the Spirit (Acts 5:3–4) are also fully God. We see additional evidence of the Trinity in Christian baptism and in Paul's benedictions to his epistles. Baptism is in the name of the Father, Son, and Holy Spirit (Matt 28:19), while Paul frequently closes his letters with a reference to all the members of the Trinity, suggesting they are equal (2 Cor 13:14; cf. Eph 4:4–6).[22]

Jesus Is God

The identification of Jesus with God was no small realization by the Jewish monotheistic writers of the New Testament. Yet they took this crucial issue head on. This was only possible because these writers identified Jesus with the one God of Israel. They maintained that Jesus was sovereign over all things (Matt 11:27; Luke 10:22; John 1:3; 3:35; 16:15; Acts 10:36; 1 Cor 15:27–28; Eph 1:22; Phil 3:21; Heb 1:2; 2:8; cf. Eph 1:9–10,22–23; 4:10; Col 1:19–20), that He had created all things (John 1:3; 1 Cor 8:6; Col 1:15–17; Heb 1:2), and that the unique name of God was to be applied to Him (Acts 2:17–21,38; 9:14; 22:16; Rom 10:9–13; 1 Cor 1:2; 2 Tim 2:22). He is worthy of worship

---

[20] G. W. Bromiley, "Trinity," *EDT* (1984), 1112–13.

[21] Many find Old Testament support for the doctrine of the Trinity in passages such as Gen 1:26 and Isa 48:16. W. Grudem, *Systematic Theology* (Leicester, England: InterVarsity, Grand Rapids: Zondervan, 1994), 226–37.

[22] See 1 Pet 1:2. R. L. Saucy, "God, Doctrine of," *EDT*, 502–3.

(Phil 2:9–11; Rev 4–5). For Jewish monotheists, these beliefs could only be true of one who was in fact God.[23] Moreover, Paul doesn't shy away from the chief Old Testament creedal statement about the oneness of God (Deut 6:4) when he identifies Jesus the Messiah as the Lord that the Shema declares to be one (1 Cor 8:6).[24] Jesus Christ is the image of the invisible God (Col 1:15). He is the express image of God (Heb 1:3) and has declared the God who had been unseen (John 1:18). Christians should not back away from the accusation that they believe in more than one God. Scripture clearly teaches the deity of each person of the Godhead.

Conclusion

In contrast with pagan and polytheistic gods, the God of the Bible is not in any way part of the creation. He is the Creator who stands outside the universe. He is wholly independent of the world He created and does not inhere in it.[25] Of modern religions, only Judaism, Christianity, and Islam affirm this truth; and these are all based on the revelation of the Old Testament, particularly the teaching of the first commandment and the Shema. The Bible is permeated by the truth that there is only one God. This doctrine is among the most important values that the biblical revelation bequeathed to the world. The first commandment could thus be viewed as the declaration of the basic principle of biblical law.[26] As the sages stated: "Whoever acknowledges a false god denies the entire Torah."[27]

God is both transcendent as He stands outside the universe, and immanent (Isa 57:15) as He is omnipresent.[28] The Jewish medieval scholar Rambam argued that faith is:

> to recognize the existence of a Being that predates the created world; that it
> was He Who brought all things, in Heaven and earth, into being; and that

---

[23] R. Bauckham, *God Crucified: Monotheism and Christology in the New Testament* (Grand Rapids: Eerdmans, 1998), 26, 32n7, 34.

[24] Ibid., 37–38.

[25] N. Sarna, *Exploring Exodus: The Origins of Biblical Israel* (New York: Schocken Books, 1996), 145.

[26] Hinneman, "אַחְדוּת הָאֱלֹהִים," 1:202,204; G. von Rad, *Deuteronomy: A Commentary* (London: SCM, 1966), 56.

[27] Wax, *The Ten Commandments*, 73.

[28] See R. Youngblood, "Monotheism," *EDT* (2001), 788–89.

there is not, anywhere in the universe, a creation that can for a moment remain in existence without the continued supply of His creative sustenance.[29]

God is absolutely supreme over the entire universe with no limitations on His sovereignty. He does not live in the processes of nature; He controls them.

Exclusive Worship

The prohibition against the worship of all but one deity was unique in religious history. The other nations of the world were polytheistic and thus innately tolerant of the views of others, as it was believed that no one god had absolute power and controlled all the phenomena of nature.[30] This same tolerance that characterized pagan cultures in the biblical period is now true of much of Western culture. Tolerance of other views, not truth, is thought to be the highest virtue in our time.[31] The biblical view of one God was not only a radical revelation in a polytheistic world, but it had positive repercussions in world history, including the possibility for modern science.[32] Of all the nations of the ancient world, Israel alone had a pervasive monotheistic outlook.[33] In the other pagan religions of the ancient Near East, the gods were dependent on the cult (religious ritual), whereas in Israel the religious deeds of the cult were only an expression of obedience to God's commandments.[34]

The demand for loyalty to agreements (covenants) in the ancient world was based on the potentate's benevolent deeds on behalf of his subjects. It was assumed that a people would be loyal to the sovereign who ruled over them. In the introduction to the Ten Commandments, God identified Himself as the sovereign who had delivered the nation

---

[29] Wax, *The Ten Commandments*, 53.

[30] The supposed gradual evolutionary progression from polytheism to monotheism has never been proven and cannot be documented. See Sarna, *Exploring Exodus: The Origins of Biblical Israel*, 150.

[31] For an exhaustive study of this modern cultural phenomenon, see D. A. Carson, *The Gagging of God* (Grand Rapids: Zondervan, 1996).

[32] F. Schaeffer, *How Should We Then Live?* (Old Tappan: Revell, 1976), 132.

[33] J. Oswalt, "Golden Calves and the 'Bull of Jacob': The Impact on Israel of Its Religious Environment," in *Israel's Apostasy and Restoration: Essays in Honor of Roland K. Harrison*, ed. A. Gileadi (Grand Rapids: Baker, 1988), 11.

[34] Kaufmann, "דָּת יִשְׂרָאֵל," 2:735–36.

from the bondage of slavery. Because God did this and because the Israelites as a consequence have a special relationship to the Lord as His people, they were not to have any other gods but the Lord.[35]

This basis for the exclusive worship of the Lord is maintained in other passages as well. For example, Judg 6:8–10 begins like the Ten Commandments in mentioning God's great deliverance of His people from Egypt and then immediately forbids any worship of the Canaanite gods. Similarly, Ps 81:9–10a begins with the command, "There must not be a strange god among you" and then states the reason, "I am Yahweh your God, who brought you up from the land of Egypt."[36] No doubt this statement is also an echo of the beginning verses of the Ten Commandments but in reverse order. This gracious act of deliverance should have been enough for Israel to submit to God's commands, as the Christian's deliverance from sin should cause the believer to live a life of commitment and obedience before the Lord (John 14:15). The first response to God's gracious provision as expressed in the first commandment is loyalty to the Lord. "Exclusivity is inherent in monotheism."[37] A person who is obedient to this command would be one whose life is dominated by his relationship to God. Every area of life and thought must be brought into obedience to the Lord.

> I, the Lord, am your God means I am *your* Creator, your Lawgiver, your Judge; the Director of your thoughts, your feelings, your words and your actions. Every one of your internal and external possessions has come to you from My hand; every breath of your life has been apportioned to you by Me. Look upon yourself and all that is yours as My property, and devote yourself wholly to Me. . . . Be the instrument of My will . . . and so join freely the choir of creation as My creature, My servant (Chorev 1:4).[38]

Jesus stated that in order for a person to be His disciple, He had to be preeminent even over one's family relations (Luke 14:26). A true follower of Christ must die to himself (Luke 14:27) and forsake what he possesses to become Christ's disciple (Luke 14:33). As Martin Luther said: "Whatever thy heart clings to and relies upon, that is properly

---

[35] According to Jewish tradition, the statement "I am the LORD your God" (Exod 20:2) is an *issur aseh* (an implied prohibition) that proscribes belief in other gods. See Wax, *The Ten Commandments*, 45.

[36] See Dohmen, *Exodus 19–40*, 104.

[37] R. A. Mohler Jr., *Words from the Fire* (Chicago: Moody, 2009), 41.

[38] Wax, *The Ten Commandments*, 53.

thy God."[39] Or as Duane Christensen has more recently stated: "Anything that relegates the relationship with God to second place functions in effect as 'another god.'"[40] A perennial chief rival to God seen in the New Testament as well as into modern times would have to be the temptation to make money into a god (Matt 6:24).

God must be acknowledged in all of our ways (Prov 3:6; 2 Cor 10:5). Even if a person were to give outward obedience to other commandments (including the Ten Commandments), if he did not obey this first commandment, his apparent obedience would be both unfounded and insincere. It is thus not an exaggeration to claim that the first commandment is the most important of all. The most rudimentary way to break the covenant is to profess allegiance to any other god.[41] Not having other gods is the chief principle of religion upon which all else depends.[42] Monotheism is generally regarded as biblical faith's greatest contribution to religious thought.[43] The ancient world believed in many gods. Our world believes in many ways to God; both are equally untrue.

Exclusive Salvation

There is only one God and only one way to know this God, through Jesus Christ. Salvation is by grace through faith (Eph 2:8–9). The notion of salvation by works is a pagan notion. One must begin with faith in the true God because apart from Him religion is nothing more than hollow moralism and humanism. When the existence of God is denied, there are no absolutes; everything becomes relative.

God desires to have an intimate personal relationship with human beings. To illustrate this intimacy, the inspired author used the imagery of marriage, the most personal of all human relationships.

[39] Quoted in M. Dunnam, Exodus, The Communicator's Commentary (Waco, TX: Word, 1987), 252–53.

[40] D. Christensen, Deuteronomy 1:1–21:9, rev. ed., WBC 6A (Nashville: Thomas Nelson, 2001), 115.

[41] T. Fretheim, Exodus, Interpretation: A Biblical Commentary for Teaching and Preaching (Louisville: John Knox, 1973), 224, and Wright, The Mission of God, 381.

[42] A. Hakam, The Book of Exodus (Jerusalem: Mossad Harav Kook, 1991) 297n34a [in Hb.].

[43] M. H. Vogel, "Monotheism," EJ 14:448.

Commandments two, five, and seven will also address the family relationship.

Excursus: *Pagan Gods in the Old Testament*

Even though other "gods" do not exist in reality, the belief in foreign gods was rampant in the ancient world. The Bible affirms that pagan gods do not exist; still, the people of God were influenced by belief in these gods. People from diverse ancient Near Eastern cultures worshipped these gods, and they became a temptation for the sons of Israel.

The god El was considered the father of the pantheon of Canaanite gods. The other Canaanite gods and goddesses were his progeny. Baal was the most popular male deity among the Canaanites. The term *ba'al,* means "lord" or "husband." Baal, known among other Semitic people groups as Hadad, was believed to be the son of El and Asherah; he is the god of the storm, war, fertility, and divination. Baal is mentioned several times in Scripture, and many local baals are mentioned such as Baal-berith (Judg 8:33; 9:4), who is also called El-berith (Judg 9:46), Baal-zebub[44] (2 Kgs 1:2,3), and Baal of Peor (Num 25:3,5).[45]

One of Baal's consorts appearing frequently in the Old Testament and in Phoenician inscriptions was known at Ugarit as Athtart.[46] She may have been known by the alternative name of Ashtoret (1 Kgs 11:5,33; see Judg 2:13). Asherah was considered the offspring of El (see 2 Kgs 21:7).[47] Fortune (Gad) and Destiny (Meni) may also have been worshipped among the Canaanites (Isa 65:11).

Dagon was a Sumerian god that was worshipped in Canaan and later by the Philistines (1 Sam 5:1-7; 1 Chr 10:10). Chemosh was the god of Moab (Num 21:29, etc.); Milcom, the god of the Ammonites (1 Kgs

---

[44] His Canaanite name was believed to be Baal-zebul.

[45] Numerous place names contain the name of Baal such as Bamot-baal (Num 22:41), Baal-gad (Josh 11:17), Baal-hazor (2 Sam 13:23; see Judg 3:7; Jer 2:23).

[46] Anat, the sister of Baal, is referred to in Ugaritic texts but is found in the Old Testament only in Hebrew names (Neh 10:19; 1 Chr 7:8; cf. 1 Chr 8:24; see Judg 3:31).

[47] The plural form of the name is rendered as Asheroth or Asherahs (see Judg 3:7; 2 Chr 24:18).

11:5; Jer 49:1,3), while Molech, whose influence was widespread in the ancient Near East, may have been worshipped among the Canaanites (Lev 18:21). Shemesh (Hb. "sun") may refer to a Canaanite deity in Deut 4:19; 17:3; 2 Kgs 23:5,11; Jer 8:2. The chief god of Edom is not mentioned in the Bible, but "the gods of Edom" are mentioned in 2 Chr 25:20. The temptation to worship the pagan gods of Canaan was perhaps the strongest because the Israelites were inhabitants of that land.

Several Mesopotamian gods are mentioned in the Bible. Bel is named in Isa 46:1; Jer 50:2; 51:44; also Succoth-benoth in 2 Kgs 17:30, Kaiwan in Amos 5:26, Marduk in Jer 50:2, Nebo in Isa 46:1,[48] Nisroch in 2 Kgs 19:37, Nergal in 2 Kgs 17:30, Sakkuth in Amos 5:26, and Tammuz in Ezek 8:14.[49]

Egyptian religion is of special interest to the study of the book of Exodus since the account of the plagues in Exod 7–12 was a validation of the Lord's supremacy and His judgment on the gods of Egypt (Exod 5:2; 7:5; 9:14–16; 12:12; Num 33:4; cf. Josh 9:9; 1 Sam 4:7–9).[50] Of the Egyptian gods, Amon is mentioned in Jer 46:25. Atum occurs in the names of the cities of Pithom (Exod 1:11) and Etham (Exod 13:20). Baset occurs in the name Pi-beseth in Ezek 30:17, the god Nut occurs in the name of Joseph's wife Asenath (Gen 41:45), and Ra in the name Rameses (Exod 1:11).

Gods of other nations include the Aramean god Ashima in 2 Kgs 17:30 and Rimmon in 2 Kgs 5:18. The Hurian god Aiah occurs as a personal name in Gen 36:24, and the Arabic god Jeush is also mentioned as a person's name (Gen 36:18).[51]

What is somewhat remarkable about this vast array of gods named in the Bible is the fact that nothing is mentioned about their alleged abilities or qualities. The Bible is purposely silent about any description of these gods. This is not important because the gods are in fact not part of reality.[52]

---

[48] The name of this god occurs in the name Nebuchadnezzar.

[49] Ishtar is believed to be the Mesopotamian (Akkadian) name for Esther.

[50] Sarna, *Exploring Exodus: The Origins of Biblical Israel*, 78–80.

[51] See M. D. Cassuto, "נְכָר אֱלֹהֵי,"*EncMiqr* 1:321–25 [in Hb.]; Clendenen, "Religious Background of the Old Testament," 283, 295–98.

[52] Kaufmann, *The Religion of Israel*, 9.

Chapter 2

THE SECOND COMMANDMENT

*Do not make an idol for yourself, whether in the shape of any-
thing in the heavens above or on the earth below or in the waters under the earth. You must not bow down to them or worship
them; for I, the LORD your God, am a jealous God, punishing the
children for the fathers' sin, to the third and fourth generations
of those who hate Me, but showing faithful love to a thousand
generations of those who love Me and keep My commands.*

Introduction

The practice of idolatry has been widespread throughout human history. Among Israel's neighbors in the ancient Near
East, both written and other material remains demonstrate
that idolatry was rampant in the cultures of Mesopotamia, Syro-
Palestine, Egypt, and the Roman Empire.[1] In paying homage to an
idol, the pagan worshipper believed that the life of a god was present
in the statue that represented the supposed deity. The gods somehow
entered every kind of stone, metal, or wooden statue. In bringing offerings of food and drink, the devotee gave evidence to the belief that
the image was alive with the spirit of the god.[2] Often and understand-
ably, the statue ceased to be thought of as a mere representation of the
god and came to be viewed as the god itself.[3]

The Meaning of the Second Commandment

The word for "idol" in the expression ("do not make an idol for
yourself") is the Hebrew *pesel*, the most common term for idol in the
Old Testament. The verbal meaning of the root is "to hew," or "carve
out." The verb is frequently used in reference to the carving of the two

---

[1] C. Dohmen, *Das Bilderverbot: Seine Entstehung und Entwicklung* (Bonn: Hanstein, 1985), 15.

[2] See P. C. Craigie, "Idolatry," *EDT* (2001), 588; E. Curtis, "Idol, Idolatry," *ABD* 3:377; and
H. Frankfort, J. A. Wilson, T. Jacobsen, and W. A. Irwin, *The Intellectual Adventure of Ancient
Man* (Chicago: The University of Chicago Press, 1946), 64.

[3] M. Halbertal and A. Margalit, *Idolatry*, trans. N. Goldblum (Cambridge, MA: Harvard University Press, 1992), 42.

stone tablets on which the Ten Commandments were written (Exod 34:1,4; Deut 10:1,3). The verb is also used to describe Solomon's and Hiram's builders who "quarried" stone to lay the foundation of the temple (1 Kgs 5:18 [32]). Thus an idol is something that is "hewn" or "carved out" of wood, stone, or even metal (Isa 40:19; 44:10).

The prohibition against the worship of idols is clarified by the phrase "whether in the shape of anything in the heavens above or on the earth below or in the waters under the earth." The word translated "shape" (*tĕmûnâ*) is another term for "idol" and occurs ten times in the Old Testament. The nature of the relationship between *pesel* and *tĕmûna* is debated. William Propp suggests that in *pesel* we find stress on the material nature of the statue or image, while in *tĕmûna* the emphasis is on the shape or form.[4] Amos Hakam, on the other hand, believes the terms are distinguished based on their perceived depth. The term *tĕmûnâ* refers to a two-dimensional object, such as a drawing on a wall or rock, while *pesel* refers to a three–dimensional object.[5] A third view is that the terms are synonymous, and their occurrence together in this passage indicates "any kind of idol." In the second commandment in Deut 5 the term *tĕmûna* also occurs, but without the *waw*, indicating the word is appositional and explains the meaning of *pesel*.[6]

Regardless, the point is clear that idols were prohibited in the God-created universe, which is divided into three open spaces. Images are not to be made that resemble anything God has created in the heavens, on the earth, or under the earth. These same three open spaces are mentioned in the creation account in Gen 1 and are a reminder that God created all things and now rules over the universe. This reminder in itself strongly suggests that no one is to be worshiped but

---

[4] W. Propp, *Exodus 19–40*, AB 2A (New York: Doubleday, 2006), 167. Propp's explanation is in harmony with the HCSB translation. The LXX translates תְּמוּנָה seven times by ὁμοίωμα (likeness), twice by δόξα (glory), and once by μορφή (form). This may indicate that physical shape was understood not to be the primary nuance of the term. See W. Kaiser Jr., "Exodus," in *The Expositor's Bible Commentary,* vol. 2, ed. F. Gaebelein (Grand Rapids: Zondervan, 1990), 422.

[5] A. Hakam, *The Book of Exodus* (Jerusalem: Mossad Harav Kook, 1991), 279n35 [in Hb.].

[6] See W. Zimmerli, "Das zweit Gebot," in *Festschrift für Alfred Bertholet* (Tübingen: Mohr [Siebeck], 1950), 551n3. It is a characteristic of Deuteronomy to add explanatory appositions to ensure that entire categories are included (see Deut 4:19; 15:21; 16:21; 17:1; 23:20). M. Weinfeld, *Deuteronomy 1–11*, AB, vol. 5 (New York: Doubleday, 1991), 290.

God alone.[7] Nevertheless, the wording of Exod 20:4 (and Deut 5:8) condemns idolatry in the most comprehensive fashion.[8]

Other Hebrew words for "idol" include *massēkâ, nesek,* and *nāsîk,* all related to the root *nāsak,* "to pour out." Not surprisingly, these words refer primarily to molten images. Another Hebrew term for an image is *gillûlîm* (e.g. Jer 50:2; Ezek 22:3–4). This noun is a cognate to the verb *gālal,* which means "roll." The noun *gēl* thus refers to something cylindrical that will roll and is often associated with "dung" (Job 20:7; Ezek 4:12,15; see 1 Kgs 14:10). Thus the idols are often referred to as "dung pellets."[9] Another term, *'ĕlîlîm,* suggests an association with the adjective *'ĕlîl,* "weak, worthless,"[10] whereas the term *hebel,* prominent in the book of Ecclesiastes, has the meaning of "vapor, mist," but is also used to refer to idols. The meaning of these terms along with their pejorative evaluation in biblical texts indicates that idols and idolatry were viewed with disdain by biblical authors. Ps 115:4–7 is illustrative:

> Their idols are silver and gold,
> made by human hands.
> They have mouths, but cannot speak,
> eyes, but cannot see.
> They have ears, but cannot hear,
> noses, but cannot smell.
> They have hands, but cannot feel,
> feet, but cannot walk.
> They cannot make a sound
>   with their throats.
> Those who make them are just
>   like them,
> as are all who trust in them.[11]

Worship of Idols

Not only are we not to make any image of a god, but we are also forbidden to bow down and worship an existing image (Exod 20:5).

---

[7] Hakam, *The Book of Exodus,* 279–80.
[8] Weinfeld, *Deuteronomy 1–11,* 291.
[9] E. Curtis, "Idol, Idolatry," *ABD* 3:378.
[10] Ibid.
[11] See 1 Kgs 18:27–29.

The word translated "bow down" (*ḥwh*) is a unique verb in that it is the only root attested in the rare *shafel* stem in the Old Testament.[12] The verb occurs 170 times in the Old Testament with the meaning of "bow down" or "prostrate oneself," whether out of respect to a human superior or in obeisance to a god. For example, the Israelites "bowed down" to the image of the golden calf (Exod 32:8). They bowed to the *ʾĕlîlîm* made by human hands (Isa 2:8) and to a carved image (Isa 44:15,17). "Bowing down" is a religious gesture that conveys homage and reverence. Idolatry involves "bowing down" in reference to the worship of the stars (Deut 4:19; Jer 8:2) and the worship in a pagan temple (2 Kgs 5:18). But it is fitting for worshippers to "bow down" to Yahweh, the true God (Gen 24:26,48,52; Ps 99:9). Many times this action of bowing down includes placing one's face to the ground (Gen 18:2; 19:1; 24:52; 42:6; Isa 49:23).

We are not only not to bow before idols but also not to "worship them" or "serve them" (*ʿbd*). The root (*ʿbd*) often occurs with *ḥwh* (bow down) in reference to the worship of other gods.[13] The verb *ʿbd* ("worship") frequently has Yahweh as its object. We see this early in the book of Exodus as we learn that the Israelites will worship God on Mount Sinai (Exod 3:12; 4:23; 7:16; 8:1[7:26]; 8:20[16]; 9:1,13; 10:3,7,8,11,24,26; 12:31).[14] For the Israelites to turn back after being delivered from Egyptian bondage (*ʿăbādîm*) and serve other gods would be to reverse the exodus.[15]

The verb *ʿbd* ("serve") can be distinguished from the verb *ḥwh* ("bow down") by the fact that *ḥwh* refers to prostration, whereas

---

[12] See *HALOT* 1:296–97, and H. D. Preuss, "חוה *ḥwh*," *TDOT* 4:249. The existence of this Hebrew root is supported by the fact that the same root occurs in Ugaritic. See H. Stähli, "חוה *ḥwh*," *TLOT* 1:398.

[13] See Exod 20:5; 23:24; Deut 4:19; 5:9; 8:19; 11:16; 29:25(26); 30:17; Josh 23:7,16; Judg 2:19; 1 Kgs 9:6,9; 2 Kgs 17:35; 21:3,21; Jer 8:2; 13:10; 16:11; 22:9; 25:6; 2 Chr 7:19,22; 33:3. None of these passages refer to bowing down and worshipping an image. This may indicate that the biblical writers did not make a distinction between the images and the gods they represented. C. Wright, *The Mission of God* (Downers Grove, IL: InterVarsity, 2006), 152.

[14] The proper "worship" of the Lord is also a central concern in the book of Deuteronomy, where it frequently is mentioned in the context of "loving" (*ʾāhab*) God (Deut 6:13; 10:12,20; 13:4[5]).

[15] E. Merrill, *Deuteronomy*, NAC (Nashville: B&H, 1994), 147–48. The direct object "them" (Exod 20:5) is most commonly taken as referring to the idols, although it is not impossible that the suffix includes not only the idols but the other gods in Exod 20:3.

ʿbd often refers to making offerings (Exod 10:26; Isa 19:21). As with ḥwh ("to bow down"), the word for worship (ʿbd) has a nontheological usage as it refers to serving kings and political suzerains, which may involve paying tribute (Gen 27:29; Ps 72:11).[16]

What must be clarified in any discussion of the second commandment is whether this prohibition refers to making an idol of the Lord (Yahweh), or whether it prohibits making images in general (to any other so-called god). The first commandment teaches that Yahweh is the only God, and no others are to be tolerated, or even thought of. The second commandment either declares how this God is to be worshipped, or more generally prohibits the manufacture and worship of any kind of image. Worshipping an image of Yahweh would be blasphemous in the sense that one would confuse the Creator with part of His creation.[17] God is infinitely greater than any attempt to portray Him in His creation.

Many scholars who take the former position suggest that the golden calf incident, which occurs shortly after the giving of the Ten Commandments, is a narrative commentary on the second commandment. The people, demoralized by Moses' delay in returning from the top of Mount Sinai, demanded that Aaron make them an idol in place of Yahweh. It is argued that the golden calf was an image of Yahweh, the God of Israel.[18] The golden calf is often viewed as "the epitome of idolatry in the Bible."[19] Much of the content of Exodus 34 at the conclusion of the golden calf incident in fact looks back on the Ten Commandments.

Yet I believe the stronger position is the more general and broader view that the prohibition is against the worshipping of images not only of Yahweh but of other gods as well. The Bible does not distinguish between idols of the Lord and idols of other gods.[20]

---

[16] The form appears to be a Hophal imperfect verb. According to Nielsen, this analysis is confirmed by the reading from the DSS (E. Nielsen, *Deuteronomium*, HAT [Tübingen: J. C. B. Mohr, 1995]), 72, 77. Dohmen believes that the nuance of the Hophal suggests the seduction of the cult of the foreign god. C. Dohmen, *Exodus 19–40* (Freiburg: Herder, 2004), 109. Similarly, see Weinfeld, *Deuteronomy 1–11,* 277, and GKC § 60b.

[17] M. Noth, *Exodus*, OTL (Philadelphia: Westminster, 1962), 162–63.

[18] Y. Kaufmann, "דָּת יִשְׂרָאֵל," *EncMiqr* 2:745 [in Hb.].

[19] Halbertal and Margalit, *Idolatry,* 3. The golden calf incident, which occurs after the seven sections that pertain to the construction of the tabernacle, is in this way like the fall of man in Genesis 3, which occurs shortly after the seven-day creation.

[20] Y. Kaufmann, *The Religion of Israel: From Its Beginnings to the Babylonian Exile,* trans. and

God is a Jealous God

The reason the Israelites were not to engage in this idolatrous activity was "for (*kî*)[21] I, the LORD your God, am a jealous God" (20:5). The particle *kî* ("for") creates a link between two clauses stating the reason an action or situation takes place, or providing the reason or motivation something should be done.[22] The latter seems to be in view in Exod 20:5.

The root of the adjective "jealous" is *qn'*, which appears about 85 times in the Old Testament. It is often argued that the concrete, non-theological use of the term came from the realm of marriage when a spouse might become "jealous" of his partner who is suspected of adultery. This usage is found in two biblical contexts, Num 5:14,30 and Prov 6:34–35. Exodus 20:5 qualifies as a theological usage, as the term depicts God's reaction to Israel's violation of the *běrît* ("covenant").

This link to the marriage relationship echoes the first commandment in that the covenant between God and his people Israel is comparable to the marriage covenant between a man and a woman, and it prepares for the fifth commandment as well as the seventh.[23] God will be jealous when His people worship another god, like a man who is jealous over his wife because of her lover.[24] God becomes jealous when His people worship other gods and idols (Exod 34:14; Deut 4:24; 6:15; 32:16,21; Ps 78:58; cf. Josh 24:19; 1 Kgs 14:22).[25] We may understand the jealousy of God as his fervent and passionate protection of what is rightfully His. He will not transfer the honor

---

abridged by M. Greenberg (New York: Schocken Books, 1960), 9–20, 236–37, and M. Greenberg, "The Tradition Critically Examined," in *The Ten Commandments in History and Tradition*, ed. B. Z. Segal (Jerusalem: Magnes, 1990), 100.

[21] The causal use of the particle כִּי is its most common usage in Hebrew. See *IBHS* § 38.4.

[22] B. Arnold and J. Choi, *A Guide to Biblical Hebrew Syntax* (New York: Cambridge, 2003), 149.

[23] Hakam, *The Book of Exodus*, 280. See Hos 1–3; Jer 2:32; 3:1–13,20; Isa 50:1; 54:4–7; 62:4–5. Thus the marriage bond functions as an implied metaphor in descriptions of the relationship God has with His people. Moreover, the Hb. term for covenant (בְּרִית) is also used of the marriage bond (Prov 2:16–17; Ezek 16:8; Mal 2:14). See chapter 1 of this work.

[24] A. Ehrlich, "Exodus," in *Miqrâ Ki-Peshutô* (New York: KTAV, 1969), 172 [in Hb.]. Weinfeld suggests that the basic meaning of the root קָנָא applies to passionate love (*Deuteronomy 1–11*, 295–96).

[25] Jealousy could be defined as a passionate zeal to protect a relationship. J. Vines, *Basic Bible Sermons on the Ten Commandments* (Nashville: Broadman Press, 1992), 25.

that is due Him to something else (Isa 42:8; 48:11) nor tolerate the worship of any other god (Exod 34:14). Just as a husband refuses to share his wife with another man, God refuses to share His people with another god. This act of unfaithfulness on the part of God's people is as repugnant as adultery. The relationship between a husband and wife is the principal image used by the prophets for the explication of idolatry.[26]

At the conclusion of the phrase that refers to God as a "jealous God," Werner Schmidt has observed the following chiastic pattern in Exod 20:2–5a:

> I am Yahweh, your God . . .
>> You shall have no other gods before me.
>>> You shall not make an image or any form
>> You shall not serve them or worship them;
> For I, Yahweh, your God am a jealous God.[27]

According to this layout, the central point of these verses is in the phrase "not make an image or any form." The interconnectedness of this structure would lend support to the position that the prohibition against worshipping other gods and idols is part of the same commandment.[28] If this analysis is accepted, the phrase "for I, the LORD your God, am a jealous God" would then function as the grounds of obedience in the first two commandments. Alternatively, the phrase "I am the LORD your God" (Exod 20:2) would serve as the incentive to obey the first commandment while "for I, the LORD your God" would serve as the motivation for not worshipping idols.[29]

Repercussions of Idolatry

As a jealous God (Exod 34:14; Deut 6:15; Josh 24:19), the LORD punishes the idolatrous acts of the fathers to the third and fourth generations[30] of those who hate Him. The verb "punish" is a translation

---

[26] Halbertal and Margalit, *Idolatry*, 11.

[27] *Die Zehn Gebot im Rahmen alttestamentlicher Ethik* (Darmstadt: Wissenschaftliche Buchgesellschaft, 1993), 65 (author's translation).

[28] Ibid. Similarly, G. André, *Determining the Destiny: PQD in the Old Testament* (Lund, Sweden: CWK Gleerup, 1980), 93.

[29] Weinfeld, *Deuteronomy 1–11*, 294.

[30] The word "generations" is not in the Hebrew text but is supported by the LXX, Vulgate,

of the Hebrew root *pāqad,* which occurs in contexts describing the covenant relationship between God and Israel. The term is used to describe God's response to the covenant people's obedience or disobedience. It can be translated "care for, attend, help" as a reward for obedience (Gen 50:24–25; Exod 4:31; Ruth 1:6; Jer 15:15; Zeph 2:7) or "punish" as here for sins of disobedience (see Exod 32:34; Lev 18:25; 1 Sam 15:2; Isa 13:11; Hos 4:14).[31] In the book of Exodus, the term has been used to describe God's visitation on behalf of Israel in order to punish Egypt (Exod 3:16; 4:31; 13:19). Now, however, God will "visit" the Israelites if they are disobedient to His command.[32]

The punishment is for the "fathers' sin" of idolatry. The word translated "sin" in this passage is the Hebrew *ʿāwōn,* attested about 230 times in the Old Testament. The verb related to this term means "bend, curve, turn aside, or twist." The verb is used in Ps 38:6(7) in the phrase "I am bent over (*naʿăwêtî*) and brought low." It refers to something that is not straight or as it should be. In the moral realm the idea is that of perversion that leads to a long-lasting consequence.[33] In the theological sense the word refers to moral aberrations and is often translated as "transgress, incur guilt, sin."[34]

Idolatry will have a long-lasting effect on a person's descendants, even on great-grandchildren and great-great-grandchildren.[35] The text does not say that God holds one's descendant, a son or a grandson, personally responsible for his father's sins (Ezek 18:20). Nor does this text say that the generational extension of punishment has anything to do with the legal administration of justice. But the text does hold out the threat that one's descendants may suffer for their parents' sin.[36] As Walter Kaiser has well stated: "No *external* condemnation can be laid

Targum Onqelos, Targum Neofiti, and Syriac versions. A similar omission of the equivalent to "generation" in referring to the "fourth generation" occurs in 2 Kgs 15:12.

[31] T. Williams, "פקד," *NIDOTTE* 3:658–59. Over one-third of the usages of the term refer to military preparation or tax censuses.

[32] P. Enns, *Exodus,* The NIV Application Commentary (Grand Rapids: Zondervan, 2000), 415.

[33] The first occurrence of the term, in Gen 4:13, illustrates the close connection between the transgression and the enduring punishment.

[34] K. Koch, "עָוֹן *ʿāwōn,*" *TDOT* 10:546–47.

[35] The language of this verse is echoed in Exod 34:7 and Num 14:18, which refer to the third and fourth "generation."

[36] The sins of Solomon were visited upon his son Rehoboam, as the kingdom was taken from him (1 Kgs 11:11–13).

on either the parents or the children by the other party, even though God does often allow some *temporal* punishments to come to children for the sake of parents."[37] This type of punishment may take place when the sin involves: (1) national guilt and shame (1 Sam 15:2), (2) rejection of a message or the messenger (Matt 23:35), (3) fraud and extortion of another person's good name and property (2 Kgs 10:1,7,10), and (4) causing the enemies of God to blaspheme His name (2 Sam 12:14).[38]

This threat of harm to one's descendants functions as a powerful deterrent as one naturally grieves over the affliction of his children and grandchildren more than his own hardship.[39] The notion that others are affected by one's sins is not foreign to the Old Testament (Lev 26:29; Josh 7:22–26; Lam 5:7).[40]

Those who are guilty of idolatry are further described as those who "hate" God. Since the Lord demands exclusive loyalty, those guilty of idolatry are in effect rejecting Him.[41] Those who hate God are those who have transgressed His will as they do not keep His commandments.

Repercussions for Faithfulness

By sharp contrast, those who refuse to bow the knee to an idol and remain loyal to the true God find that God shows "faithful love to a thousand generations of those who love Me and keep My commands." "Faithful love" is a translation of *hesed*, an important theological word

---

[37] W. Kaiser Jr., *Toward Old Testament Ethics* (Grand Rapids: Zondervan, 1983), 87 (italics his).

[38] Ibid. The Jewish medieval commentator Nahmanides argued that such a passage as Isa 14:21 does indicate that God punishes children for their parents' sins. See M. Carasik, מקראות גדולות. *The Commentators' Bible: The JPS Miqráot Gedolot. Exodus* (Philadelphia: Jewish Publication Society, 2005), 158.

[39] See U. Cassuto, *A Commentary on the Book of Exodus,* trans. I. Abrahams (Jerusalem: Magnes, 1974), 243. The fourth generation may have shared the same basic residence as the grandfather in Israelite society (Job 42:16; see Gen 50:23).

[40] See for example, D. J. Wiseman, "Law and Order in Old Testament Times," *Vox Evangelica* 8 (1973): 16; and J. Tigay, *Deuteronomy*, JPS Torah Commentary (Philadelphia: Jewish Publication Society, 1996), 66. There is a strong Jewish tradition as reflected in the Aramaic Targumim that the retribution is extended to subsequent generations if they too are guilty of idolatry. Among Christians, Douglas Stuart agrees that the successive generations who continue the sins of their parents are those who are to be punished. See D. Stuart, *Exodus*, NAC (Nashville: Broadman & Holman, 2006), 454.

[41] Tigay, *Deuteronomy*, 66, 357.

that speaks of God's faithfulness to those with whom He has a covenant relationship. It is often rendered by English terms such as "goodness," "grace," or "kindness." The word *ḥesed* describes the love of God toward His people within the relationship of the covenant (Deut 7:9,12; see also 1 Kgs 8:23; Neh 1:5; 9:32; Dan 9:4).[42] When the people of God are in need of deliverance, there is a particular appeal to God's *ḥesed* (Neh 13:22; Ps 6:4[5]; 44:26[27]; 109:21,26; 119:149).

The word *ḥesed* is so associated with God's faithfulness that the term can refer to God Himself (Ps 144:2; cf. Jon 2:8[9]). Because the Lord is omnipresent, His *ḥesed* fills the earth (Ps 33:5; 119:64). Moreover, because at the heart of the term *ḥesed* is its use in the covenant relationship, the term also expresses what God expects from His people (Mic 6:8; see Hos 6:6). In this context of the Ten Commandments, God's *ḥesed* could be considered the opposite, as well as remedy, to man's *ʿāwōn*. The contrast continues with regard to the faithful God and unfaithful action of the idolater.

Whereas man's sin may have negative repercussions unto the fourth generation, God's faithfulness extends to a thousand generations "of those who love Me and keep[43] My commands" (20:6). "A thousand generations" may be a figurative expression for the end of time or "forever."[44] As a result of the good deeds that men do, God will reward their offspring for all time, whereas the retribution on those who do evil deeds will continue only until the fourth generation. Good families can last until a thousand generations but bad families often do not make it to the fifth generation (Gen 15:16; 2 Kgs 15:12).[45] A holy and righteous God cannot wink at sin, but this verse

---

[42] P. Craigie, *The Book of Deuteronomy* (Grand Rapids: Eerdmans, 1976), 155n7. The occurrence of חסד in the phrase עשׂה חסד indicates the tangible nature of the concept associated with חסד. See H. Stoebe, "חסד ḥesed," *TLOT* 2:453.

[43] The verb שׁמר that occurs in the phrase "keep My commands" has the meaning of "paying careful attention to." The verb was first used in reference to Adam's responsibility to "keep" the garden (Gen 2:15) but was also commonly used in the expression of "keeping" the Sabbath as well as other feast days. See K. Schoville, "שׁמר," *NIDOTTE* 4:182, and G. Sauer, "שׁמר šmr," *TLOT* 3:1382.

[44] A. S. Hartom and M. D. Cassuto, "Exodus" and "Leviticus" in *Torah, Prophets, Writings* (Tel Aviv: Yavneh, 1977), 71 [in Hb.]. The term "generation" is once again not in the text but is understood based on parallels with the phrase. See Deut 7:9, where דור ("generation") does occur with the word "thousand."

[45] Thus Bekhor Shor. See M. Carasik, מקראות גדולות. *The Commentators' Bible*, 158.

stresses God's magnanimous grace, as the blessings for obedience are infinitely greater than His judgments for disobedience.

We also see the biblical truth that love for God is demonstrated in the keeping of His commands (Deut 5:10; 6:1–5; 10:12–13; 11:1,22–23; 26:18; Neh 1:5; Dan 9:4; John 14:15). The "love of God continues to mean in essence faithfulness to Yahweh's covenant, which must be made real by keeping the commandments."[46] Thus loving God and keeping His commandments are one and the same. The behavior of those who love God is characterized by obedience to God's laws, while a man cannot be considered to love God if he does not keep His commands.[47] The fact that love can be commanded of the believer (Deut 6:5; 10:12; 11:1,13,22; 19:9; 30:16,19–20; Josh 22:5; 23:10–11) proves that love is not an emotional feeling but a behavior characterized by obedience and commitment to the Lord.[48]

The term for law or command in this verse is the Hebrew *miṣwâ*.[49] This term has a relatively wide range of meaning as it can refer to "laws" in a general sense (Gen 26:5) or to the Mosaic legislation (Neh 1:5,7,9). In Deuteronomy, *miṣwâ* refers to the contents of the entire book as well as the total legal contents of the covenant (Deut 4:2; 6:1; 11:8; 15:5; 19:9).[50] In the DSS it refers to the Torah as a whole.[51] Keeping God's commandments would characterize a person who loves God, who lives a life of consistency in obedience to God's commands including not worshipping idols. The Pentateuch emphasizes the admonition to observe the commandments and decrees of the Lord

---

[46] P. Els, "אהב," *NIDOTTE* 1:286.

[47] See Hakam, *The Book of Exodus*, 281.

[48] See Els, "אהב," 1:287.

[49] Whereas in Exod 20:6 we find the reading מִצְוֹתַי "my commandments," in Deut 5:10 we read מִצְוֺתָו "His commandments." There is external evidence, including the Qere reading of the MT, that the reading מִצְוֹתַי "my commandments" is the best and the original. Nielsen prefers the Deuteronomy reading based on the text-critical principle that the more difficult reading should be preferred. See Nielsen, *Deuteronomium*, 72.

[50] The LXX almost always translates מִצְוָה with ἐντολή. In Deut 4:2; 11:8; 15:5; 19:9; Neh 1:5,7,9, the term also occurs with the verb שמר as in Exod 20, with the idea of "keep My commandments." The term also refers to the cultic regulations in the book of Leviticus (4:2,22,27; 5:17). The technical phrase אֶת שַׁבְּתֹתַי תִּשְׁמֹרוּ "observe My Sabbaths" (Exod 31:12[13]; Lev 19:3,30; 26:2; see also Isa 56:4), also contains the verb שמר. See discussion in chapter 4 of this work.

[51] See G. von Rad, *Old Testament Theology*, 2 vols. (New York: Harper & Row, 1962) 1:220; B. Levine, "מִצְוָה *miṣwâ*," *TDOT* 8:513–14; P. Enns, "מִצְוָה," *NIDOTTE* 2:1070.

(Lev 22:31; Deut 4:40; 6:2; 26:17), and this admonition is repeated in the Prophets (Josh 22:5; 1 Sam 13:14; 1 Kgs 2:3; 11:34; 2 Kgs 17:37; Jer 35:18; Ezek 18:19), and the Writings (Ps 119:8; Prov 4:4).[52]

One who loves God walks in His ways (Deut 10:12; 11:22; 19:9; 30:16; Josh 22:5). We find in Deut 8:6 that the expression "keep His commandments" is parallel to the phrase "to walk in His ways." "Love the Lord" is also parallel to the expression "keep His commandments," demonstrating the intrinsic equivalence of loving God and keeping His commands (e.g., Exod 20:6; Deut 5:10; Neh 1:5; Dan 9:4). Those who refrain from paying homage to idols are described as those who love God.

Three passages in the Pentateuch echo the terminology and teaching of the second commandment. Exodus 34:7 and Num 14:18 refer to the iniquity of the fathers that brings punishment for the third and fourth generations, and God's loyal love (*ḥesed*) to thousands, while Deut 7:9 refers to God's loyal love (*ḥesed*) for a thousand generations (*dôr*) to those who love Him and keep His commandments (*miṣwâ*).[53] The contrast is "between God's boundless beneficence and the limited extent of His punishment."[54]

The Second Commandment in the Old Testament

There are numerous parallels or echoes of the prohibition against worshipping images in the legal literature of the Old Testament (Exod 20:23; 34:17; Lev 19:4; 26:1; Deut 4:15–19,25; 27:15). One context that helps shed light on the meaning of the second commandment occurs in Deut 4 before Moses gives the Ten Commandments to the new generation that is about to enter the promised land. Deuteronomy 4:9–20 expands on the rationale for the prohibition against idolatry. In that passage Moses informs the Israelites that when God appeared to the

---

[52] See Schoville, "שמר," 4:183.

[53] The guilty in ancient Israelite society would be likely to see their grandchildren and great-grandchildren in their own lifetimes. The reference to "a thousand generations" is another way of saying "to the end of all generations." The use of the word for generation in Deut 7:9 (דור) as the object of "thousand" may support the idea that "third," "fourth," and "thousand" referred to generations in the Ten Commandments.

[54] N. Sarna, *Exodus*, JPS Torah Commentary (Philadelphia, New York: Jewish Publication Society, 1991), 110–11.

people on Mount Horeb, He did not reveal Himself in a physical form; rather, the only tangible manifestation of God was His voice (Deut 4:12). Because the people saw no shape (*tĕmûnâ*) but only heard God's word, they were not to make an image (*pesel*) in the shape (*tĕmûnat*) of any idol (Deut 4:15–16). God makes Himself known through His voice, not through any physical form. Thus, images are inappropriate ways to represent God.[55] Any symbolic representation of God by its very nature must be both inadequate and a distortion. God cannot be depicted in any material form because He is separate from and far superior to the material world. The legal literature prohibits all forms of idolatry; indeed, the Israelites were instructed to eradicate both idolaters and their idols when they arrived in Canaan (Deut 7:16,25).

The war against idolatry in the Old Testament is part of the story of the struggle against the foreign nations who tried to seduce the Israelites to follow their idolatrous practices.[56] Idolatry was the primary form of temptation for the Israelites throughout their history.[57] The welfare and destiny of the nation was directly connected to the avoidance of the sin of idolatry (1 Sam 12:20–25; 1 Kgs 11:1–12:33; 2 Kgs 21:1–17; 24:3–4).[58] This sin, along with the worship of other gods, led to the collapse of the northern kingdom by the hand of the Assyrians (2 Kgs 17:7–23).

War Against Idolatry in Israel's Early History

In the book of Judges, a man named Micah possessed an image (*pesel*), and apparently he and the Danites advocated the worship of this idol in a private shrine (Judg 18:1–31).[59] Earlier in Judges, Gideon's ephod became an idol, an object of worship (Judg 8:26–27). A similar

---

[55] B. Childs, *The Book of Exodus: A Critical-Theological Commentary* (Louisville: Westminster John Knox, 1974), 407. The prohibition against worshipping the terrestrial bodies may lend support to the notion that the prohibition of idolatry included idols of other "gods," not only images of the real God. In addition, the reversal of the created order in Deut 4—human beings, land animals, birds, fish, and heavenly bodies—may reflect on the serious nature of idolatry, as the whole created order appears to be turned upside down. See Wright, *The Mission of God*, 382.

[56] Halbertal and Margalit, *Idolatry*, 69.

[57] P. Craigie, "Idolatry," *EDT*, (2001), 589.

[58] Y. Kaufmann, "דָּת יִשְׂרָאֵל," 2:753.

[59] E. Curtis, "Idol, Idolatry," *ABD* 3:379.

occurrence took place with regard to the bronze serpent that Moses made in the wilderness (2 Kgs 18:4; Num 21:4–9). Jeroboam I (1 Kgs 12:28–33) introduced at Bethel and Dan a form of Yahweh worship that included images of bulls. This practice was meant to counter the influence of the temple at Jerusalem and orthodox worship. The description of the images echoes the language used in describing the worship of the golden calf (Exod 32:8), indicating that this was idolatrous and illicit worship.[60] It was recognized as a covenant violation, and was viewed by the prophets and the faithful as an act of idolatry (1 Kgs 13:33–34; see 1 Kgs 16:32–33; 2 Kgs 3:2).[61]

War Against Idolatry in the Prophetic Literature

The time of the classical prophets was the period of the universal reign of idolatry. This is seen time after time during the reigns of Assyrian, Babylonian, and Persian kings. The people of Israel allowed themselves to be assimilated to these foreign cultures and were overtaken by the universal reign of idolatry.[62] The prophets, based on their belief in the only true God and inspired by their commission from God, declared war on idolatry. The Israelites of the northern kingdom were guilty of erecting images (Hos 3:4; see 2 Kgs 17:16). But the southern kingdom was guilty as well. Isaiah denounced idolatry in the southern kingdom in the eighth century BC (40:18–20; 41:21–29; 42:8,17; 44:9–20; 45:16,20; 46:1,6–7). In Isa 44:9–17 the prophet mocks both the manufacturer of an idol and the confidence the idolater has in idol worship:

> All who make idols [pesel] are nothing,
> And what they treasure does not profit.
> Their witnesses do not see
>   or know |anything|,
> so they will be put to shame.
> Who makes a god or casts
>   a metal image [pesel]

[60] See C. Carmichael, *The Origins of Biblical Law: The Decalogues and the Book of the Covenant* (Ithaca and London: Cornell University Press, 1992), 28–29.

[61] The description of Jeroboam's cultic images as other gods and cast images may indicate that these are separate violations and thus favor the division of Exod 20:3–6 as referring to two commandments.

[62] Kaufmann, "דָּת יִשְׂרָאֵל," 757–58.

for no profit?
Look, all its worshipers will be
    put to shame,
and the craftsmen are humans.
They all will assemble and stand;
they all will be startled
    and put to shame.
The ironworker labors over the coals,
Shapes the idol with hammers,
And works it with his strong arm.
Also he grows hungry
    and his strength fails;
he doesn't drink water and is faint.
The woodworker stretches out
    a measuring line,
he outlines it with a stylus;
he shapes it with chisels
and outlines it with a compass.
He makes it according to
    a human likeness,
like a beautiful person,
to dwell in a temple.
He cuts down cedars for his use,
Or he takes a cypress or an oak.
He lets it grow strong among the trees
    of the forest.
He plants a laurel, and the rain
    makes it grow.

It serves for fuel for man.
He takes some of it and warms himself;
also he kindles a fire and bakes bread;
he even makes it into a god
    and worships (*ḥwh*) it;
he makes it an idol [*pesel*] and bows down to it.
He burns half of it in a fire,
and he roasts meat on that half.
He eats the roast and is satisfied.
He warms himself and says, "Ah!
I am warm, I see the blaze."
He makes a god or his idol [*pesel*) with the rest
    of it.
He bows down to it and worships (*ḥwh*);
He prays to it, "Save me, for you are
    my god."

In the sixth century, Jeremiah (50:2; 51:17–18,44,47,52) and Daniel leveled attacks on specific idols.[63] Shadrach, Meshach, and Abednego preferred to be cast into a blazing fire rather than to prostrate themselves before the statue of Nebuchadnezzar (Dan 3). The prophets are unified in their announcement that all idols are nothing more than a human fabrication (Isa 40:18–20; 42:8,17; 43:10; 44:8–20; 45:20; 46:5–7; Jer 1:16; 51:17–18).[64] They are powerless to save (Isa 45:20), and in fact are nothing (Jer 51:17–18). They cannot hear, smell, walk, or talk (Deut 4:28; Ps 115:4–7; Hab 2:18–19).[65]

Idolatry and National Collapse

Idolatry reached its height in Judah during Manasseh's reign. Manasseh instituted public idolatry as he turned the sanctuary into an idolatrous pantheon (2 Kgs 21:1–7; 2 Chr 33:7,15). Idolatry had penetrated virtually every town (Jer 2:28; 11:13). Idols were erected in the temple itself (Jer 32:34; Ezek 8:5–11). As with the northern kingdom, idolatry led to the fall of the southern kingdom (2 Kgs 21:1–7; 24:3–4). God could be reconciled to Israel only if the nation established the Torah in all of life, and they needed to purge from their midst all idols, even the dust of idols, since idolatry was the sin of sins.[66] Only with the Babylonian exile was idolatry dealt a fatal blow.

The Second Commandment in the New Testament

In New Testament times, idolatry was practiced throughout the Roman Empire similarly to its extensive practice in the ancient Near East in the Old Testament period. When Paul arrived at Athens, he found it replete with idols (Acts 17:16). Paul confronted the people about their idolatry with words that reflect the teaching of the Old Testament prophets: "Being God's offspring, then, we shouldn't think that

---

[63] Teraphim, perhaps household images, were used for divination (Ezek 21:21; Zech 10:2; see Gen 31:30–35), although they were prohibited (1 Sam 15:23; 2 Kgs 23:24).

[64] J. Watts, "Babylonian Idolatry in the Prophets as a False Socio-Economic System," in *Israel's Apostasy and Restoration: Essays in Honor of Roland K. Harrison*, ed. A. Gileadi (Grand Rapids: Baker, 1988), 117, 120–21.

[65] R. Spencer, "Idol, Idolatry," *EDBT*, 364.

[66] Kaufmann, "דָּת יִשְׂרָאֵל," 2:760; Rabbi D. Wax, ed., *The Ten Commandments* (Lakewood, NJ: Taryag Legacy Foundation, 2005), 141.

the divine nature is like gold or silver or stone, an image fashioned by human art and imagination" (Acts 17:29). He also confronted idolatry in Ephesus (Acts 19:23–41). Paul shared the Old Testament conviction that idols were nothing at all (1 Cor 8:4; Acts 19:26), although he acknowledged that demonic influences could be behind their worship (1 Cor 10:20; see Ps 106:35–38). Idolatry was a sign of human folly and thus perverted the true faith (Rom 1:22–23). Believers were admonished to flee idolatry (1 Cor 10:14) because it was a sin (1 Cor 6:9–10; Gal 5:19–21; Eph 5:5; Col 3:5; 1 Pet 4:3; Rev 21:8), and not to associate with idolaters (1 Cor 5:11).[67] The Thessalonian believers are commended for turning from idols to the true God (1 Thess 1:9).

The New Testament also teaches that there will be idolatry in the future, as we learn in Rev 13 that the image of the beast will be worshipped before the return of Christ. This act of rebellion will be in violation of Scripture, which says that God is Spirit and is to be worshipped in spirit and in truth (John 4:24). A material image cannot represent a spiritual God.

Conclusion

The second commandment prohibits any crafted or sculptured image for worship. This applies to images of both pagan gods and the Lord. No one can make an image of the Lord because no one knows what He looks like. Any representation of Him would be false since it could not possibly represent the reality of the true God.[68] The powerful suzerains in the ancient Near East wanted their images everywhere. The true God wants just the opposite because any image would diminish His power and glory. An idol that is manufactured and thus inherently finite could not possibly represent God, who alone is infinite. The danger of the localization and materialization of God is thus ruled out. Moreover, the focus on idolatry was diametrically opposed to the biblical faith. In idolatry, worshippers attempt to manipulate

---

[67] See D. Horrell, "Idol-Food, Idolatry and Ethics in Paul," in *Idolatry: False Worship in the Bible, Early Judaism and Christianity*, ed. S. Barton (London: T&T Clark, 2007), 139.

[68] Idolatry is an attempt to represent the immanence of God.

the gods to accomplish their selfish goals; in the biblical faith, Yahweh controls human destiny to accomplish His own goals.[69]

No image is to be used in worship. Artistic expressions for decoration such as the cherubim were displayed in the tabernacle as God commissioned them. However, this kind of artistic rendering did not constitute an image of God as it was not made to represent Him. The same principle would apply to Christian art. Art that is intended to be an object of worship is prohibited. No artistic depiction should ever be offered as a way to understand something of God's glory. Any attempt to understand an aspect of God's glory in this way would present a false impression and a distortion. "In a similar way, the pathos of the crucifix obscures the glory of Christ, for it hides the fact of His deity, His victory on the cross, and His present kingdom."[70] As Jerry Vines has stated:

> When you make a graven image of God, you fix God. An image is limited. God is unlimited. An image is local. God is universal. An image is temporal. God is eternal. An image is material. God is spiritual. When you make a graven image, it distorts God.[71]

But the prohibition against the erecting and worshipping of images involves more than the physical act of paying homage to a statue or idol. The worship of images often is accompanied by a decadent lifestyle. Idolatry has never been connected to ethical behavior. In fact, sexual immorality often has accompanied the practice of idolatry (2 Kgs 23:6–7; see Exod 32:7).[72] The Talmud describes a direct connection between sexual immorality and idolatry.[73] Wrong thoughts about God lead to wrong behavior. The rabbis considered idolatry as one of three sins for which a person should suffer martyrdom rather than commit (*Sanh.* 74a).

---

[69] Watts, "Babylonian Idolatry in the Prophets as a False Socio-Economic System," 115.

[70] J. I. Packer, *Knowing God* (Downers Grove, IL: InterVarsity, 1973), 40–41. Similarly, C. S. Lewis has Screwtape advise his nephew to influence the young Christian to concentrate on a religious object so the Christian may keep praying "to the thing he has made, not to the Person who has made him." See C. S. Lewis, *The Screwtape Letters* (New York: The Macmillan Company, 1943), 27.

[71] J. Vines, *Basic Bible Sermons on the Ten Commandments* (Nashville: Broadman, 1992), 24.

[72] See D. Stuart, *Exodus,* NAC (Nashville: B&H, 2006), 451, 453.

[73] See Halbertal and Margalit, *Idolatry,* 25, 209. In Gal 5:20, "idolatry" immediately follows sexual sins.

The New Testament associates idolatry with greed (Col 3:5; Eph 5:5). Brian Rosner explains why idolatry is an appropriate metaphor for greed. Greed leads to a strong desire to acquire more and more money and other material things. This mind-set "is an attack on God's exclusive rights to human love and devotion, trust and confidence, and service and obedience."[74] Idolatry, like greed, involves "trusting, loving, and serving gold and silver objects rather than the true and living God."[75]

> Just as the reverence of a pagan symbol inevitably dilutes one's dedication to the service of God, it is likewise impossible to invest time and effort into one's spiritual calling while being consumed by the scramble for possessions and wealth.[76]

Idolatry is putting anything between you and God. As Martin Luther stated in his larger catechism: "Whatever your heart clings to and relies upon, that is your God."[77] As with idolatry, those who are greedy ignore their Creator; they have left their first love (Rev 2:4). The failure to acknowledge God as sovereign Creator leads to idolatry as well as spiritual blindness.[78] Idolatry is deleterious to others. The consequences of committing idolatry are far-reaching, affecting not just the guilty party but his descendants to the third or fourth generation. You reap what you sow (Gal 6:7).

Furthermore, Christians are not to make images because they understand that God has been revealed in the flesh in the incarnation of Jesus Christ. Jesus Christ is the image of the invisible God (Col 1:15) and the express image of God's person (Heb 1:3). Those who beheld Jesus in the flesh had seen the Father (John 14:9).

Even though the characteristic of pagan nations is to bow down and worship the image of false gods, in the messianic age they will come to know and worship the true God of Israel (Ps 100:1–2; Isa 19:21; Zeph 3:9). At that time they will be ashamed of their idols (*pesel*) (Ps 97:7). This transformation will not occur until God acts on His "jealousy" (*qin'â*) for Israel and delivers His people (Zeph 1:18; 3:8).

---

[74] B. Rosner, *Greed as Idolatry: The Origin and Meaning of a Pauline Metaphor* (Grand Rapids: Eerdmans, 2007), 173.

[75] Ibid., 174.

[76] Wax, *The Ten Commandments*, 103.

[77] Rosner, *Greed as Idolatry*, 173.

[78] See D. Spender, "Idol, Idolatry," *EDBT*, 364.

Both the saving of the remnant (2 Kg 19:31) and the sending of the Messiah (Isa 9:7 [Hb. 9:6]) are prompted by God's jealousy (*qin'â*) for Israel.[79] Here God's jealousy signifies the realization of the reign of the Prince of peace and the peace He will bring. Thus *qin'â* refers to God's powerful, effective striving for attainment of the goal.[80] Because of His loyalty (*hesed*) to the covenant, He bears human iniquity (*'āwōn*) (Pss 32:5; 85:2[3]; 89:32 [33]; 103:3,10; 106:43; 107:17–21; 130:8).[81] Wright summarizes the role of divine jealousy over idolatry:

> Divine jealousy is in fact an essential function of divine love. It is precisely because God wills our good that he hates the self-inflicted harm that our idolatry generates. God's conflict with the gods is ultimately for our own good as well as for God's glory. This further highlights why idolatry is such a primary sin in the Bible—identified as such by the primacy of the first two commandments of the Decalogue. It is not merely that idolatry steals God's glory but it also thwarts God's love—the love that seeks the highest good of all God's creation. Idolatry therefore contradicts the very essence, the Goodness, of God, for "God is love."[82]

The sin of idolatry existed in Israel to the end of the First Temple period.[83] Isaiah predicted the end of idolatry in the entire world.[84] The Gentiles will come to recognize the God of Israel (1 Kgs 8:41–43,60; Pss 22:28; 47:2; 68:30–33). The Lord is the living God who made all things, and He intends that all nations turn from idolatry and worship Him (Isa 17:7–8). God has created all people for His glory and that they might serve Him (Isa 43:7). One day all people will turn from their idols, "bow down" (*hwh*) and "worship" (*'bd*) in reverence and submission (Ps 72:11; cf. Ps 22:29[30]; Rom 14:11; Phil 2:10). In the meantime, God expects His covenant people to be loyal and to act faithfully (*hesed*) because of God's gracious redemption. Put differently, God's people should respond to Him in love (*'hb*) and endeavor to keep His commands (*miṣwâ*) (Exod 20:6; Deut 5:10; 26:18; Neh 1:5; Dan 9:4).[85]

---

[79] H. Peels, "קָנָא‎‎," *NIDOTTE* 3:939.

[80] A. Jepsen, "Beiträge zur Auslegung und Geschichte des Dekalogs," *ZAW* 79 (1967): 288.

[81] See Koch, "עָוֹן‎ *'āwōn*," 554.

[82] Wright, *The Mission of God*, 177.

[83] Kaufmann, "דָּת יִשְׂרָאֵל‎," 2:747; id., *The Religion of Israel*, 3, 133.

[84] Kaufmann, "דָּת יִשְׂרָאֵל‎," 2:758.

[85] Hakam argues that the expression of loving God and keeping His commands should make us recall the life of Abraham; see Gen 26:5 (*The Book of Exodus*, 281).

Chapter 3

THE THIRD COMMANDMENT

Do not misuse the name of the LORD your God, because
the LORD will punish anyone who misuses His name.

Introduction

In the ancient world, serious matters such as treaties and contractual obligations derived their binding character by the use of solemn oaths. These oaths normally included the invoking of an individual's god, often at a temple or before a representation of that god. It was believed that the gods would attest to the oath transactions as well as serve as potential avengers of their violation. The fear of divine retribution would compel the oath taker to speak the truth. So real was this threat that a person might refuse to take an oath even if he had to pay a fine.[1]

The critical issue in the oath taking is the calling on or evoking a deity's name. We see this in a prayer by an Egyptian man:

> I am a man who swore falsely by Ptah, lord of Maat,
> And he made me see darkness by day.
> I will declare his might to the fool and the wise,
> To the small and great:
> Beware of Ptah, Lord of Maat!
> Behold, he does not overlook anyone's deed!
> Refrain from uttering Ptah's name falsely.
> Lo, he who utters it falsely, lo he falls![2]

It was thus no light matter to utter a false oath using the name of a deity. There is widespread evidence in the ancient Near Eastern documents that invoking a god in a frivolous manner or without serious intent could lead to serious repercussions.[3]

---

[1] R. Westbrook, ed., *A History of Ancient Near Eastern Law*, 2 vols. (Leiden; Boston: Brill, 2003), 1:12–13, 24, 34, 84; 2:831.

[2] M. Lichtheim, *Ancient Egyptian Literature*, 3 vols. (Berkeley: University of California Press, 1973–80), 2:110.

[3] H. Huffmon, "The Fundamental Code Illustrated: The Third Commandment," in *Pomegranates & Golden Bells*, ed. D. Wright, D. N. Freedman, and A. Hurvitz (Winona Lake, IN: Eisenbrauns, 1995), 368.

The Meaning of the Third Commandment

The first phrase of the third commandment warns us not to "misuse the name of the LORD your God." The verb of this phrase, translated "misuse," comes from the root *nāśā᾽*, which occurs more than 650 times in the Old Testament. The verb has a wide range of meaning and is rendered in English by such verbs as "lift, raise, carry, take, pardon."[4] The phrase *lō᾽ tiśśā᾽ ᾽et šēm* "do not misuse the name" is rare, occurring outside the Ten Commandments (Exod 20:7; Deut 5:11) only in Ps 16:4 ("I will not speak their names," *ûbal ᾽eśśā᾽ ᾽et šēmôtām*).

The verb used in this formula (*nāśā᾽*, lit., "raise") occurs in the expression "raise the hand." Raising the hand was a common gesture accompanying a solemn oath (Exod 6:8; Num 14:30; Deut 32:40; Neh 9:15; Ezek 20:5–6,15,23,28,42; 36:7; 44:12; 47:14).[5] The expression "do not misuse the name" (lit. "do not raise the name") in the Ten Commandments may be a shortened formula for this gesture when it accompanied an oath.[6] "To swear in God's name" (*nišbaʿ bĕšēm*) is a common biblical phrase (Lev 19:12; Deut 6:13; 10:20; Isa 48:1; Jer 12:16; 44:26; Zech 5:4).[7]

What's in a Name?

In the ancient Near East, nothing was thought to exist unless it had a name. We see this most vividly in the Mesopotamian creation account, *Enuma Elish*, which begins: "When on high heaven had not been named." The name of a deity was thought to be equivalent to that deity and was believed to express something of the deity's essence

---

[4] V. Hamilton, "נשׂא," *NIDOTTE* 3:160.

[5] K. Van Der Toorn, *Sin and Sanction in Israel and Mesopotamia: A Comparative Study* (Assen, The Netherlands: Van Gorcum, 1985), 166n187. In 1 Kgs 8:31 the verb (נשׁא; *nāśā᾽*) is used but has oath (אלה) rather than "hand" (יד) as its object. A similar phrase, "raise the hand," with a different verb (*rûm*), has the same function in Gen 14:22 and Dan 12:7. There is a Jewish tradition that a person made an oath or swore by holding a Torah scroll in his hand (*b. Sebu.* 38b).

[6] Huffmon, "The Fundamental Code Illustrated: The Third Commandment," 366. D. Freedman and B. Willoughby understand this phrase in the Ten Commandments as the oath formula. "נשׂא *nāśā᾽*," *TDOT* 10:38. The omission of the term "hand" would be analogous to the biblical covenant formula which omits the object "sacrifice" in the expression "make a covenant," literally "cut a covenant."

[7] It should be noted that the JB, NEB, and NRSV similarly refer to "misusing the name."

or character.[8] This idea appears to be true to the Old Testament concept of understanding God's name and other names.

In the Old Testament we learn that by giving a name to someone or something, a person had a certain control over what he had named. We see this in Genesis 1 where God names the light "day" and the darkness "night" (Gen 1:5). Moreover, He calls the expanse "sky," the dry land "earth," and the gathering of the water "seas" in Gen 1:8,10. In Genesis 2, man made in the image of God gives names to the animals God had made (Gen 2:19–20). When Isaac reopens the wells his father Abraham had dug, he renames them with the same names that his father had given them (Gen 26:18). When the Danites conquer Leshem they rename the city Dan, after the name of their ancestor (Josh 19:47). A name may be evoked as a token of possession in capturing cities (Num 32:38; 2 Sam 12:28) or to express the Lord's legal claim over people (Amos 9:11–12).

We find that some individuals' names were changed. Abram became Abraham (Gen 17:5) to mark a new stage for his life, Sarai became Sarah (Gen 17:15), and Jacob became Israel (Gen 32:28). These changes announced a new work of God in their lives.[9] In 2 Kgs 23:34/2 Chr 36:4, the Egyptian Pharaoh Neco installed Eliakim as king of Judah and changed Eliakim's name to Jehoiakim. In 2 Kgs 24:17 the king of Babylon made Mattaniah king and changed his name to Zedekiah. These name changes are an illustration of the foreign king's power. The king of Babylon had the power to rename a national ruler and control his destiny. The person renamed is thus subject to the one who gives the name. This may also be seen in the name changes for Daniel and his friends in Dan 1:7. This notion of having a certain control over someone by knowing the person's name may also be illustrated in Jacob's wrestling with the angel in Gen 32:28–31 (where Jacob's name is changed). On the other hand, "blotting out" or "cutting off" a name referred to a person's destruction (2 Kgs 14:27; Isa 14:22; Zeph 1:4; cf. Ps 83:4[5]).

---

[8] J. Walton, *Ancient Near Eastern Thought and the Old Testament* (Grand Rapids: Baker Academic, 2006), 88, 156; A. Ross, "שֵׁם," *NIDOTTE* 4:147.

[9] The person who will not raise up an heir in his deceased brother's name is not worthy to have his name mentioned (Deut 25:10; cf. Ruth 4:5,10).

The effect that a name had depended on the power or reputation of the person who bore the name. Thus, the Hebrew word *šēm* ("name") refers to "fame, honor, power, or reputation" of a person or persons (Deut 26:19; 2 Sam 8:13; Pss 66:2; 102:21[22]; 145:21; Jer 13:11; Ezek 23:10; Zech 13:9; Isa 48:9; Jer 33:9).[10] The name of God stands for far more than the mere pronouncing of His title of address. It includes His nature, being, and person (Ps 20:1; Luke 24:27; John 1:12; cf. Rev 3:5), as well as His teaching or doctrine (Ps 22:22; John 17:6,26).

The queen of Sheba heard of Solomon's "fame" (*šēm*) (1 Kgs 10:1). In the tower of Babel incident, the people wanted to "make a name (*šēm*) for" themselves, so they built a tower to guarantee their fame or power (Gen 11:4). God promised to make Abraham's and David's *šēm* ("reputation") great (Gen 12:2; 2 Sam 7:9; 1 Chr 17:8).

The Name of Yahweh

We find an intimation of the meaning of the name Yahweh in Exod 3:14 when Moses asked God about His name. God responded that His name was *'ehyeh*, "I AM," using the first person of the verb "to be" (*hāyâ*). The name Yahweh is also from the root illustrating the more ancient spelling *hwh*. In the immediately succeeding verse, Exod 3:15, the name Yahweh occurs without explanation, suggesting that it has been explained by the previous verb of the same root, *'ehyeh*. Thus Yahweh means "He causes to be," or "He brings into existence."[11]

The use of the noun *šēm* in reference to the Lord (Yahweh) has the same connotations that were demonstrated in the previous section of the Old Testament usage. The Hebrew term *šēm* is used with reference to Yahweh to refer to his fame (Exod 9:14–16; Deut 26:19; Jer 32:20; Dan 9:15; cf. 2 Sam 7:22). The Lord's "name" is often associated with His attributes. Most striking is the virtual identification of *YHWH* (Yahweh) with his *šēm* (name). In Ps 143:11–12, the Lord's name is parallel to His righteousness (*ṣĕdāqâ*) and his lovingkindness (*ḥesed*). In Isa 30:27 the word "name" is used as an alternative term for Yahweh. In Isa 42:8, *šēm* and *YHWH* are identified;

---

[10] See F. Reiterer, "שֵׁם *šēm*," *TDOT* 15:172; A. S. van der Woude, "שֵׁם *šēm*," *TLOT* 3:1356.

[11] See L. Hartman and S. Sperling, "God, Names of," *EJ* 7:675.

they are also interchangeable in Deut 28:10,58; Pss 83:16(17); 96:1–
2; 100:4; 135:3; Isa 63:16; Jer 10:6; Ezek 39:25; Mal 2:5; 3:16.[12] In
1 Kgs 8:41–42, *šēm* refers to Yahweh's personal name. In Isa 52:5, to
blaspheme the name is to blaspheme Yahweh Himself.[13] The majesty
given to *šēm* is the same majesty given to Yahweh (Ps 8:1,9[2,10]. In
Ps 103:1 and 145:21 the name is associated with holiness, an attribute
which specifically applies to God.[14] The creation of the universe is attributed to "the name" *(šēm)* (Ps 89:12[13]).

Since the temple cannot contain Yahweh, He is present in His name
(šēm).[15] The temple is the place God has chosen to place His name
(Deut 12:5,21; 14:24; 16:2,6,11; 26:2; cf. 2 Chr 6:20). Eugene Merrill
says the name is an alter ego for God in Deuteronomy.[16] Where
Yahweh is, His name is present (Pss 99:6; 116:4).

Improper Use of God's Name

The prohibition of the third commandment is to refrain from misusing *(laššāwʾ)* "the name of the LORD."[17] While the root meaning of
the term is up for debate, it is clear from usage in the Old Testament
that the nuance of the noun carries the negative connotation of "deceit" or "falseness, wickedness or ineffectiveness."[18] Similarly, Moshe
Weinfeld argues that we should understand the term to refer to what
is "groundless" or "unreal" (Ps 127:1; Jer 2:30; 4:30; 6:29; 46:11; Mal
3:14) as well as false (Job 31:5; Pss 12:2[3]; 41:6[7]; 144:8,11; Prov
30:8; Isa 59:4; Hos 10:4).[19] The term is used to refer to a "false" report

---

[12] In Pss 74:10 and 145:1, שֵׁם "name" is parallel to אֱלֹהִים "God."

[13] Reiterer, *TDOT* 15:142–43.

[14] According to Origen, the most characteristic feature of God's name is holiness. See J. T.
Lienhard, ed., *Exodus, Leviticus, Numbers, Deuteronomy*, ACCS (Downers Grove, IL: InterVarsity,
2001), 100.

[15] Reiterer, *TDOT* 15:156.

[16] E. Merrill, *Deuteronomy*, NAC (Nashville: B&H, 1994), 149.

[17] The preposition לְ is used for marking the aim, object, or consequence of an action or
thing. BDB defines the phrase here as "for a vain or frivolous purpose" (515). It is unclear
whether the noun שָׁוְא is related to the root נָשָׁא II "to deceive" (J. Sawyer, "שָׁוְא *šāwʾ*," *TLOT*
3:1311; F. Reiterer, "שָׁוְא *šāwʾ*," *TDOT* 14:447), שָׁוְא I "treat badly," or שָׁוְא II "to make desolate
or waste" (J. Shepherd; "שָׁוְא," *NIDOTTE* 4:53).

[18] The connotation of "evil" or "deceitfulness" distinguishes שָׁוְא from other Hb. terms such
as חִנָּם and רִיקָם that convey the meaning of "in vain." See Sawyer, *TLOT* 3:1311.

[19] M. Weinfeld, *Deuteronomy 1–11*, AB 5 (New York: Doubleday, 1991), 300. The major
versions reflect this same meaning of "empty, worthless, untruth, falsehood" as seen in the use

(Exod 23:1), a "false" witness (Deut 5:20; Isa 59:4; Hos 10:4; cf. Ps 144:8,11; Prov 30:8), "false" worship (Ps 31:6[7]); Isa 1:13; Jer 18:15; Hos 12:11[12]; Jon 2:8[9]), and "false" prophecy (Lam 2:14; Ezek 12:24; 13:6–9,23; 21:23[28], 29[34]; 22:28; Zech 10:2).[20] This general understanding finds complete support from the ninth commandment in Deut 5 where *šāw'* is used to describe a false witness. In Exod 20, the close synonym *šeqer,* "deception, disappointment, falsehood," is used in the ninth commandment.[21] The terms *šāw'* and *šeqer* are parallel in Ps 144:8; Prov 30:8; Hos 10:4; and Zech 10:2. In Isa 59:4, *šāw'* is parallel to *tōhû,* a term that refers to nonexistence or chaos in the creation account (Gen 1:2).[22] Any invocation of the Lord or calling on His name that is insincere or needless is simply perfunctory and constitutes taking God's name in vain.[23]

The reason one must make all efforts to refrain from misusing God's name is "because the LORD will punish anyone who misuses His name."[24] The critical word translated "punish" is the translation of the clause *lō' yĕnaqqeh.* The verbal root *nāqâ* may be rendered "be free from punishment," and thus the literal translation of the phrase in Exod 20:7 is "let him not be free from punishment." In five of the occurrences of the term, it appears in what is almost a refrain in the phrase: "God shows mercy but does not leave the guilty *unpunished*" (Exod 34:7; Num 14:18; Jer 30:11; 46:28; Nah 1:3). The verb occurs in the Piel stem in 18 places in the Old Testament, and only in one passage (Ps 19:12[13]) is it not negated; otherwise, it is negated just as in Exod 20:7.[25] The verb is frequently used in what might appear

---

of μάταιος in the LXX (LEH, 385) and in the Peshitta (Payne-Smith, 83), and by the use of מנן in Targum Neofiti.

[20] Sawyer, *TLOT* 3:1311.

[21] See BDB, 1055.

[22] The close synonym שֶׁקֶר occurs in Isa 59:3.

[23] See Jewish medieval commentator David Kimchi in M. Carasik, מקראות גדולות. *The Commentators' Bible: The JPS Miqráot Gedolot. Exodus* (Philadelphia: Jewish Publication Society, 2005), 159.

[24] Both syntactically and grammatically the conjunction כִּי could be understood either as a coordinate or as a subordinate conjunction. In the first case it means "for," and in the second "because." The HCSB has translated the particle as introducing a subordinate (causal) clause. For discussion, see T. Elssner, "Das dekalogische Namensmissbrauch-Verbot (Ex 20,7/Dtn 5,11)," *BN* 114/115 (2002): 62.

[25] See G. Warmuth, "נָקָה *nāqâ,*" *TDOT* 9:553–56.

to be legal or forensic contexts (Gen 24:8,41; Num 5:19; Josh 2:17,20; Zech 5:3).[26]

Thus in the subordinate clause the prohibition is repeated to make a deeper impression as well as to make the teaching of the command more memorable. God will not allow the violator of this command to go unpunished because He will not allow His character to be defamed through misuse of His name. Thomas Elssner graphically shows how the effect of this repetition creates a chiastic structure:

> you shall not lift up the name of the LORD your God in vain
>> for the LORD will not acquit
> whoever lifts up his name in vain.

This symmetrical structure (aba) places the grounds for the proposition in the middle with the stress on assonance at the end. The first part of the third commandment announces a violation of the sanction, while the third part repeats the prohibition but in the form of a final causal statement. The commandment has three primary parts: (1) the prohibition [Exod 20:7a; Deut 5:11a], (2) a causal sentence with a sanction threat [Exod 20:5b; Deut 5:11b], and (3) a dependent object sentence that is a final reinforcement in the form of a terminal prohibition [Exod 20:7c; Deut 5:11c].[27]

The Misuse of God's Name

Just what is prohibited by the third commandment? Three primary but distinct positions have been presented. These include misuse of the Lord's name in a magical incantation, false swearing, or a general inappropriate use.

The first view of what constitutes misuse of God's name is that what is prohibited in the third commandment is the use of the Lord's name in magic. We have seen in discussions of the first two commandments that Israel was not only surrounded by paganism that was characterized by the use of magic to influence the gods but also that Israel was tempted throughout its history to adapt to pagan beliefs. Eichrodt identified the problem of magic:

[26] The legal use of the term is common in rabbinic literature (Weinfeld, *Deuteronomy 1–11*, 301).

[27] Elssner, "Das dekalogische Namensmissbrauch-Verbot (Ex 20,7/ Dtn 5,11)," 61, 70.

Magic, however, is the hidden malignancy in all pagan religions, on account of which genuine reverence for the holy is nullified; since it was the means for bringing the sovereign will of God under human control and of using it for egotistical purposes.[28]

It would not be too much of a stretch to suggest that the third commandment, like the first two, is primarily addressing Israel's temptation to follow pagan beliefs and practices.[29] If this interpretation is correct, the Israelites would be using God's name for their own benefit, perhaps as Balaam did (Num 22–24).[30] To resort to such actions would be an assault on the distinctiveness of Israel's God, primarily His sovereignty.

The second major interpretation of the "misuse of God's name" understands the phrase to describe the swearing of a false oath in the name of the Lord (Lev 19:12; see Deut 10:20; Josh 23:7; Isa 19:18). In everyday life as well as in court statements, claims were often backed up by evoking God's name (1 Kgs 17:12).[31] Men must swear by someone greater than themselves (Heb 6:16). When a person evoked God's name, he called God as a witness to the truth of his word. Assertions made in court, in public affairs, or even in ordinary conversation were often backed up with conditional self-curses that would take effect if the swearer's assertion proved false or his promise unfulfilled.[32] Thus the commandment addresses a warning against a witness who swears contrary to what is known or is later discovered to be the truth.[33] According to Ibn Ezra: "The reason for mentioning God's name in an oath is to emphasize to man that just as God's name is Truth, so

---

[28] W. Eichrodt, "The Law and the Gospel," *Int* 11 (1957): 30.

[29] Staples believed the commandment prohibited giving the name "Yahweh" to an idol. See W. Staples, "The Third Commandment," *JBL* 58,4 (1939): 329. For a further explanation of this view, see M. Noth, *Exodus*, OTL (Philadelphia: Westminster, 1962), 163; H. Betz, *The Sermon on the Mount* (Minneapolis: Fortress, 1995), 260–61, 265; Merrill, *Deuteronomy*, 149.

[30] Advocates of this position include A. Phillips, *Ancient Israel's Criminal Law: A New Approach to the Decalogue* (Oxford: Basil Blackwell, 1970), 54; W. Keszler, "Die Literarische, Historische und Theologische Problematik des Dekalogs," *VT* 7 (1957): 9; P. Craigie, *The Book of Deuteronomy* (Grand Rapids: Eerdmans, 1976), 156.

[31] J. Tigay, *Deuteronomy*, JPS Torah Commentary (Philadelphia: Jewish Publication Society, 1996), 67, 357n80.

[32] JSB, 149.

[33] A. Hakam, *The Book of Exodus* (Jerusalem: Mossad Harav Kook, 1991), 282 [in Hb.]. This position is predominant among Jewish interpreters and can be seen in the Aramaic Targum and Syriac Peshitta as well as in the English JPS translation. This understanding is similar to Philo's definition of an oath: "For an oath is nothing else than to call God to bear witness in a disputed matter" (Philo, *Spec.* 2:10).

should his own words be true; and that if he does not fulfill his word then it is as if he had denied God Himself."[34] To speak a falsehood in an oath when Yahweh's name is invoked is to associate the Lord's name with something that is fraudulent. Maligning God's name misrepresents Him and thus bears false witness to Him.[35] The mention of "swearing falsely" (wĕhiššābē(a)ᶜ laššeqer) in Jer 7:9 after listing violations of the Ten Commandments such as "stealing, killing, and committing adultery" is understood by some to identify "swearing falsely" with the third commandment.[36] A false oath would demonstrate disrespect if not contempt for God as the offender would be expressing his lack of faith in God's power to execute His punishment for this offence.[37] In swearing without cause or with evil intent, the person would be submitting his words and deeds to the judgment of God who holds the oathtaker's fate in His hands. Additional support for this approach comes from the occurrence of the verb nāqâ "not punish," which we saw above as a technical term for being free from punishment in the forensic sense.

The third position regarding the meaning of the third commandment is not as specific as the other two as it views the prohibition as being against use of the name of the Lord in any inappropriate or frivolous way. This prohibition is more general and thus could include the other two positions, namely, that use of God's name for magic or in false swearing as well as for any frivolous purpose is prohibited. Any attempt to manipulate God for one's personal benefit would fall under this prohibition.[38] The name of the Lord should not be used for any pointless or unproductive purpose. This would include idly mentioning Him, invoking His name for no good reason, or imploring Him in a matter in which He is unlikely to respond.[39] The Talmud

---

[34] S. Albeck, "The Ten Commandments and the Essence of Religious Faith," in *The Ten Commandments in History and Tradition,* ed. B. Z. Segal (Jerusalem: Magnes, 1990), 268–69.

[35] R. A. Mohler Jr., *Words from the Fire* (Chicago: Moody, 2009), 70.

[36] A. Jepsen, "Beiträge zur Auslegung und Geschichte des Dekalogs," *ZAW* 79 (1967): 292. See also Hos 4:2.

[37] Tigay, *Deuteronomy,* 67, 357n81.

[38] Craigie, *Deuteronomy,* 156. As the Jewish medieval commentator Hizkuni observed, "One who is accustomed to swear needlessly by God's name will end up, out of familiarity, swearing falsely by it." Carasik, מקראות גדולות. *The Commentators' Bible,* 159.

[39] W. Propp, *Exodus 19–40,* AB 2A (New York: Doubleday, 2006), 174.

says that whoever says a blessing that is not necessary transgresses the third commandment (*b. Ber.* 33a).

The commandment prohibits any misuse of the Lord's name, from making light of it to blatantly mocking it. Every mention made of the Lord with our mouths is to be made with the highest sincerity and reverence. The Peshitta (Syriac) translation and Josephus (*Ant.* 3.91) support the third position, namely, that the third commandment prohibits the misuse of the Lord's name by using it thoughtlessly.[40] Those who use God's name in this way assume that God is nothing and possesses no power or authority in life.[41] The warning about the misuse of God's name is not only about the protection of God's name, this admonition warns against an illicit or thoughtless contact with God.[42] God's name is also rendered cheap and common when used in needless oaths. According to rabbinic theology: "The greatness of God transcends all existence, and His name should be uttered only amid feelings of awe, and strictly for matters of utmost importance. To invoke His name for a needless oath is a serious affront to the honor of God."[43]

The Third Commandment in the Old Testament

It was a common practice in the Old Testament period to verify a statement by an oath (1 Kgs 17:12). Thus this commandment does not exclude legitimate oaths, as they are relatively common in the Old Testament (Deut 6:13; Jer 4:2) as well as the New (Rom 1:9; 9:1).[44] Occasions for oathtaking range from the personal (Gen 21:23; 1 Sam 20:42) to the most solemn public undertakings (Judg 21:1; 1 Sam 14:28; 20:3; 2 Sam 14:19; 1 Kgs 17:1; 2 Kgs 2:2; cf. 2 Chr 36:13). Alliances and agreements were solemnized by oaths.[45] Not only do the

---

[40] Payne-Smith, 83. See A. Jepsen, "Beiträge zur Auslegung und Geschichte des Dekalogs," 291.

[41] See J. Holbert, *The Ten Commandments* (Nashville: Abingdon, 2002), 38.

[42] Dohmen believes the focus is on the latter. C. Dohmen, *Exodus 19–40* (Freiburg: Herder, 2004), 115. It appears that Childs also holds this third view. B. Childs, *The Book of Exodus: A Critical-Theological Commentary* (Louisville: Westminster John Knox, 1974), 410–11.

[43] Rabbi D. Wax, ed., *The Ten Commandments* (Lakewood, NJ: Taryag Legacy Foundation, 2005), 160.

[44] See also Ps 63:11; Isa 45:23; Jer 12:16; 1 Cor 15:31; Phil 1:8; Rev 10:5–6.

[45] M. Greenberg, "Oath," *EJ* 15:359.

leaders of Israel swear oaths (Gen 14:22; 21:24; 47:31; Josh 2:12), but God does as well (Gen 22:16; 26:3; Isa 45:23; Ezek 17:19; Amos 6:8; 8:7).[46] The taking of an oath was to be accompanied by sincerity and truthfulness (Deut 6:13; Jer 4:2; 12:16; Ps 63:11).[47]

Out of an expression of allegiance and loyalty to the Lord, the Israelites were commanded to take their oaths in Yahweh's name (Deut 6:13; 10:20). To swear and take an oath in the name of another god was to commit apostasy (Josh 23:7; cf. Exod 23:13; Jer 5:7; 12:16; Amos 8:14). When taking an oath in Yahweh's name, the people were not to give a false statement (Lev 19:12; Jer 7:9; Hos 4:2; cf. Zech 5:4). They were prohibited from making a false report (Exod 23:1) and committing perjury (Zech 8:17).

A prophet who represented the Lord and spoke for Him was to speak nothing but the truth in the name of the Lord (1 Kgs 22:16; 2 Chr 33:18; Jer 26:16). False prophets spoke lies in God's name, only pretending they had received a word from the Lord (Jer 14:14; 23:25; Ezek 13:8). Those who delivered the prophetic word in the names of other gods were to be put to death (Deut 18:20; cf. Zech 13:3).

But the third commandment, as we have seen, is broader than just making an oath; it is also applied to any frivolous or fraudulent use of the Lord's name. Swearing in the name of the Lord with an evil intention (Zech 5:4) or the utterance of allegiance by a person with an intransigent lifestyle in rebellion against God (Hos 4:15) would bring disrepute on the name of the Lord.[48] Thus the result of fraudulent use of the Lord's name is comparable to offering a child in sacrifice to the pagan god Molech, an action which profanes (*ḥālal*) the name of the Lord (Lev 20:3). Anyone who would blaspheme (*nāqab*) the name of the Lord was to be put to death (Lev 24:16).

The third commandment addresses not only speaking truthfully in an oath and treating the name of the Yahweh with respect but also the more general issue of speaking truthfully. Numbers 30:2(3) states that when a man makes a vow to the Lord or swears an oath, he must

---

[46] See D. Garland, "Oaths and Swearing," *DJG*, 577.

[47] N. Sarna, *Exodus*, JPS Torah Commentary (Philadelphia, New York: Jewish Publication Society, 1991), 111.

[48] Those guilty of stealing "profane" or "abuse" (חָמַס: Prov 30:9) the name of the Lord. See Childs, *The Book of Exodus*, 411–12.

not break his word. A similar law is recorded in Deut 23:21–23(22–24), where focus again is on exhibiting truthfulness by fulfilling a vow (see also Ps 50:14). Moreover, in Neh 5:12–13, we find an additional warning for a person to fulfill his word. In Eccl 5:1–6 the reader is warned against taking an oath and addressing God in a casual manner. From this Old Testament perspective it is but a step to Philo's recommendation to avoid taking oaths entirely:

> To swear not at all is the best course and most profitable to life, well suited to a rational nature which has been taught to speak the truth so well on each occasion that its words are regarded as oaths; to swear truly is only, as people say, a "second-best voyage," for the mere fact of his swearing casts suspicion on the trustworthiness of the man.[49]

When God swears with an oath to confirm His promises, His own truthfulness and faithfulness to the vow is the focus (Ps 132:11; Heb 6:17–18). The man who enters the sanctuary and walks with his God must be a righteous man who speaks truthfully and is free from deceitful swearing (Pss 15:2; 24:3–6). He fulfills his vows to the Lord (Ps 65:1[2]).

The Third Commandment in the New Testament

There appears to be an application of the third commandment in the Sermon on the Mount (Matt 5:33–37). In Matt 5:33, Jesus said to His disciples, "You must not break your oath [lit. "swear falsely"], but you must keep your oaths to the Lord." When a person makes a vow or an oath to the Lord, he has to really mean it and be faithful to carrying it out (see Deut 23:21–23[22–24]; Ps 50:14). "Every assertion accompanied by an oath must be true; every promise accompanied by an oath must be kept."[50] The reference to oaths and vows is not a precise reference to the third commandment but appears to combine the teaching of Lev 19:12 and Num 30:2(3),[51] both of which appear to be extensions of the third commandment. To the extent that "swearing falsely" may be a

---

[49] Philo, *Decal*, § 84, 49. See also Philo, *Spec. Laws, II*, §§ 1–8, 307–11. Sir 23:9–11 also strongly discourages swearing.

[50] J. Broadus, *Commentary on the Gospel of Matthew* (Philadelphia: American Baptist Publication Society, 1886), 114.

[51] See for example R. Lenski, *The Interpretation of St. Matthew's Gospel* (Minneapolis: Augsburg, 1961), 235; R. Gundry, *Matthew: A Commentary on His Literary and Theological Art* (Grand Rapids: Eerdmans, 1982), 92.

way one "misuses" the name of the Lord, the teaching of the third commandment does apply. Hellenistic Judaism saw perjury as a violation of the third commandment.[52] David Garland argues that the teaching of Jesus in Matt 5:33–37 as well as Matt 23:16–22 probably arose in response to the issue of "profaning the holy name"[53] and in all probability was thought of as violating the third commandment.

In keeping with His demand for a greater righteousness (Matt 5:20), Jesus prohibits all swearing in Matt 5:34. The best way to avoid false swearing, and thereby the misuse of God's name, is not to swear at all. A valid oath was supposed to be taken in the name of God (Deut 6:13; 10:20), but in the first century AD the Jews would avoid using God's name at all costs based on a misinterpretation of the third commandment.[54] To avoid misusing God's name, the Pharisees developed some rather casuistic practices, thinking they could avoid the use of God's name but still express a serious oath. They calculated ways to express an oath by avoiding the use of God's name. Jesus corrects this misunderstanding of the third commandment. Jesus appears to be addressing popular practices in which an oath was taken by swearing by something significant but not invoking God's name. The Pharisees thought that in swearing by heaven, earth, Jerusalem, or by one's own head, they could avoid mention of God's name (Matt 5:33–36).[55] However, oaths invoking heaven, earth, Jerusalem, and the hairs of one's head would in fact bear some reference to God. Since God's authority is universal over all creation, even substitutions for His name stand in association and connection with Him.[56] Jesus stated that all oaths are made to God, and to swear by anything is to swear to God.[57] An oath is an oath regardless of how oblique the reference to God might be.[58] All oaths are binding

---

[52] Betz, *The Sermon on the Mount,* 265.

[53] D. Garland, "Oaths and Swearing," *DJG,* 577.

[54] D. Turner, *Matthew,* BECNT (Grand Rapids: Baker Academic, 2008), 173.

[55] See Betz, *The Sermon on the Mount,* 262. Swearing by heaven, earth, Jerusalem, or one's head are mentioned in *m. Šebu.* 4:13; *m. Ned.* 1:3; *m. Sanh.* 3:2.

[56] Gundry, *Matthew,* 93.

[57] D. A. Carson, *Jesus' Sermon on the Mount. An Exposition of Matthew 5–10* (Toronto: Global Christian Publishers, 1987), 51.

[58] Turner, *Matthew,* 173.

and cannot be revoked. Substitute oaths, where God's name is not explicitly evoked, are a legal mirage.[59]

Moreover, all oaths are pledges to speak and act out the truth.[60] But the use of this religious sophistry and false motives of getting away with not fulfilling an oath or vow led Jesus to command that one who offered an oath with this attitude would be better not to offer an oath at all (see Jas 5:12).[61] To the extent that this attitude trivialized God's name, it would constitute a violation of the third commandment. Philo, a first-century AD Jew, was well aware of the abuse of swearing among his people when he wrote:

> There are some who without even any gain in prospect have an evil habit of swearing incessantly and thoughtlessly about ordinary matters where there is nothing at all in dispute, filling up the gaps in their talk with oaths, forgetting that it were better to submit to have their words cut short or rather to be silenced altogether, for from much swearing springs false swearing and impiety.[62]

Jesus instructed His disciples to avoid frivolous swearing. Rather, they should be known for their integrity; their yes should be yes, and their no should be no (Matt 5:37). This transcends the issue of oathtaking, swearing, or keeping vows, and addresses the heart of the issue: sincerity, honesty, and truth. For disciples of Christ, truth should reign supreme in the heart.[63] Honesty and truthfulness are demanded by Christ, and there should no longer be any occasion for an oath. Followers of Christ should be characterized as exhibiting a straightforward speaking of the truth. "It is the condition of the heart that decides whether the 'yes' is really a 'yes' and the 'no' really a 'no.'"[64] The root of perjury is a disobedient heart. Those who would frequently swear or resort to oaths imply that they cannot be trusted to speak the truth unless they speak

---

[59] Garland, "Oaths and Swearing," 578. See J. Calvin, *Institutes of the Christian Religion*, ed. J. McNeill, 2 vols. (Philadelphia: Westminster, 1975), 1:392–93.

[60] Carson, *Jesus' Sermon on the Mount*, 51.

[61] J. Calvin, *Commentary on a Harmony of the Evangelists Matthew, Mark, and Luke*, trans. W. Pringle (Grand Rapids: Baker, 1979), 294–95. This behavior is also demonstrated by the religious leaders in Matt 23:16–22.

[62] Philo, *Decal.* § 92, 53.

[63] W. Hendriksen, *Exposition of the Gospel of Matthew* (Grand Rapids: Baker, 1973), 308.

[64] Betz, *Sermon on the Mount*, 274.

under oath.[65] "By inserting oaths we imply that our statements are not truthful, that we really cannot be believed except under oath."[66]

Jesus rebukes the hypocritical and flippant oaths that characterized many Jewish leaders and instead exhorted His followers to a life of truthfulness in thought, word, and deed.[67] In harmony with Jesus' application of the Old Testament teaching is the command in Deut 23:21–23(22–24) to be true to one's word by carrying out a vow (see Ps 50:14).[68] Disciples of Jesus are expected to speak the truth on all occasions as a matter of course. They are accountable for every idle word (Matt 12:34–37). Jesus was concerned not only about truthfulness in keeping a pledge but also about proper use of God's name, the unstated yet critical issue in Matt 5:33–37.

The New Testament is not silent about this broader application of the third commandment, the frivolous use of God's name. Reverence for God and His name is still prevalent in the New Testament. However, the stress is often shifted to the name of Jesus, God incarnate. We are now to believe in the name of Jesus (John 1:12), be baptized in the name of Jesus (Acts 8:16), and worship in the name of Jesus (Acts 9:14). There is no other name by which we are saved (Acts 4:12). For His is the name above all names. Every knee will bow and every tongue confess that He is Lord (Phil 2:9–11).[69]

Conclusion

In Jewish tradition, the ban on misuse of God's name led to the prohibition on even pronouncing His name. However, we know that the name Yahweh (Lord) was pronounced until the destruction of Solomon's temple in 586 BC, according to the Lachish Letters.[70] Avoiding pronunciation of the divine name was thought to be a sign of reverence, but it was actually a misinterpretation of the third

[65] Lenski, *Matthew*, 238.

[66] Ibid.

[67] Hendriksen, *Exposition of the Gospel of Matthew,* 309.

[68] Garland, "Oaths and Swearing," 577.

[69] The language of Phil 2 is taken from Isa 45:23, which addresses the future worship of Yahweh. Thus Paul equates Jesus with Yahweh. Moreover, the verb "confess" is a translation of the Hebrew word תִּשָּׁבַע "swear," from Isa 45:23.

[70] For the text, see J. C. L. Gibson, *Textbook of Syrian Semitic Inscriptions,* 3 vols. Vol. 1: *Hebrew and Moabite Inscriptions* (Oxford: Clarendon, 1971), 37.

commandment.[71] But the third commandment has also been misunderstood in more modern times.

The popular American view that the words "misuse the name of the Lord" or "take the Lord's name in vain" refer only to profanity cannot be substantiated from the text. The teaching of the passage cannot be reduced to such a limitation. But if God's name is used in any kind of profane way, this would constitute a violation of the third commandment. This applies as well to an inappropriate use of Jesus' name.

To pray in Jesus' name is to pray in accord with His purpose, His person, and His will. Unfortunately, a real danger in our day—similar to the Old Testament period—is the temptation to use the formula "in Jesus' name" as a form of magic. However, the third commandment warns against the manipulation of God for purely personal reasons, the attempt to hitch the Lord to your own wagon. Every reference we make to the Lord, whether verbal or mental, should be made with the highest reverence.[72] Not to do so would violate the command to fear the Lord (Deut 6:13). It would be better for a person to have never been born than to utter God's name for no good purpose (*Zohar, Shemot* 87b).[73] "Hallowed be thy name" (Matt 6:9 KJV) should be the prayer of the saints of all generations. At its core, this commandment is meant to instill reverence for the reality of the Lord.[74] But is swearing or taking an oath ever permissible for the Christian?

There has been a difference of interpretation among Christians with regard to the appropriateness of swearing. Anabaptists and other Protestants such as William Penn understood Jesus' statement "But I tell you, don't take an oath at all (Matt 5:34)" to apply comprehensively to all situations. Other Christian interpreters believe that as loyal and obedient subjects of the state, Christians should be willing to take an oath if required by civil law.[75] Hendriksen noted:

---

[71] The pronunciation of the special name of Israel's God as "Yahweh" is supported by the abbreviation *Yah* (e.g., Exod 15:2) and the ending of *–ya* or *–yahu* attached to many Hebrew names. See Dohmen, *Exodus 19–40*, 116; L. Hartman and S. Sperling, "God, Names of," *EJ* 7:675.

[72] C. Houtman, *Exodus* (Leuven: Peeters, 2000), 3:36–38.

[73] Wax, *The Ten Commandments*, 174.

[74] R. Collins, *Christian Morality: Biblical Foundations* (Notre Dame, IN: University of Notre Dame Press, 1986), 54.

[75] This was the position of Calvin, Luther, and Broadus. See Calvin, *Commentary on a*

In this world of dishonesty and deception the oath is at times necessary to add solemnity and the guarantee of reliability to an important affirmation or promise. Nothing either here in Matt 5:33–37 or anywhere else in Scripture forbids this. Heb 6:16 confirms this practice without a word of adverse criticism.[76]

The taking of an oath is made necessary because of the dishonesty and deception that exists in society. It is a means whereby justice can be carried out. In everyday communication, Christians will not need to use oaths; they speak and act as if in God's presence. This would leave the swearing under oath to the jurisdiction of the state alone.[77] Christian interpreters who affirm this position point out that Paul swore or took an oath in passages such as Rom 1:9; 2 Cor 1:23; Gal 1:20; 1 Thess 2:5,10.[78] In the second advent of Christ, non-Israelites will express their allegiance to the true God by an oath (Isa 19:18; 45:23). God stressed the absolute trustworthiness of His word in Ps 132:11 and Heb 6:17–18 as He confirmed His promises by oath.

To trivialize the name of the Lord is to diminish His person and His glory. To trivialize God's name is to show the utmost disrespect for the God to whom we owe everything, not only in this world but also in the world to come. This commandment addresses any insincere reference to the Lord, as His name is the revelation of His person. This would include offering praise or singing to God out of routine without any thought to what one is singing or praying. In the thinking of the ancient world, the name of a person was linked to his character. The name Lord (Yahweh) was a revelation of God's nature, and thus to use this name in an inappropriate manner would be an affront to the character of God. Making God an accomplice to anything that is false or unsuitable shows the utmost disrespect.[79]

Harmony of the Evangelists, 297; Broadus, *Matthew,* 115; U. Luz, *Matthew 1–7: A Continental Commentary,* trans. W. Linss (Minneapolis: Fortress, 1989), 319.

[76] Hendriksen, *Matthew,* 309.

[77] Lenski, *Matthew,* 239. Vines also affirms that the third commandment does not forbid the taking of an oath in a court of law but rather the attaching of the name of God to a dishonest, untruthful statement. J. Vines, *Basic Bible Sermons on the Ten Commandments* (Nashville: Broadman Press, 1992), 40.

[78] It is a matter of debate whether Jesus took an oath in Matt 26:63. Those who believe that Jesus consented to take an oath include Broadus, *Matthew,* 114, while Luz and Turner maintain that Jesus did not answer with an oath. See Luz, *Matthew 1–7,* 318; Turner, *Matthew,* 173.

[79] See Huffmon, "The Fundamental Code Illustrated: The Third Commandment," 370.

While the third commandment is a warning to human beings, it is greatly concerned with God's reputation and honor. As the source of truth, God cannot be associated with falsehood and deceit.[80] The aim of the third commandment is to protect the name of Yahweh—which was entrusted to His people (Exod 3:13–14; 6:3)—from any kind of disrepute. A central theme of the book of Exodus is the promulgation of the Lord's name throughout the earth (Exod 9:16). The plan of God and the mission of God for this world are interrelated in making known God's name.[81] The concern for God's reputation, that He be associated with truthfulness, is also the concern of the first two commandments, that the Lord who brought His children out of Egypt be recognized in truth as the only true God, and that no image or idol be thought to be a substitute for Him.

The third commandment is similar to the ninth commandment but should be distinguished from it for several reasons. First, the third commandment is placed in the first section of the Decalogue, which focuses on one's relationship to God, while the ninth commandment occurs in the second section of the Decalogue, which emphasizes one's relationship to his fellow man. Second, while the ninth commandment would focus on legal issues within the community, the third commandment focuses directly on how one relates to God and would thus be considered extralegal. God will directly sanction and punish those who violate the third commandment and will not leave them to human courts. The third commandment is aimed at untruthfulness in general while the ninth commandment is more directly connected with perjury in a legal court.[82] The third commandment finds its source in the first commandment, the unique and exclusive God who alone is to be worshipped. And whereas the second commandment has to do with visible representations of God (or gods), the third commandment is concerned with the use of His name as an extension of His person.[83]

---

[80] Childs, *The Book of Exodus*, 68.

[81] See T. Fretheim, *Exodus,* Interpretation: A Biblical Commentary for Teaching and Preaching (Louisville: John Knox, 1973), 227–29.

[82] Huffmon, "The Fundamental Code Illustrated: The Third Commandment," 371n36.

[83] J. Gordon McConville, "God's 'Name' and God's 'Glory,'" *TynBul* 30 (1979): 149–63.

Chapter 4

THE FOURTH COMMANDMENT

*Remember to dedicate the Sabbath day: You are to labor six
days and do all your work, but the seventh day is a Sabbath to the LORD your God. You must not do any work—you,
your son or daughter, your male or female slave, your livestock, or the foreigner who is within your gates. For the LORD
made the heavens and the earth, the sea, and everything in
them in six days; then He rested on the seventh day. Therefore the LORD blessed the Sabbath day and declared it holy.*

Introduction

The fourth commandment is unparalleled among the laws of
the ancient Near East. While many scholars have attempted
to connect the observance of the Sabbath with the Akkadian
word *šapattu*, a festival term associated with a phase of the moon, this
attempt has fallen out of favor among both biblical and ancient Near
Eastern scholars. There is a growing consensus that the two words
are not etymologically related and the Hebrew term cannot be derived
from the Akkadian term.[1] The Sabbath day has nothing to do with
the alignment of the moon or other heavenly bodies. It is merely the
seventh day of the week in perpetual sequence.[2]

Some scholars have argued that the Sabbath was borrowed from
the Kenites (Num 10:29–32; Judg 4:11,17), others from the Phoeni-
cians of Ugarit, for whom the number seven appeared to be significant. These views have had few proponents.[3] No quest for the origin

---

[1] Among other difficulties is the fact that the Hb. term שַׁבָּת doubles the second letter while
the Akkadian term doubles the third letter.

[2] U. Cassuto, *A Commentary on the Book of Exodus*, trans. I. Abrahams (Jerusalem: Magnes,
1974), 244. See N. Andreasen, *The Old Testament Sabbath: A Tradition-Historical Investigation*
(Missoula, MT: Society of Biblical Literature, 1971), 6; W. Schmidt, *The Faith of the Old Testament*, trans. J. Sturdy (Philadelphia: Westminster, 1983), 89.

[3] The number *seven* and the noun *Sabbath* have the same two first letters but have a different
third consonant. The association of the two terms based on this connection is not valid, however. See Andreasen, *The Old Testament Sabbath: A Tradition-Historical Investigation*, 9,103.

of the Sabbath outside the Old Testament has forged a consensus.[4] There is no clear evidence of a Sabbath day outside the Old Testament tradition.[5]

The Masoretic scribes clearly wanted to distinguish the fourth commandment from the previous three as they placed a *Parashot* paragraph division (represented by the Hb. letter פ) before the fourth commandment. This paragraph division marker in Exod 20 occurs elsewhere only at the end of the Ten Commandments (Exod 20:17). Based on the location of the *Parashot* paragraph marker, it may be argued that its placement here marks a major division within the Ten Commandments. This commandment is furthered distinguished in that it is the first one presented as a positive formulation rather than a prohibition. In addition, it is the longest of the commandments.

It is also with the Sabbath commandment that one begins to find more significant differences between the Exodus and Deuteronomy formulations of the Ten Commandments. These differences can be accounted for based on the different settings, the Exodus account from Mount Sinai and the Deuteronomy account delivered on the plains of Moab. These accounts have audiences separated in time by forty years. The events that had taken place since the giving of the law at Mount Sinai called for a new understanding of the Sabbath as the new generation was ready to enter the promised land.[6]

The Meaning of the Fourth Commandment

As mentioned, the fourth commandment begins not with a prohibition but with a positive command, "Remember to dedicate the Sabbath day" (Exod 20:8). While the verb "remember" (Hb. *zākar*) is often contrasted with *šākaḥ* ("to forget"),[7] *zākar* is not primarily about recalling something from the past but refers to the presence of

---

[4] See Andreasen, *The Old Testament Sabbath*, 93; B. Childs, *The Book of Exodus: A Critical-Theological Commentary* (Louisville: Westminster John Knox, 1974), 413–14; G. Hasel, "Sabbath," *ABD* 5:849–51; P. Barker, "Sabbath, Sabbatical Year, Jubilee," *DOTP*, 699.

[5] P. Craigie, *The Book of Deuteronomy* (Grand Rapids: Eerdmans, 1976), 157, 157n19.

[6] See E. Merrill, *Deuteronomy*, NAC (Nashville: B&H, 1994), 149.

[7] See Gen 40:23; Deut 8:18–19; 19:7; 1 Sam 1:11; Job 24:20; Pss 9:12(13); 74:18–19; Prov 31:7; Isa 17:10; 54:4. It may be significant that Hb. זכר ("remember") begins with the seventh letter of the Hb. alphabet, the letter ז (*zayin*).

something in the mind. The verb does not refer to a mere recollection but includes the consequences or actions the memory demands.[8] The verb is often used as a synonym for various actions (Josh 1:13; Esth 9:28; Ps 109:16; Isa 17:10; Amos 1:9; Mal 4:4[3:22]).[9] The verb is often used in the sense of remembering the law and the commandments with the idea of doing them (Num 15:39–40; Mal 4:4[3:22]).

The verb, in the same grammatical form (Qal infinitive absolute), is also used in reference to "remembering" the exodus deliverance from Egypt in Exod 13:3. In this context, remembering the exodus inspires the ritual celebration of the Passover festival. In a similar manner, "to remember the Sabbath is to observe it by abstaining from work."[10] The stress on remembering or calling to mind might be especially important with regard to the Sabbath as it is the only religious festival whose observance is not tied to a phase of the moon. The Sabbath relies on human record keeping.[11] In order to remember the Sabbath, a person had consciously to calculate when the next Sabbath would take place.[12]

The Sabbath commandment in Deuteronomy has the verb *šāmar* rather than *zākar*, although both are grammatically equivalent (Qal infinitive absolutes). The verb *šāmar* occurs 468 times in the Old Testament, and its range in meaning includes "watch, guard, observe, fulfill, keep, keep watch, spy out." It may convey the underlying meaning of "pay careful attention to."[13] This root is frequently used in conjunction with "keeping" the commandments (Gen 26:5; Lev 8:35; 18:26,30; 22:9,31; Num 9:19,23; Deut 4:40; 6:2; 11:1; 26:16–17; Josh 22:3,5; 1 Kgs 2:3; 11:34; 2 Kgs 17:37; 2 Chr 13:11; 23:6; Jer 35:18; Ezek 11:20; 18:19; Mal 3:14). The verb is characteristic of the Deuteronomy expression for "observing the Law."[14] The verb is also used

---

[8] See H. Eising, "זָכַר *zākhar*," *TDOT* 4:65–67; and T. Fretheim, *Exodus,* Interpretation: A Biblical Commentary for Teaching and Preaching (Louisville: John Knox, 1973), 229. See Exod 2:24.

[9] L. Allen, "זכר," *NIDOTTE* 1:1,103.

[10] Ibid., 1103.

[11] W. Propp, *Exodus 19–40,* AB (New York: Doubleday, 2006), 175.

[12] Thus A. Hakam, *The Book of Exodus* (Jerusalem: Mossad Harav Kook, 1991), 283 [in Hb.]. See also C. Dohmen, *Exodus 19–40* (Freiburg: Herder, 2004), 119.

[13] G. Lopez, "שָׁמַר *šāmar*," *TDOT* 15:283, 286; Schoville, "שׁמר," *NIDOTTE* 4:182.

[14] E. Nielsen, *Deuteronomium,* HAT (Tübingen: Mohr [Siebeck], 1995), 73.

in the semantically similar concept of "keeping" the ways of the Lord (Gen 18:19; 2 Sam 22:22), and occurs particularly in the phrase "keep or observe the Sabbath" as in Deut 5:12 (Exod 31:13; Lev 19:3,30; 26:2; Isa 56:4).[15] The verb is also used in reference to observing other holy feast days such as the Passover (Exod 12:17) and other festivals (Exod 23:16).[16]

The fact that *šāmar* is put in place of *zākar* in Deut 5 indicates that the two verbs overlap in meaning. One way to illustrate the interchange of these verbs may be observed in the instruction to observe the Passover. In Exodus the verb *zākar* is used (Exod 13:3), while in Deuteronomy we find the verb *šāmar* (Deut 16:1). These verbs are in the same grammatical form (Qal infinitive absolute), just as they occur in the Sabbath law in the two versions of the Ten Commandments. The fact that *šāmar* is used in reference to keeping the Sabbath in Exod 31:13, as well as the fact that *zākar* and *šāmar* occur in parallel in Ps 103:18, suggests that they are not far apart in meaning. As Martin Noth said: "There is hardly any difference in content, as 'remember' means that the Sabbath day is not to be overlooked, not to remain unnoticed, and this comes to the same thing as 'observe,' 'keep.'"[17]

The Meaning of the Word "Sabbath"

The word "Sabbath" (Hb. *šabbāt*) occurs more than 100 times in the Old Testament, primarily in legal passages and later passages that address observance of the Sabbath. The term "Sabbath" is related to the verb *šābat* as indicated by the frequent combination of these two terms as well as the clear assonance (similarity of sound) that exists between this noun and verb.[18] The verbal meaning of *šābat* means "to cease." The use of the verb with this meaning may be illustrated in such passages as Gen 8:22; Josh 5:12; Neh 6:3; Isa 14:4; 24:8; and Jer 31:36. The relationship and connection of the verb with the noun Sabbath is

---

[15] In more than 200 verses, the verb is used with "commandments" as its object. See Lopez, *TDOT* 15:290–91.

[16] The root has "festivals" as its object on at least 20 occasions, according to Sauer. See G. Sauer, "שׁמר *šmr*," *TLOT* 3:1382.

[17] M. Noth, *Exodus*, OTL (Philadelphia: Westminster, 1962), 164. Furthermore, in Gen 37:11, שׁמר seems to mean "to remember" (see Isa 47:7; Lam 1:9).

[18] See F. Stolz, "שׁבת *šbt*," *TLOT* 3:1297; E. Haag, "שַׁבָּת *šabbāt*," *TDOT* 14:388.

clear in such passages as Exod 23:12; 34:21; and Lev 23:32, where the notion of Sabbath is related to "ceasing" or "desisting" activities, i.e., not working.[19] The relationship between the two words is suggested in the Exodus verses even though the noun *šabbāt* is not present. In these texts, the seventh day is mentioned in context with the verb *šābat*.[20] But the clearest and perhaps most significant connection between the noun and the verb may be understood from the first occurrence of the verb in Gen 2:2 when God "ceased" (*wayyišbōt*)[21] from his work on the seventh day; from this point on, the seventh day is the Sabbath (*šabbāt*), from the same root. Thus, the Sabbath is the day when a person suspends or ceases his normal routine of labor.

The related term *šabbātôn* ("complete rest") occurs 11 times in the Old Testament, most often in the same phrase with *šabbāt*. The combined designation of *šabbāt šabbātôn* refers to the Sabbath day (Exod 16:23; 31:15; 35:2; Lev 23:3), the Day of Atonement (Lev 16:31; 23:32), and the sabbatical year (Lev 25:4).[22] The occurrence of the two terms together indicates something of a superlative, conveying and stressing the idea that all forms of labor are prohibited. At the Feast of Trumpets (Lev 23:24) and the first and eighth days of the Feast of Booths (Lev 23:39 [2x]), the word *šabbātôn* occurs by itself.[23] But the term *šabbātôn* conveys the idea that these festive days share features of the Sabbath. Thus, the terms are related by form and meaning as they refer to the idea of sacred time.

These nouns are related, and *šabbātôn* is based on and is perhaps a nominal extension of *šabbāt*.[24] The term *šabbātôn* seems to

---

[19] J. Tigay, "שָׁבַת," *EncMiq* 7:505.

[20] Barker, "Sabbath, Sabbatical Year, Jubilee," 695.

[21] See HCSB note. Childs and Andreasen argue that the noun was derived form the verbal form, which has the meaning of "to rest, cease from work" (Childs, *The Book of Exodus: A Critical-Theological Commentary*, 413; Andreasen, *The Old Testament Sabbath*, 121).

[22] In Lev 25:5, in reference to the sabbatical year, the word שַׁבָּתוֹן (*šabbātôn*) occurs without the noun שַׁבָּת.

[23] The distinction between the terms Sabbath and שַׁבָּתוֹן (*šabbātôn*) is not completely clear. Bosman suggests that "Sabbath" conveys total abstinence from work with a focus on rest, while שַׁבָּתוֹן occurs with the annual festivals where again no work is to be carried out but one may still participate in the festival (H. Bosman, "Sabbath," *NIDOTTE* 4:1160).

[24] Gesenius suggests the ending of שַׁבָּתוֹן *šabbātôn* is indicative of an abstract noun, thus שַׁבָּתוֹן should be thought of as "restfulness" (GKC 86f, 240); similarly Andreasen, *The Old Testament Sabbath*, 113.

indicate that other religious festivals were "Sabbath-like," and thus the observance of the weekly Sabbath, which included the cessation of work, was an example for how other religious festivals were to be observed.[25]

The fourth commandment calls for one to remember and "to dedicate" the weekly Sabbath. The important term translated "dedicate" is from *qdš*, which is the root for holiness or holy things, and refers to things that belong to God. One is to dedicate the Sabbath by making it distinct from other days. God declared that the first six days of creation were good; only the Sabbath day He declared to be holy. As a holy day, the Sabbath is removed from the mundane sphere of secular time and reflects the divine dimension. In this way the Sabbath could be seen as a suspension of time as it prohibits all work on that day.[26] The Sabbath belongs to the Lord, and it must be used for God's purposes, not ours (Isa 58:13). It is God's day (Exod 16:23,25; 31:15).[27]

After this initial command for remembering or keeping the Sabbath, Deut 5 adds "as the LORD your God has commanded you" (Deut 5:12b). This phrase, which also occurs in the following commandment regarding the honoring of parents, refers back to the initial giving of the Ten Commandments on Mount Sinai (Exod 20).[28]

No Work on the Sabbath Day

Beginning in Exod 20:9, the law starts to explain more fully not only Sabbath observance but the correct understanding of the root *šbt*, upon which the noun "Sabbath" is based. The commandment begins by addressing what is to be the work pattern for man: "You are to labor (*ʿābad*) six days and do all your work" (Exod 20:9). The root *ʿābad* occurred in the second commandment, where it had the meaning of worship, in the sense of worshipping or serving other

---

[25] See Bosman, *NIDOTTE* 4:1160.

[26] N. Sarna, *Exploring Exodus: The Origins of Biblical Israel* (New York: Schocken Books, 1996), 148.

[27] Human activities that may have been prohibited for human benefit are permitted in the temple as they were part of the setting apart of this special worship day to the Lord (see Exod 27:20–21; 29:38–42; Num 9:9–10). J. Tigay, *Deuteronomy*, JPS Torah Commentary (Philadelphia: Jewish Publication Society, 1996), 68.

[28] Craigie, *The Book of Deuteronomy*, 156.

gods. Here in the fourth commandment the term refers not to man's spiritual work but rather his physical labor. The focus on the root referring to physical labor is especially apparent in texts such as Gen 29:27; Lev 25:39; Ezek 29:18, where the verb *'ābad* occurs with its cognate *ăbōdâ* in the sense of physical, nonreligious work.[29] The verb *'ābad* is used with the meaning of physical labor in other texts such as Exod 1:13–14; 5:18; Deut 15:19; 21:3 (Pual), 4 (Niphal); 2 Chr 2:17 (Hiphil); Jer 22:13; Ezek 48:18–19 (Qal). The common use of the cognate noun *'ebed* for a slave reduced to a life of physical labor in the socioeconomic realm is harmonious with this view.[30] As noted above, we see that this important verb with its wide scope of meaning refers to both religious and profane work. Thus work (*'ābad*), whether in the spiritual or physical sense, expresses the scope of all mankind's activity. It is "an essential and inalterable characteristic of human life."[31]

The stress on physical labor is reinforced or qualified by the subsequent phrase "and do all your work" (Exod 20:9b). Both of these expressions describing what is to be done on six days of the week are in contrast with the Sabbath day, which calls for ceasing all labor.

The noun *mělā'kâ* ("work") occurs 166 times in the Old Testament, but the root of the noun never occurs as a verbal form.[32] The noun has a wide range of meaning that can be grouped into four basic categories: (1) skilled work, craftsmanship; (2) general work (including physical labor); (3) the result of work; and (4) mission, commission, errand, or business.[33] While the term often refers to skilled labor, including work on the tabernacle and the performance of cultic tasks, its use here is for work in general or occupational work in physical labor.[34] This understanding is supported not only from the context

---

[29] The combination occurs in the cultic or religious sense as well (Exod 13:5; Num 3:8; 4:23,27; 7:5; 8:22; Josh 22:27).

[30] See C. Westermann, "עֶבֶד *'ebed*," *TLOT* 2:822.

[31] Ibid., 824. In the Qal stem the root is often used with respect to the cult of Israel in her service and care for the tabernacle and temple as well as for those who served there.

[32] According to other Semitic languages, the meaning of the verbal root is "to send" (J. Milgrom and D. Wright, "מְלָאכָה *mělā'kâ*," *TDOT* 8:325).

[33] Ibid., 326.

[34] In the LXX, the noun is most often translated by ἔργον (127 times). This Greek term has the same basic range of meaning, as it may refer to sacred or secular work (S. Hague, "מְלָאכָה," *NIDOTTE* 2:944). The term is an antonym of שַׁבָּת "Sabbath."

but also by the types of work that are subsequently prohibited on the Sabbath. These include "leaving one's place" (Exod 16:29), agricultural activities (Exod 34:21), kindling fire (Exod 35:3), gathering wood (Num 15:32–36), conducting business (Neh 10:31; 13:15–18; Isa 58:13; Amos 8:5), carrying burdens (Jer 17:21,24,27), and treading the winepress and loading donkeys (Neh 13:15).[35] The Israelite is not to "work" *mělāʾkâ* on the seventh day because God brought all His "work" *mělāʾkâ* to an end by the seventh day (Gen 2:2).

Thus man is to do his work for six days in the week. This is in harmony with the instruction that Adam received when he was placed in the garden of Eden "to work *(ʿābad)* it and watch over *(šāmar)* it" (Gen 2:15). As the concern for nourishment is essential for existence, cultivation of the land that produces nourishment is a necessary part of being human.[36]

> Gen 2:5 indicates clearly that one of the purposes for the creation of adam, humankind, was to till *(ʿbd)* the ground *before* the Fall. So it was always God's design that humans would work the ground the Lord/God had created in Eden, an inherent religious act when done to fulfill the Creator's purposes. Working the ground became a burdensome task after the rebellion of humankind (3:17–19). Work in the sense of the kinds of duties carried out to earn one's living becomes subsumed in the word. Ecclesiastes can even assert that the sleep of the laborer *(ʿbd)* is sweet (Eccl 5:12 [11]).[37]

So even though the focus of the fourth commandment is on the cessation of work on one day a week (see Exod 20:11), it also affirms that man's life is to be characterized by work, and he is to be about his labor for six days of the week.[38]

But the seventh day of the week "is the Sabbath to the LORD your God" (Exod 20:10). The Sabbath day belongs to the Lord. This reinforces the initial command in Exod 20:8 that the Sabbath day is to be dedicated (Hb. *qdš*) to the Lord, the Holy One. The expression underlines the holiness of the Sabbath.[39] No work is to be done on this day.

---

[35] N. Sarna, *Exodus*, JPS Torah Commentary (Philadelphia, New York: Jewish Publication Society, 1991), 112.

[36] See Westermann, *TLOT* 2:824.

[37] E. Carpenter, "עבד," *NIDOTTE* 3:305.

[38] As Dohmen observed, these statements put work in a new light. See Dohmen, *Exodus 19–40*, 120.

[39] Andreasen, *The Old Testament Sabbath*, 208.

This applies to the addressee as well as his son or daughter, his male or female slave, his livestock, or the foreigner who is within his gates. The prohibition of work on the seventh day also applies to those who may be under one's authority, including animals.[40] Thus animals are to be given a break from labor like humans.[41] The kindness to be exercised to animals is the theme of several passages in the Pentateuch (see Exod 22:30[29]; Lev 22:27–28; Deut 22:6–7,10; 25:4). The stranger is also exempt from work on the seventh day. The foreigner or stranger (Hb. *gēr*) is one who lives in a foreign land among people who are not his blood relatives, and lacks the protection and support that would usually come from a blood relationship. The foreigner would not possess land and would be in the service of and under the authority of an Israelite as his master (Deut 24:14). Quite possibly as a result, he may be subject to abuse in the sense of hard labor. The stranger, who may be particularly vulnerable to abuse, is also to enjoy the respite from work one day a week (see Exod 23:9).[42] Every human being, irrespective of social class, has the inalienable right to a day of complete rest every seven days.[43]

This concern not to exploit workers is brought out even more forcefully in the Deuteronomy version of the Ten Commandments, where the stated reason is not following God's example in creation (see below) but rather recalling that the Israelites' ancestors had been enslaved in Egypt.[44] This remembrance of the nation's experience in

---

[40] The list of those addressed begins with "you," the masculine singular independent pronoun. As the list goes on to mention "your son or daughter, your male or female slave," the pronoun "you" should be understood as addressing both males and females. Tigay, *Deuteronomy*, JPS Torah Commentary 68, 375n91,92; M. Weinfeld, *Deuteronomy 1–11*, AB 5 (New York: Doubleday), 308. Alternatively, the omission of wives could indicate that the prohibitions do not apply to wives engaging in domestic activities. A. Phillips, *Ancient Israel's Criminal Law: A New Approach to the Decalogue* (Oxford: Basil Blackwell, 1970), 69.

[41] In Deut 5, two animals are added, oxen and donkeys (Deut 5:14). They are to experience a Sabbath rest (Exod 23:12). This prohibition may refer to all the work men might do with animals and thus still focus on the prohibition of human labor. See Tigay, "שָׁבַת," 506.

[42] The foreigner was not to be oppressed (Exod 22:21[20]; 23:9). For texts that give insight on the life of a foreigner, see Gen 23:4; Exod 2:22; 12:19; Ruth 1:1; 1 Chr 22:2. The LXX translates גֵּר by προσήλυτος ("proselyte"). See D. Kellerman, "גּוּר *gûr*," TDOT 2:442; A. Konkel, "גּוּר" NIDOTTE 1:837; R. Martin-Archard, "גּור *gûr*," TLOT 1:309.

[43] Sarna, *Exploring Exodus*, 148.

[44] The humane treatment of servants is the subject of many biblical laws (Exod 21:20–21,26–27; Deut 15:12–15,18; 16:11–12; 23:15–16).

Egypt is a common theme in Deuteronomy. Because the Israelites were mistreated in Egypt, they should act charitably and kindly toward slaves and the needy (Deut 15:15; 16:12; 24:18,22). "This is not to be understood as suggesting that the Sabbath day was instituted because of the Exodus; rather, because of the deliverance from Egypt, Israel is urged to observe the Sabbath, which means letting the slaves and other dependents rest on this day."[45]

Seven categories of people are listed as beneficiaries of the Sabbath rest: you, your son, your daughter, your male slave, your female slave, your livestock, the foreigner. This sevenfold list not only suggests completion and comprehensiveness but is another way to emphasize the concept of the Sabbath, the seventh day.

God Did Not Work on the Seventh Day

The rationale for obedience to the fourth commandment is provided in Exod 20:11.[46] The reason man is not to work on the seventh day is that this is what took place during the creation week when God[47] made "the heavens and the earth, the sea, and everything in them" (Exod 20:11a). The phrases describing God's work mirror the Genesis creation account as God made the heavens, the earth, and the sea on the first three days, and "everything in them" on the fourth through sixth days.[48]

God made all that exists in six days and then "rested *(wayyānaḥ)* on the seventh day" (Exod 20:11a). The verb *nwḥ*, translated "to rest," conveys the notion of "settling down" and coming to a rest. The verb is used of Noah's ark and of the ark of the covenant as settling down, or coming to rest, in Gen 8:4 and Num 10:36.[49] In the creation account God "ceased" *(šbt)* from his labor on the seventh day (Gen 2:2), and now in the Ten Commandments we are informed that this

---

[45] Weinfeld, *Deuteronomy 1–11*, 309.

[46] The use of the particle כִּי to indicate cause or reason was noted in Exod 20:5 in discussion of the second commandment, which is the second-longest commandment.

[47] In the creation account of Gen 1:1, the Hb. name אֱלֹהִים is used, but here in the Ten Commandments we have the name יהוה as the One who made the heavens and the earth. This shows that the true God has various names, each of which indicates a purpose.

[48] Hakam, *The Book of Exodus*, 285.

[49] The term is frequently used to refer to those who have been threatened by enemies but now enjoy peace (Esther 9:17–18; Neh 9:28; Isa 23:12). See F. Stolz, "נוח nûaḥ," *TLOT* 2:722–24.

completion of the creation work also means that He "rested" from His work.[50] The Israelites also are to toil for six days but like God "rest" on the seventh day. All types of work are forbidden including plowing and harvesting, gathering food and firewood, lighting fires, and commercial activities (Exod 16:23–30; 34:21; 35:3; Num 15:32–36; Neh 13:15–21; Amos 8:5; Jer 17:21–22).[51] Work was also forbidden on religious days and festivals (Exod 12:16; Lev 16:29; 23:8,28).

The reason man is called to work six days and rest on the seventh is that in doing so he imitates the pattern of God during the creation week and thereby is reminded of God's work in creation. As the obedient Israelite imitated God, he would be reminded that he was created in the image of God (Gen 1:26). Man's divinely appointed task to have dominion over God's created order (Gen 1:26) carried with it the privilege of sharing in God's rest.[52] This reason for Sabbath observance in Exod 20 is one of the major differences with the parallel account in Deut 5.

In Deut 5, the motivation for keeping the Sabbath is deliverance from Egyptian bondage. "The motive-clause in Exodus centers on the Sabbath as creation celebration (Exod 20:11) whereas that in Deuteronomy is concerned with the Sabbath as redemption celebration (Deut 5:15)."[53] In Exod 20 the Sabbath is grounded in a sacred commemoration, the purpose of which was to reenact the divine rest on the seventh day. Like God, humans are to do their work in six days and rest on the seventh. In Deut 5, the Sabbath is grounded in historical recollection, as the Israelites recall that they were slaves in Egypt.[54] The different basis for the motivation to obey the Sabbath

---

[50] When we think of God resting, we are not to conclude that He ceased work because of fatigue. Rather, as Isa 40:28 states, our God "never grows faint or weary."

[51] The commandment is not prohibiting any sort of exertion, or the preparing of food, or the feeding or watering of animals, or anything else necessary to get through the day in an agrarian culture. It prohibits duplicating on the Sabbath any of the usual labor of the other six days that can be stopped without causing harm to someone or something. D. Stuart, *Exodus*, NAC (Nashville: B&H, 2006), 449.

[52] Craigie, *The Book of Deuteronomy*, 157 and 157n18.

[53] E. Merrill, *Deuteronomy*, 151. Interestingly, in 4QDeut 5:15 from the Dead Sea Scrolls, the motive clause is taken from the Hb. text of Exod 20:11.

[54] According to Augustine, the reason the memory of slavery in Egypt was evoked was that the Sabbath law, unlike others of the Ten Commandments, was not as clearly defined in the human conscience. J. Lienhard, S. J., ed., *Exodus, Leviticus, Numbers, Deuteronomy*, ACCS (Downers Grove, IL: InterVarsity, 2001), 105.

command helps to explain the difference between the verbal forms
zākar and *šāmar*. The verb *zākar* focuses on the historical recollection (of creation in Gen 1:1; 2:3), while with *šāmar* the focus is on
keeping the commandment.[55] In Exod 13:3 the verb *zākar* is again
employed with reference to remembering the exodus from Egypt so
as to motivate the people to keep the religious festivals. Here in Exod
20 it is employed to remember the most frequently occurring festival,
the Sabbath.

The memory of Israel's servitude in Egypt (Deut 5:15) was to
arouse empathy in the Israelites for the needs of the servants who
would work for them.[56] As the Israelites looked around at these workers, they would remember their harsh labor in Egypt and in gratitude for God's deliverance would allow them to enjoy a Sabbath rest.
Because the people are about to move from an essentially nomadic
economy to one that will include farming and trade, oxen and donkeys are specifically mentioned in Deut 5:14. In another indication of
the coming move from a nomadic life to a more sedentary existence,
the Deuteronomy version of the commandments mentions the fields
where crops will be grown.[57] Israel kept the Sabbath law in order to
remember God's work both in creation and in deliverance.

The Sabbath Day Is Unique

The cessation of creative activity on the seventh day by God made
this day distinct in comparison with the first six days of creation.
God "blessed *(bārak)* the Sabbath day and declared it holy" (Exod
20:11b).[58]

"Bless" is an important word from the creation account (Gen
1:22,28; 2:3). God blessed His creation and also the Sabbath as He

---

[55] M. Weinfeld, "The Uniqueness of the Decalogue and its Place in Jewish Tradition," in *The Ten Commandments in History and Tradition*, ed. B. Z. Segal (Jerusalem: Magnes, 1990), 7. See Dohmen, *Exodus 19–40*, 119.

[56] D. Christensen, *Deuteronomy 1:1–21:9*, rev. ed., WBC 6A (Nashville: Thomas Nelson, 2001), 120.

[57] R. Youngblood, "Counting the Ten Commandments," *BR* 10,5 (1994): 33.

[58] The Deuteronomy version of the Sabbath law adds a phrase to the end of the fourth commandment: "That is why the LORD your God has commanded you to keep the Sabbath day" (Deut 5:15b). The formula "to keep the sabbath day" (cf. Exod 31:16) occurs in a similar fashion with reference to keeping the Passover (Exod 12:47–48; Num 9:1–5; Deut 16:1; 2 Kgs 23:21).

blesses the Sabbath in the fourth commandment. The Hb. word "bless" *(bārak)* occurs 327 times in the Old Testament. It is a continuous, present power that affects the future.[59] The bestowal of blessing results in vitality, prosperity, abundance, or fertility. God's blessing causes the heavens to give rain, the subterranean water to sustain arable land, the womb and breasts to give birth and suckle, and the people to eat in the presence of the Lord and rejoice in everything they do (Gen 49:25; Deut 12:7; 15:4). It is a direct act of God that causes what is blessed to perform and produce at the optimum level and to fulfill its purpose.[60] God's blessing is a bestowal of His kindness that results in success. With the call of Abraham, the possibility of blessing counteracts the curse that had burdened humanity.[61] The blessing of the Sabbath, according to Josef Scharbert, indicates that God bestows a blessing on the person who observes the Sabbath.[62] God blessed the Sabbath day because He sanctified it.

God also announces that the Sabbath is "holy," as He did in the creation account (Gen 2:3). The basic meaning of "holy" *(qdš)* is "distinct, withheld from ordinary use, treated with special care, to belong to the sanctuary." It denotes something of the sphere of the sacred. It may be used of people (Jer 1:5), places (Exod 29:37), things (Exod 30:29), and times (Lev 25:10) that were separated from the mundane affairs of everyday life and dedicated to the service of the Lord. The antonym of "holy" is "profane" or "common," something existing in its natural state. Thus holiness is associated with God and is an expression of His perfection. Holiness is not inherent in creation, but an entity is determined to be holy only as God dictates. It requires an act of God to bring something from its normal state into the sphere of holiness.[63]

It is significant that the word "holy" occurs at the beginning (Exod 20:8)[64] and now at the end of the Sabbath law (Exod 20:11).[65] Its

---

[59] C. Westermann, *Genesis 1–11*, trans. J. Scullion (Minneapolis: Fortress, 1994), 161.

[60] See J. Scharbert, "בְּרַךְ *brk,*" *TDOT* 2:287, 294, 298–99; C. Keller and G. Wehmeier, "בְּרַךְ *brk,*" *TLOT* 1:270–71, 277; M. Brown, "בְּרַךְ," *NIDOTTE* 1:759.

[61] The Hb. word "בְּרַךְ" ("bless") occurs five times in the call of Abraham (Gen 12:1–3) to correspond with the five occurrences of the Hb. word "אָרַר" ("curse") in Gen 3–11.

[62] Scharbert, "בְּרַךְ *brk,*" 295.

[63] J. Naude, "קָדַשׁ," *NIDOTTE* 3:877–79, 883–84.

[64] In Exod 20:8 the root קָדַשׁ, "holy," is translated "dedicate" in the HCSB.

[65] In the Deuteronomy account, the word "Sabbath" occurs prominently at the beginning

connection to the creation account is emphasized as the root *qdš* first occurs in Scripture in the account of the Sabbath (Gen 2:1–3). This root now is repeated at the beginning and end of the Sabbath law to stress the uniqueness of this day. The Sabbath was withdrawn from ordinary days, with no labor taking place on that day. Its distinctiveness and consecration to God is also expressed by the special religious activities that were to take place on the Sabbath. Umberto Cassuto commented on the worshippers' response to the fact that God dedicated the Sabbath day:

> Rise on this day above the plane of ordinary activities, liberate yourself from the burden of work of the six preceding days, and dedicate it not to your body but to your soul, not to material things but to things of the spirit, not to your relationship to nature, but to your relationship to the Creator of nature. Thereby you will imitate the ways in which the Lord your God works, and you will bear constant witness to the fact that He alone created the whole world in all its parts, and that He is not to be identified with any portion of the world or with any of the forces of nature, but he transcends the sphere of nature.[66]

As a day sacred to the Lord, the Sabbath was meant as a time of religious observance (Isa 1:13; 58:13; Jer 17:19–27). On the Sabbath day an Israelite might visit a sanctuary or a prophet (2 Kgs 4:23; Isa 1:13). Special sacrifices as well as additional spiritual matters and religious ceremonies were to take place on this holy day (Lev 24:8; 1 Chr 23:31; 2 Chr 8:12–13; 31:2–3).[67] However, it is not only a festive time but a weekly time for God. [68] "Thus as God originally declared the Sabbath day itself holy, the reception of the Sabbath command as well as its observance indicated that the Israelites also were holy before God."[69] Like other festal occasions on the worship calendar (see Lev 23), the Sabbath is called a holy convocation *(miqrā' qōdeš)*. But as apparent in Lev 23, the Sabbath is distinct from other sacred assemblies because it is the most frequently occurring holy convocation.

and end of the fourth commandment, which creates an envelope around the Sabbath legislation (Deut 5:12,15).

[66] Cassuto, *A Commentary on the Book of Exodus*, 246.

[67] See J. Tigay, *Deuteronomy*, 68; id., "שַׁבָּת," 511. In addition, Psalm 92 was to be read every Sabbath day.

[68] A. Jepsen, "Beiträge zur Auslegung und Geschichte des Dekalogs," ZAW 79 (1967): 293. See D. Christensen, *Deuteronomy 1:1–21:9*, 119.

[69] Barker, "Sabbath, Sabbatical Year, Jubilee," 698.

The Fourth Commandment in the Old Testament

In addition to its occurrence in the Ten Commandments, the Sabbath law was a part of all Old Testament legal codes (see Exod 23:12; 34:21; 35:2–3). The authority of the Sabbath law was acknowledged in both the northern and southern kingdoms (2 Kgs 4:23; Isa 1:13; Jer 17:21–27; Hos 2:11[13]; Amos 8:5). Ezekiel in particular seems to stress obedience in regard to the Sabbath as more important than the rest of the commandments (Ezek 101 22:8,26; 23:38). The Sabbath belongs to the Lord,[70] and its violation puts the nation at risk of going into exile (Ezek 20:12–13,20–21,24; 22:26; 23:38; 44:24; see Neh 13:18). The author of 2 Chronicles clearly believed that it was the neglect of the Sabbath that led the nation into exile (2 Chr 36:21). Banishment from the homeland would be the inevitable result of violation of the Sabbath law, Lev 26:32,35 prophesied. God vowed that His children would be sent into captivity in order that the land would experience the rest it did not enjoy when the Israelites lived there. The importance of the Sabbath law is seen in the postexilic priorities of Nehemiah (Neh 10:32–34; see 2 Chr 31:3). Nehemiah seemed to view obedience to the Sabbath as the paramount command for the nation's continued existence (Neh 13:15–22; cf. Neh 9:14; 10:31[32]).[71] The reason observance of the Sabbath was singled out as the barometer for Israel's covenant obedience was that the Sabbath was understood as the sign of the Mosaic covenant (Exod 31:13,17; Ezek 20:12,20).[72]

The odiousness of the violation of the fourth commandment is indicated by the punishments rendered to those who did so. The Israelite who did not keep the Sabbath command was subject to death by stoning (Exod 31:14–15; 35:2; Num 15:32–36). This law had to be kept at all times, even in the busy times of plowing and reaping as well as the service of the tabernacle (Exod 31:12–17; 34:21; 35:1–3).

---

[70] This is emphasized in the Hb. text by the *waw* adversative ("but") that begins Exod 20:10.

[71] The books of Chronicles link the rest the Lord has brought to His people with the theology of Zion and the temple (see also Isa 14:3–4; 32:18). See H. Preuss, "נוּחַ *nuaḥ*," *TDOT* 9:281; Stolz, *TLOT* 2:724.

[72] G. Hasel and W. G. C. Murdoch, "The Sabbath in the Prophetic and Historical Literature of the Old Testament," in *The Sabbath in Scripture and History,* ed. K. Strand (Washington, D.C.: Review and Herald, 1982), 47. The importance of the Sabbath for the life of Israel is also apparent in religious songs (Ps 92; Lam 2:6).

The placement of the Sabbath laws in Exod 31 directly adjacent to the instructions for building the tabernacle suggests that even the labor involved in construction of the most holy place was prohibited on the Sabbath.[73]

Additional support for preeminence of the Sabbath law may be found in the commandment for the sabbatical year (Exod 23:10–12; Neh 10:31[32]), which is formulated with the language of the Sabbath (cf. Exod 20:9–10; Lev 23:3; 25:1–5). The Sabbath was the foundation for all festal times as it is the first-mentioned holy day in Lev 23. As such it served as a model for how other festive days were to be observed.

The association of the sanctuary and priestly ritual with the Sabbath day indicated the special holiness of the Sabbath. The priests had special duties on the Sabbath (Neh 13:22; cf. Ezek 44:24), which included changing the shewbread (Lev 24:5–9). It was the responsibility of the priests to instruct the people regarding the holiness of the Sabbath (Ezek 22:26).[74] Additional sacrifices were also offered on the Sabbath (Num 28:9–10; 1 Chr 23:31; 2 Chr 2:4[3]; 8:13; 31:3; Ezek 45:17; 46:4–5). The Sabbath day was the time for the changing of the temple guard (2 Kgs 11:5–9; 1 Chr 9:25–27,32; 2 Chr 23:8). Furthermore, the Sabbath was a *miqrā' qōdeš*, a "holy convocation" ("sacred assembly," HCSB Lev 23:3).[75] This phrase was used as a fixed expression for Israelite feasts. The Sabbath is the first-mentioned feast in Lev 23 because it was the only feast that repeated through the year; the rest were celebrated only once a year.[76] The expression *miqrā' qōdeš* was used to refer to the first and last days of Passover (Lev 23:7–8). The expression was also used for the Feast of Firstfruits (Lev 23:21), the beginning of the year (Lev 23:24), the Day of Atonement (Lev 23:27), the beginning of the Festival of Booths (Lev 23:35), and the eighth day of the Feast of Booths (Lev 23:36). On all of these occasions, no work *(mělākâ)* was to be done; i.e., these feast days are

---

[73] C. Slane, "Sabbath," *EDBT*, 698.

[74] Hakam, *Exodus*, 283.

[75] Andreasen maintains that *miqrā' qōdeš* presupposes a sacred assembly. See Andreasen, *The Old Testament Sabbath*, 147.

[76] Tigay, "שַׁבָּת," 507; Andreasen, *The Old Testament Sabbath*, 237.

all "Sabbath-like."[77] The inclusion of the Sabbath in this list, indeed at the beginning, indicates there was a special religious dimension to the Sabbath observance.[78] The often-repeated notion that the Sabbath was originally only a day of rest without any worship activity is unfounded.[79]

Another indication of the sacredness of the Sabbath and its distinctiveness as a special day is that it was a day of worship. After Jerusalem had been established as the special place for God to be worshipped (Deut 12), the people came to the tabernacle to worship on the Sabbath (2 Kgs 11:4–20 = 2 Chr 23:4–11; Isa 1:12–13; cf. Isa 66:23; Ezek 46:3),[80] and took occasion to inquire of a man of God (2 Kgs 4:23). The worship of Yahweh and the celebration of the Sabbath are inseparably linked (2 Kgs 16:17–18; Isa 1:13; Hos 2:11[13]). However, as with the Passover, we learn more about what characterized the Sabbath over time (see Lev 23:3; 24:8,9; Num 28:9–10; 1 Chr 9:32; 23:31; 2 Chr 2:4; 23:8; 2 Kgs 11:5–9; Psalm 92; Lam 2:6; see Ezek 45:17; 46:1–4). Initial Sabbath celebrations were in homes, but later the religious community gathered on the Sabbath to worship in the temple.[81] It was a day of holiness and joy when work stopped and the people and priests celebrated both in the sanctuary and outside it as it was, like other special days, a festive assembly.[82] For the Israelites, the Sabbath was a day of worship and service to the Lord their God, and it testified to His sovereignty over creation and their dependence upon Him.

In contrast with the rest of the Ten Commandments, the Sabbath law alone was considered a sign for ancient Israel (Exod 31:12–17). Just as the rainbow was a sign of the Noachian covenant (Gen 9:13,17) and circumcision was a sign of the Abrahamic covenant (Gen 17:11), so the Sabbath was the sign of the Mosaic covenant. The same expression

---

[77] See J. Licht, "מִקְרָא קֹדֶשׁ," *EncMiq* 5:437–38 [in Hb.].

[78] Barker, "Sabbath, Sabbatical Year, Jubilee," 696.

[79] Andreasen, *The Old Testament Sabbath,* 237; W. Schmidt, *The Faith of the Old Testament,* trans. John Sturdy (Philadelphia: Westminster, 1983), 88–92.

[80] Andreasen, *The Old Testament Sabbath,* 241.

[81] C. Houtman, *Exodus 20–40* (Leuven: Peeters, 2000), 3:45; Andreasen, *The Old Testament Sabbath,* 241–42.

[82] See Tigay, "שַׁבָּת," 507–8; G. Hasel, "The Sabbath in the Pentateuch," in *The Sabbath in Scripture and History,* ed. K. Strand (Washington, D.C.: Review and Herald, 1982), 33.

"between me and you" (Exod 31:13,17), occurs as a formula in the covenants established with Noah (Gen 9:12) and Abraham (Gen 17:11). The Sabbath was a perpetual reminder of the covenant relationship God had established with His people on Mount Sinai.[83] It was a sign that the Lord revealed His day of holiness to Israel alone, and by observing this day it becomes a sign of Israel's holiness.[84] As the Israelites shut down their normal work routine and worshipped God on the Sabbath, they demonstrated that they were keeping the covenant.

Observance of the Sabbath became the standard for Israel's obedience to its covenant with God in the prophetic literature.[85] Keeping the Sabbath meant holding fast to "My (God's) covenant" (Isa 56:6; cf. Lev 26:42,45). Just as the firstfruits and the tithe were offered to God as a recognition that the whole produce of the earth belongs to the Lord, the dedication of one day in seven is an expression that every minute of man's life belongs to God who gave him life (see Exod 20:10; 35:2).[86] Just as one sacrifices a valuable animal to the Lord, forgoing use of the animal for oneself, so one must relinquish a seventh of one's time, offering the value of the time to God.[87] Von Rad noted that, as "signs of the covenant," circumcision and the Sabbath observance were decisive in showing that a Jew belonged to Yahweh and His people.[88]

For these reasons the Sabbath law has been viewed by many as the most important OT law (Neh 9:14).[89] Observing the Sabbath was not meant to be legalistic or ritualistic but was to bring joy and delight (Isa 58:13–14).

Unlike the previous commands, the fourth is stated positively. It is dependent on the creation account of Gen 1–2, which also describes the cessation of the Creator's work and affirms that the Sabbath is sanctified (*qdš*). The motivation for obedience in Deut 5 is humanitarian, focusing on allowing rest for one's household. This altruistic

---

[83] See Hasel, "The Sabbath in the Pentateuch," 34, 36. Ezekiel also mentions that the Sabbath was a sign for Israel (Ezek 20:12,20).

[84] Tigay, "שַׁבָּת," 508.

[85] Slane, "Sabbath," 698.

[86] A. McNeile, *The Book of Exodus*, 3rd ed. (London: Methuen, 1931), 118.

[87] Propp, *Exodus 19–40*, 176.

[88] See G. von Rad, *Old Testament Theology*, 2 vols, trans. D. M. G. Stalker (New York: Harper & Row, 1962–65), 1:84.

[89] Stolz, *TLOT* 3:1301.

basis is not lacking from Exodus, since it is mentioned in Exod 23:12. But Deut 5 adds a motivation for Sabbath obedience—that the Israelites knew what it was like not to enjoy rest as they served as slaves in Egypt.[90] This reminder, already mentioned in the introduction to the commandments by the phrase "I am the LORD your God, who brought you out of the land of Egypt," should create in the Israelite a desire to obey the One who has given them life and freedom. "The covenant relationship demands Israel's sanctification, and by keeping the Sabbath holy Israel is reminded continually that the God who sanctified the seventh day also sanctifies her."[91]

The fates of the house of David, the city of Jerusalem, and the children of Israel were connected to the nation's observance of the Sabbath law (Neh 9:14; 13:15–18; Ezek 20:12–24; 22:8,26; 23:38). Observance of the Sabbath applied to the future as well, with the messianic promise that all flesh would one day worship the true God on the Sabbath (Isa 56:6; 66:23; Ezek 44:24; 45:17; 46:1,3–4,12). The Sabbath will play a prominent role in the worship of the new era of salvation (Ezek 45:17; 46:1–5). The Sabbath required a day be set aside to the Lord for something that was truly special. It was a day that "belonged to the Lord."

The Sabbath was not given to Israel for the first time at Mount Sinai. The special status of the day as well as its name were disclosed to Israel with the giving of the manna (Exod 16:22–23). God provided a day's supply of manna for each of five days, but on the sixth day a double portion was given, so gathering would not have to be done on the Sabbath. In this episode the nation learned that the Sabbath belonged to the Lord and work was forbidden. Thus barely one month after the departure from Egypt and one month before the arrival at Mount Sinai, it was assumed that the Sabbath law was in force.[92] However, at Mount Sinai Israel was commanded to honor this day that was established at the beginning (Gen 2:1–3). The Sabbath com-

---

[90] M. Greenberg, "The Tradition Critically Examined," in Segal, *The Ten Commandments in History and Tradition*, 103.

[91] Slane, "Sabbath," 697.

[92] Sarna, *Exploring Exodus*, 146–47.

mandment is to be read in light of the Genesis creation account that focuses on sanctification of the seventh day.[93] As Craigie stated:

> The rest on the Sabbath day was to remember that man, as part of God's created order, was totally dependent on the Creator; man's divinely appointed task to have dominion over the created order (Gen 1:26) carried with it also the privilege of sharing in God's rest. The Exodus, too, was a type of *creation* and thus forms an analogy to the creation account in Genesis. The Exodus from Egypt makes in effect the creation of God's people as a nation, and the memory of that event was also a reminder to the Israelites of their total dependence upon God (see Exod 15:16b).[94]

In the creation account blessing and holiness stand on a cosmic plane, and nothing is mentioned about man keeping a commandment. Here we learn of the name of the day, its holiness, and the prohibition against work. In the Ten Commandments, Israel is commanded to remember the day that has been revealed to them. The prohibition is repeated in the account of the manna (Exod 16:23–26), and in the Ten Commandments the reason for the Sabbath is revealed (Exod 20:8–11).[95]

Because of the significance of the Sabbath commandment, the longest commandment and the center of the Decalogue, Phillips maintains that the Sabbath commandment is *the* law of the Decalogue.[96] Moreover, its importance may be seen by the fact that it is often juxtaposed with the prohibition against idolatry (Lev 19:3–4; Ezek 20:16–24).[97] Violation of the Sabbath law was tantamount to breaking the covenant.[98] According to the Midrash, the Sabbath was equal to all other legal precepts (*Exod. Rab.* 25:12). Added to this is the fact that in the observance of the Sabbath the worshipper emulates the activity pattern of God.

The Fourth Commandment in the New Testament

At the close of the Old Testament period, Sabbath-keeping and Jewish identity had virtually become one concept in normative Juda-

---

[93] Childs, *The Book of Exodus: A Critical-Theological Commentary,* 416.

[94] Craigie, *The Book of Deuteronomy,* 157 and 157n18.

[95] Tigay, "שַׁבָּת," 510.

[96] A. Phillips, *Ancient Israel's Criminal Law: A New Approach to the Decalogue* (Oxford: Basil Blackwell, 1970), 70 (emphasis his).

[97] Tigay, *Deuteronomy,* 68.

[98] M. Unger, "The Significance of the Sabbath," *BSac* (1966): 58.

ism.[99] Jews met in synagogues on the Sabbath day for prayer, Scripture readings, and edifying discourses.[100] In the Judaism of the Second Temple period, as well as in the rabbinic sources, the Sabbath was conceived as a day for contemplating God and studying the Torah. We hear Josephus saying that Moses enjoined "that every week men should desert their occupations and assemble to listen to the Law" (*Ag. Ap.* 2.175; see also *Ant.* 16.43). Reading of the Torah on the Sabbath is also mentioned in Acts 15:21.[101]

The prohibition of work on the Sabbath was embraced to such a degree among many Jews that they chose death rather than to defend themselves against Antiochus IV on the Sabbath (1 Macc 2:31–38). According to the book of Jubilees (2:17–32; 50:6–13), the death penalty was maintained for any Sabbath transgression. However, the Sabbath commandment could be ignored if a life was at stake (1 Macc 2:40–41).[102]

In the first century AD, the role and institution of the Sabbath had become extremely significant in the religious practices of Jewish Palestine. In New Testament days the discussions about what it meant to work on the Sabbath came to a head. This preoccupation with the Sabbath is reflected in the Mishnah where 39 activities are expressly forbidden on the Sabbath day (*m. Šabb.* 7:2). These 39 activities may not have been arbitrary but rather correspond to the 39 occurrences of the word *mĕlā'kâ* ("work") in the Torah. By the time of Jesus, the intent of the Sabbath had been distorted, and the Sabbath had become a burden rather than a time for worship and celebration.[103]

However, we find in the New Testament evidence of Sabbath observance. The Sabbath continued to be thought of as a day set aside to worship God. This is seen first of all by the consistent practice of worship taking place on the Sabbath in the New Testament. We find that Jesus remained faithful to the Old Testament Scripture, as it was His custom to attend the synagogue each Sabbath (cf. Mark 1:21,29; 3:1;

---

[99] Hasel, "Sabbath," 854.

[100] S. Westerholm and C. Evans, "Sabbath," *DNTB*, 1032.

[101] See Weinfeld, *Deuteronomy 1–11*, 306–7.

[102] The service of the temple as well as the rite of circumcision also took precedence over the Sabbath (cf. Num 28:9–10; 1 Chr 23:31). Westerholm and Evans, "Sabbath," 1031.

[103] M. Dunnam, *Exodus*, The Communicator's Commentary (Waco, TX: Word, 1987), 260.

Luke 4:44; 13:10).[104] This was not an occasional or sporadic practice of Christ, but Luke tells us that this characterized His religious life (Luke 4:16). The same consistency was also exhibited by Paul as he routinely entered synagogues on the Sabbath, where he took the opportunity to preach the Christian gospel (e.g., Acts 13:14,42,44; 17:2; 18:4).[105]

Worship on the Sabbath is in harmony with the teaching of the fourth commandment from the Old Testament. But the prohibition against work is also apparent. In Mark 1:32, the people wait until the Sabbath is over to carry the sick to Jesus. Moreover, in Mark 16:1, the women wait until the Sabbath has passed before attending to the body of Jesus.[106]

Jesus and the Sabbath

The Gospels record six occasions where there was a controversy over the Sabbath. These include the picking of grain by the disciples (Matt 12:1–8), the healing of a man with a withered hand (Matt 12:9–14), the healing of a crippled woman (Luke 13:10–14), the healing of a man with dropsy (Luke 14:1–6), the healing of a sick man by the pool of Beth-zatha (John 5:1–14), and the healing of a man born blind (John 9). Jesus maintained consistently, against the rabbinic position, that it was "lawful to do good on the Sabbath" (Matt 12:12).[107] Jesus' healing on the Sabbath was in line with the true intention that the Sabbath be a benefit to all creation. This was even recognized in Jewish tradition, which called for suspension of all Sabbath prohibitions when human life might be in danger.[108] Jesus could not be legally accused of violating the Sabbath, nor was He officially charged with this transgression at His trial.[109] "Jesus freed the Sabbath from human restrictions and encumbrances and restored it by showing its universal

---

[104] Hasel, "Sabbath," 854.

[105] See Westerholm and Evans, "Sabbath," 1035.

[106] Ibid., 1032.

[107] Hasel, "Sabbath," 855.

[108] See Sarna, *Exodus,* 112.

[109] For a fuller discussion, see H. Basser, *Studies in Exegesis: Christian Critiques of Jewish Law and Rabbinic Responses 70–300 C.E.* (Leiden: Brill, 2000), 15–49. See also Slane, "Sabbath," 698.

import for all men so that every person can be the beneficiary of the divine intentions and true purposes of Sabbath rest and joy."[110]

Sabbath Rest

The theme of rest created by God is seen in New Testament texts such as Matt 11:28–30 and Hebrews 4.[111] In Christ we have entered fulfillment of the Sabbath already as we have spiritual rest, but the ultimate rest is yet to come. (Ps 95).[112] Thus the Sabbath is a type of Christ. The controversy with the Pharisees was generally about how to obey the Sabbath. Jesus addressed these issues head on and rejected their tradition.[113] Jesus spoke authoritatively about the intention of the Sabbath law, as He was Lord of the Sabbath (Matt 12:8; Mark 2:28; Luke 6:5).

In Acts 15, the Gentiles who had come to believe in Jesus Christ as the Messiah did not have to become Jews; they were not required to be circumcised. However, they were obligated to obey some legal instructions. Observance of the Sabbath was not among the legal instructions they were required to keep. The Sabbath law was no longer binding on the people of God (Acts 15:28–29).

In his letters Paul showed concern for restrictions placed on his converts, which undoubtedly included the Sabbath (Rom 14:5; Gal 4:10; Col 2:16). In his characteristic refusal to allow such things to become a basis for judging fellow believers, Paul supported the believers' freedom either to observe or not observe the Jewish Sabbath (Rom 14:5).[114] Paul showed tolerance toward those who had a special conviction about Sabbath observance, while still affirming that rest should be given to workers. Rest could come on virtually any day, but it must not be denied. Even though tolerance was stressed, the era of placing one day above another was over. Paul announced that everyone had to be convinced in his own mind. He doesn't say this

---

[110] Hasel, "Sabbath," 855.

[111] Stolz, *TLOT* 2:724.

[112] See J. Calvin, *Institutes of the Christian Religion*, ed. J. McNeill, 2 vols. (Philadelphia: Westminster, 1975), 1:396–97; R. A. Mohler Jr., *Words from the Fire* (Chicago: Moody, 2009), 86.

[113] Hasel, "Sabbath," 855.

[114] Evidently Paul continued to obey the Sabbath law himself (Acts 17:2).

about other laws. From what is known about Jewish Sabbath observance in the first century AD, such a statement was revolutionary. It is
clear that something had changed. The Lord of the Sabbath had come
and gave its true meaning. The Sabbath law is the only law of the Ten
Commandments that is not repeated in the New Testament.[115]

Excursus: Did Sunday Replace the Sabbath?

In the New Testament era, Jewish worship on the Sabbath appears to
reflect a long-standing tradition. On the Sabbath day Jews gathered in
synagogues to study and read the Torah (law).[116] This practice apparently was carried over into the Christian church. Early Jewish and non-
Jewish Christians apparently continued to worship on the seventh day,
as evidenced in the book of Acts (1:12; 13:14–44; 15:21; 17:2; 18:4).[117]

But there is evidence in the New Testament that Christian believers were worshipping on the first day of the week in order to com-
memorate Christ's resurrection (Acts 20:7; 1 Cor 16:2; Rev 1:10). Yet,
although the New Testament mentions Christian worship on the first
day, it gives no indication that Sunday had anything to do with the
fourth commandment, nor was there any attempt to make Sunday the
new Sabbath day.

Early church fathers such as Ignatius (35–107) and Barnabas (before AD 135) argued for exclusion of Sabbath observance, but they did
not attempt to make Sunday the new Sabbath. Tertullian appears to
be the first of the church fathers to suggest that business be deferred
on Sunday so as to enhance worship, but still Sunday was a workday,
not a day of rest. In the third century Cyprian argued that additional
activities be avoided on Sunday, but even with Cyprian no attempt
was made to connect Sunday to the fourth commandment.

Ambrose and Chrysostom (347–407) firmly attached the rest
of Sunday to the fourth commandment. Following the fourth century, there was a steady move toward identifying the Sabbath with

---

[115] See Unger, "The Significance of the Sabbath," 57.

[116] See H. McKay, *Sabbath and Synagogue: The Question of Sabbath Worship in Ancient Judaism*
(Leiden; New York: Brill, 1994), 208.

[117] See Hasel, "Sabbath," 855; Slane, "Sabbath," 699.

Sunday.[118] Early in the fourth century AD, Constantine issued an edict that no work be performed on the Lord's day.[119] Puritans such as Jonathan Edwards argued that in light of the new covenant blessings in Christ, Sunday had replaced Saturday.[120]

According to the NT there are no grounds for treating the Old Testament Sabbath as a continuing legal requirement for believers. While there is solid evidence that the early Christians were beginning to worship on Sunday in honor of the resurrection, there is no evidence that Sunday was to be considered the new Sabbath day of rest and the way Christians would now keep the fourth commandment. Thus, Sunday did not replace the Sabbath, but it is clear from the NT that Christians began to worship on Sunday, the Lord's Day (Rev 1:10), because of the transcendent significance of Christ's resurrection.[121]

Conclusion

The fourth commandment occupies a unique place in the Decalogue. It is the only day of observance mentioned in the Ten Commandments. It is the only commandment specified in the creation account and the only commandment said to be a sign for Israel (Exod 31).[122] In addition, it is the only one of the Ten Commandments that is not repeated in the New Testament. The New Testament instead speaks of its typical nature. As a shadow, it was fulfilled in Christ's ministry in giving rest, but it also awaits a future fulfillment.[123] Yet the fourth commandment is not without relevance for the modern Christian. The principles involved in observance of the Sabbath law are applicable today. The principles of work, rest, and worship that emerge

---

[118] J. Laansma, "Lord's Day," *DLNTD*, 684.

[119] J. Holbert, *The Ten Commandments* (Nashville: Abingdon, 2002), 51.

[120] See R. Caldwell III, "Call the Sabbath a Delight: Jonathan Edwards on the Lord's Day," *SwJT* 47,2 (2005): 191–205.

[121] For a fuller treatment of this question, see D. A. Carson, ed., *From Sabbath to Lord's Day.* (Grand Rapids: Zondervan, 1982). S. McKinion, ed., *Life and Practice in the Early Church: A Documentary Reader* (New York: New York University Press, 2001).

[122] Nielsen asserts that the Sabbath law is the chief law of the Ten Commandments. See E. Nielsen, *Deuteronomium*, HAT (Tübingen: Mohr [Siebeck], 1995), 76.

[123] Augustine stated that the Sabbath law was typical in nature, whereas the other nine commandments are to be literally followed.

from the Sabbath law are extremely meaningful in their application to the contemporary Christian.

The first principle of the Sabbath law is that of the responsibility to work. While there is a focus on rest in the commandment, the law also endorses the principle that human beings should be about work six days in a week. As Abraham Heschel observed: "The duty to work for six days is just as much a part of God's covenant with man as the duty to abstain from work on the seventh day."[124] When one engages in work for six days a week, he follows God's example in the creation. As we follow the lead of the consummate Craftsman, our work should be characterized by integrity and produce a quality product (see Exod 31:6; 35:35). "Work is a God-ordained activity and was set forth from the beginning, sometimes called one of the creation ordinances, to fill, subdue, and rule the earth (Gen 1:28), to keep the garden, and to labor (2:5,15)."[125] Even though work has been affected by the fall, we should work with a zeal and industriousness that is honoring to God and not be characterized by idleness, laziness, and slothfulness (Prov 6:6–11; 21:25). All work and all occupations (providing they do not promote illicit activity) are significant and honorable before the Lord. The fourth commandment affirms human labor and exalts the dignity of our work. As we imitate Him in rest, we should imitate Him in work.

The fourth commandment teaches that for six days you will engage in work to provide for your needs, but on the Sabbath all work should be brought to an end as the seventh day is set apart for the Lord. The commandment teaches that the Lord should be sovereign over our time, and in ceasing to work one day a week, we show our faith and offer our praise to the One who is the true ruler of time (Ps 74:16). We express our belief that ultimately we are not dependent on our own work but that God is sovereign in our lives and our work, and our lives are under His control. "In ceasing from labor one is reminded of one's true status as a dependent being, of the God who cares for and sustains all his creatures, and of the world as a reality be-

---

[124] A. Heschel, *The Earth Is the Lord's and the Sabbath* (New York: Harper & Row, 1966), 28.
[125] Hague, "מְלָאכָה," 943.

longing ultimately to God."[126] Sabbath observance places a clear limit on human autonomy. The fact that we should work, our ability to do work, and the work we have been assigned are all part of His plan for us (Gen 2–3; 1 Thess 5:14; 2 Thess 3:10).

Finally, the fourth commandment calls for a day to offer worship and praise to God, a day set aside that we might remember His creation and His redemption. It is a day in which we acknowledge God's ownership not only of ourselves but of all creation. As we enter a time of deep reflection on this day of worship, we turn "from the world of creation to the creation of the world."[127] We turn in worship to God to celebrate those of His acts whereby our lives have come to be valued.[128] It is a day wherein we reflect on the fact that God is the Creator, Redeemer, and Lord of all.[129] It is a day to be still and know that He is God.

The book of Hebrews anticipates an eschatological Sabbath rest *(sabbatismos)*[130] that remains for the people of God (Heb 4:1–11). This coming "rest" and restoration will be marked by the cessation of labor patterned after God's rest on the seventh day of creation (Gen 2:2; see Ps 95:11).[131] "As the Sabbath was the climax of the first creation and destined for all mankind (Gen 2:1–3), so the Sabbath will again be the climax of the new creation and destined again for all mankind in the new heaven and the new earth."[132] This rest was inaugurated with the coming of Jesus (Heb 1:1–3) and will be fully realized at His second advent. With the dawning of the second advent there will be a new world when life reverts to creation bliss. The world will once again be "very good" (Gen 1), no longer adversely affected by the fall, and the people of God will experience His rest. This eternal rest was implied from the creation account because the seventh day, unlike

---

[126] Slane, "Sabbath," 697.

[127] Heschel, *The Earth Is the Lord's and the Sabbath*, 10.

[128] See R. Collins, *Christian Morality: Biblical Foundations* (Notre Dame, IN: University of Notre Dame Press, 1986), 55.

[129] Barker, "Sabbath, Sabbatical Year, Jubilee," 698.

[130] This Greek term occurs only here in the NT and may thus indicate the superiority of this coming eschatological rest.

[131] Slane, "Sabbath," 699.

[132] Hasel and Murdoch, "The Sabbath in the Prophetic and Historical Literature of the Old Testament," 49.

the previous six days of creation, was not described with the evening and morning formula. It was in a sense an endless day, anticipating the ideal for God's creation. It is to this that Exod 20 appeals by inviting Israel to participate in a weekly Sabbath modeled on the original, "very good" creation (so also Exod 31:12–17).[133]

What should not be lost in the fourth commandment is the gracious and kind God who established this law. We worship a God who does not desire that we have a yoke too heavy to bear; we are in need of a time of reflection and rest. The Sabbath was made for man. The fact that the work and rest pattern was established in the work of God Himself indicates that this principle for mankind has universal significance and application.[134] As we follow God's example we endeavor to avoid making life too difficult for others. This humanitarian concern of the Sabbath is a bridge to the commandments concerned with inter-human relationships in commandments 6–10.[135]

---

[133] Barker, "Sabbath, Sabbatical Year, Jubilee," 697.

[134] See W. Eichrodt, *Theology of the Old Testament.* 2 vols, trans. J. A. Baker, OTL (Philadelphia: Westminster, 1961), 1:133.

[135] See Fretheim, *Exodus,* 230.

Chapter 5

THE FIFTH COMMANDMENT

*Honor your father and your mother so that you may have a
long life in the land that the LORD your God is giving you.*

Introduction

I n the ancient civilizations of world history, the first evidence
of a hierarchical structure began with the husband and wife in
the family. The family structure laid the foundation for all other
forms of authority and obedience within culture. But it is only within
the biblical faith that the authority of parents was founded on a divine
sanction (Exod 20:12).[1] The need for cohesion and solidarity, especially within the family bond, characterized the world of the ancient
Orient and especially the Old Testament.[2]

The care of parents was also a common theme, particularly in
the ancient Near East. In Middle Assyrian law, children were legally
bound to support their impoverished widowed mothers or stepmoth-
ers. A widowed mother was to reside with one of her sons. At Nuzi,
the main rationale behind adoption laws was to secure the service and
support of a younger person when the parent (adopter) was older.
Babylonian adoption records stipulated that the adoptee show reverence and honor to the adoptive parents by providing them with cloth-
ing, food, and other essentials.[3]

Since relationships between parents and children (biological or
adopted) were governed by legal prescriptions, violations resulted in
punitive measures. If a person cursed, struck, or flagrantly disobeyed
a parent, measures including mutilation, disinheritance, and death

---

[1] See K. van der Toorn, *Sin and Sanction in Israel and Mesopotamia: A Comparative Study* (Assen, The Netherlands: Van Gorcum, 1985), 13; S. Paul, *Studies in the Book of the Covenant in the
Light of Cuneiform and Biblical Law* (Leiden: Brill, 1970), 64.

[2] See Lipit-Ishtar §§ 20–33: in *ANET* 160; Hammurabi §§ 196–214: in *ANET* 175; Hittite
Laws §§ 189–94: in *ANET* 196 (see Lev. 18:6–23; Deut 22:21–24); J. Gamberoni, "Das Elterngebot im Alten Testament," *BZ* 8 (1964): 182.

[3] R. Westbrook, ed., *A History of Ancient Near Eastern Law*, 2 vols. (Leiden; Boston: Brill,
2003), 1:50, 539, 544–45, 595, 710; Van Der Toorn, *Sin and Sanction in Israel and Mesopotamia*,
14. See *b. Qidd.* 31b; G. Blidstein, *Honor Thy Father and Mother: Filial Responsibility in Jewish
Law and Ethics* (New York: KTAV, 1975), 38.

could ensue.[4] Assaulting a parent—as well as general disobedience—was punished in the Old Testament period, not only because of the demonstration of disrespect for parents but also because of the psychological damage rendered to the community.[5]

The fifth commandment is viewed by many as transitional. Its transitional nature is evident from the fact that the first four commandments focus on a person's responsibilities to God while the sixth through tenth commandments address how a person is to live in covenant community with his fellow man. The fifth commandment is viewed as a bridge between these two sections. It is transitional because a person's relationship to his parents, while not on the same level as his relationship to God, is still addressing an authority higher than himself, and that authority should be respected similarly to God. Moreover, if the fifth commandment occupied the last position of the first tablet of the Decalogue, as many affirm, this in itself would indicate its intermediary role.[6]

On the other hand, the fifth commandment is the first one that addresses how an individual is to relate to his fellow man. The fifth is the pivotal commandment that moves man from his contemplation of the divine to human society. Beginning with the fifth commandment, we are to draw our attention to created things. This transition begins with the human father because the father, like God, is the creator to his progeny. Like God (our first father) the human father (our last father) is a participant in our making.[7]

The first arena where one encounters the world is the family, the foremost area of our obligation outside our relationship with God.[8] In the family we first encounter not only our "neighbor" but also parents who partnered to bring us into the world (b. Qidd. 30b). Through the parents our attention is directed back to God (commandments

---

[4] Westbrook, A History of Ancient Near Eastern Law, 1:77.

[5] J. Fleishman, Parent and Child in Ancient Near East and the Bible (Jerusalem: Magnes, the Hebrew University, 1999), 268 [in Hb.].

[6] H. Kremers, "Die Stellung des Elterngebotes im Dekalog," ET 21 (1961): 157; Blidstein, Honor Thy Father and Mother, 22.

[7] Blidstein, Honor Thy Father and Mother, 6.

[8] See J. Motyer, The Message of Exodus (Downers Grove, IL: InterVarsity, 2005), 227. The commandment contains the phrase "your God," which connects the fifth commandment to the previous four that regulated one's relationship to God.

1–4), by means of the everyday practices of prayer, instruction, and participation in religious activities.[9] Hence the relationship between children and parents ranks second only to one's relationship to God.

The Meaning of the Fifth Commandment

The term "honor" is from the root *kbd*, which occurs in all the Semitic languages. The root carries the idea of physical "heaviness" (see 2 Sam 14:26; Job 6:3). It is used of a large, heavy man (1 Sam 4:18) as well as a great amount of thick, heavy hair. On 13 occasions the term is used in the Old Testament in reference to the liver of an animal, perhaps because it was thought to be the "heaviest" organ. The root *kbd* is used in reference to the liver of a bull (Exod 29:13; Lev 3:4; 4:9; 8:16; 9:10,19), a sheep (Exod 29:22; Lev 3:10; 8:25; 9:19), a goat (Lev 3:15), a deer (Prov 7:23), or an animal in general (Lev 7:4; Ezek 21:21[26]).[10] Used figuratively, the root *kbd* was used to describe ears that were *dull* or *closed* (Zech 7:11), a heart that was *hardened* (Exod 9:7), or eyesight that was *poor* (Gen 48:10). The concrete meaning, on the other hand, was extended and applied to what was "heavy, weighty, severe, or important." For example, Abraham was very *rich (kbd)* in livestock, silver, and gold (Gen 13:2). The connection of "heaviness" to significance, importance, or influence may be reflected in the American expression, "He carries a lot of weight."

The nominal form of the root *kbd*, the noun *kābôd*, extends the idea of importance and weightiness to that of glory, splendor, or magnificence. This term is associated with God's majesty that appears to people (Ezek 1:28; 3:23; 8:4). The verb is often concretized in all kinds of postures, actions, and feelings that belong to good human relations such as love, obedience, regards, and support.[11] The verb can carry the connotation "to enrich" (Num 22:17,37; 24:11).[12] Honoring someone or something "carries the nuance of weighing down with

---

[9] C. Dohmen, *Exodus 19–40* (Freiburg: Herder, 2004), 121.

[10] P. Stenmans, "כָּבֵד *kābēd*," *TDOT* 7:21.

[11] Gamberoni, "Das Elterngebot im Alten Testament," 188–89.

[12] Stenmans, *TDOT* 7:18. The verb is used to describe many of the plagues (flies, locusts, hail, disease).

honor or respect."[13] It means to treat someone with the respect and deference that his position deserves.

The verb also implies submission to authority (1 Sam 15:30; Ps 86:9).[14] The subject honors the king (1 Sam 15:30), the soldier honors his officer (2 Sam 23:19,23). It is incumbent upon the nation of Israel to honor the Lord (1 Sam 2:30) and His name (Ps 86:9,12). Moreover, the royal palace honors the one who is faithful (1 Sam 22:14–15) while wisdom honors the way (Prov 4:8).[15]

The fifth commandment teaches that people have the responsibility to "honor" (kbd) their parents as they are to "honor" (kbd) the Lord (Prov 3:9). Honor has broader connotations than implied in the word "obey." Honor is frequently mentioned as the proper response to God and is consonant with worship (Ps 86:9).[16]

An additional connotation of the word "honor" may be gleaned from Lev 19:3, where we are told that parents are to be respected (lit. yrʾ; "feared"). The use of the verb yrʾ "fear/awe" is conceptually related to "honor." This association emphasizes the importance of this command, as the root yrʾ (fear) is commonly used to express one's response to God (see Deut 28:58). [17] As the relationship between Israel and God is often expressed in filial terms, the verbs "honoring" and "fearing" are used to express proper attitudes toward both God and parents (Deut 21:18–21; 27:16 with Lev 24:10–16; Num 15:30; 1 Kgs 21:12–14).[18]

In the Old Testament the word "fear" (yrʾ) is essentially limited to the sacred areas of life as an embodiment of right relationship to God. The fear of the Lord has become virtually a technical expression for the Old Testament faith. Otto Procksch stated that the fear of God expresses the lasting foundational relationship in which man

[13] E. Merrill, *Deuteronomy*, NAC (Nashville: B&H, 1994), 153.

[14] See A. Phillips, *Ancient Israel's Criminal Law: A New Approach to the Decalogue* (Oxford: Basil Blackwell, 1970), 80.

[15] Kremers, "Die Stellung des Elterngebotes im Dekalog," 159n36.

[16] See B. Childs, *The Book of Exodus: A Critical-Theological Commentary* (Louisville: Westminster John Knox, 1974), 418–19.

[17] The primary object of the verb "fear" in Deuteronomy is the Lord Himself (Deut 10:12; cf. 5:9–10; 6:2). D. Christensen, *Deuteronomy 1:1–21:9*, rev. ed., WBC 6A (Nashville: Thomas Nelson, 2001), 124.

[18] N. Sarna, *Exodus,* JPS Torah Commentary (Philadelphia, New York: Jewish Publication Society, 1991), 113, 251n48.

stands before Him. The author of the subsidiary Decalogue in Lev 19:3 stresses that the relationship between children and parents may be a religious act when he interprets "honor" by means of "fear."[19] The honoring of parents is within the realm of one's spiritual commitment to God. The parental law in the Ten Commandments is spiritual and presupposes the spiritual dignity of parents. Parents should be viewed as representatives of God. The occurrence of the term "fear" in Lev 19:3 as a response to parents is a remarkable statement about the unparalleled relationship between parent and child. This shows that "fear" has a religious foundation; it does not convey merely a noble respect for parents since fear normally expresses one's relationship to God. Scripture makes reverence to parents comparable to reverence for God.

We gain a deeper understanding of the root *kbd* when we consider the root *qll,* which functions as the antonym of *kbd* (see 1 Sam 2:30; 2 Sam 6:22; Prov 3:35; Isa 23:9; Hos 4:7; Hab 2:16). In sharp contrast with *kbd,* this root expresses cursing and contempt (Deut 27:16; see 1 Sam 2:30; 2 Sam 6:22). This root is important in determining the meaning of the fifth commandment since the root *qll* expresses the opposite of honoring parents (Lev 20:9; Prov 20:20; 30:11; Ezek 22:7).[20] The fact that God is also the object of this verb (Exod 22:28[27]; Lev 24:15), associating God with parents, establishes again the esteemed position parents have in the world. It also stresses the truth that God is honored or dishonored by man's relationship with his parents. If the fifth commandment is classified with the first section of the Decalogue, which focuses on God, we see once more a special value that is assigned to parental authority. The root *kbd* is used in the fifth commandment with reference to parents; it is never used in association with priests or prophets. Thus we find in this commandment that the relationship between child and parent is of paramount importance. This is indicated by the restricted use of the root *kbd.*

It is easier to obey than to honor. An individual may hate but still obey, whereas one cannot both hate and honor simultaneously. The

---

[19] Otto Procksch, *Theologie des Alten Testament* (Gütersloh: Bertelsmann, 1950), 612; cf. Kremers, "Die Stellung des Elterngebotes im Dekalog," 159 and 159n36,38.

[20] M. Weinfeld, *Deuteronomy 1–11,* AB 5 (New York: Doubleday, 1991), 310.

significance of parents in relation to their children indicates that parents are the first line of defense as God's representatives.[21]

In the Western world the common understanding of "honor your father and your mother" is thought to relate to the obedience of children to their parents. While the fifth commandment certainly pertains to children's obedience to their parents, this commandment may have another application, according to Jewish tradition. This understanding stresses that the fifth commandment focuses not on children being obedient to their parents but rather on care for aged parents who are beyond their productive years and cannot work.[22] The distinctiveness of this interpretation is that the commandment more specifically addresses older children. In the final analysis, however, emphases on both younger and older children should be understood as appropriate applications. As Israeli scholar Moshe Weinfeld comments:

> The filial duties are mainly twofold: reverence, which means obedience and is widely attested in the didactic sources of the Bible (Prov 1:8; 23:22; Ben Sira 3:1–16); and care, which is not specified in the Bible but is attested in external sources (Ugaritic) and in the rabbinic literature.[23]

The commandment addresses the proper treatment of the father and the mother. The combination of "father and mother" evokes memories of the creation of the first parents, Adam and Eve. By alluding to God's work in their creation, parents should be seen as representing God to their children.[24] They are seen in the Ten Commandments and even in creation to be a unity, representing the oneness and stability of the home. The moral and religious weight of parents lies fundamentally in their person and position; it never is dependent on their practical ability and performance.[25] Given the deep sense of family among the

---

[21] Gamberoni, "Das Elterngebot im Alten Testament," 174n86. The harsher punishments meted out for violations against parents than for people in general draws further attention to the parents' dignity and that obedience to parents is a holy mandate (ibid., 189).

[22] See R. Collins, *Christian Morality: Biblical Foundations* (Notre Dame, IN: University of Notre Dame Press, 1986), 73–75.

[23] M. Weinfeld, *Deuteronomy 1–11*, AB 5 (New York: Doubleday, 1991), 311. Jerome commented that parents should be supported by their children when they are old, based on the fifth commandment. See J. Lienhard, ed., *Exodus, Leviticus, Numbers, Deuteronomy*, ACCS (Downers Grove, IL: InterVarsity, 2001), 106.

[24] D. Stuart, *Exodus*, NAC (Nashville: B&H, 2006), 461.

[25] Gamberoni, "Das Elterngebot im Alten Testament," 188.

Hebrews, the father and mother are no sober legal concepts, but the centers of gravity of a rich and powerful life.[26] There is a father and a mother who lead the home.

As in the fifth commandment, other laws dealing with parent-child relations regard the father and mother as equals on equal footing (Exod 21:15,17; Lev 20:9; Deut 21:18–19; 27:16). They are mentioned together, which implies the essential unity and equality of both parents.[27]

The Motivation to Honor Parents

The reason or motivation for honoring parents is stated: "So that you may have a long life in the land that the LORD your God is giving you." The parents are the providers for every child. A person is born and has a family inheritance because of the faithful love of the parents. The one who honors his parents and thanks them for the goodness they have done for him has his reward—the Lord will provide goodness for him for the length of his days.[28] "He who so honors his parents as to provide a long life for them is to be rewarded by Yahweh with the gift of longevity."[29] It would in fact seem unjust for children who despise those who brought them into the world to be rewarded with a long life.

Some say that the promise "that you may have a long life" is mentioned at the end of the fifth commandment and placed halfway through the Ten Commandments to indicate that the promise is the reward for the one who keeps all the Ten Commandments. This understanding is related to the premise that every statute in the law clings to the whole. Every statute can be seen as motivated from the whole of the covenant. As Gerhard von Rad stated: "According to Old Testament ideas, the promise of life is attached not only to this commandment but to all

---

[26] Ibid., 179.

[27] See J. Tigay, *Deuteronomy*, JPS Torah Commentary (Philadelphia: Jewish Publication Society, 1996), 70; S. Paul, *Studies in the Book of the Covenant in the Light of Cuneiform and Biblical Law* (Leiden: Brill, 1970), 65.

[28] A. Hakam, *The Book of Exodus* (Jerusalem: Mossad Harav Kook, 1991), 287 [in Hb.]. The equivalent of the phrase לְמַעַן יַאֲרִכוּן יָמֶיךָ "so that you may have a long life" (Exod 20:12) with virtually identical wording may be found in Deut 6:2; 17:20; 22:7.

[29] Collins, *Christian Morality*, 56.

of them" (Deut 4:1; 8:1; 16:20; 30:15–16).[30] The extending of days is a frequent biblical reward (Exod 23:26; Deut 4:40; 5:33; 6:2; 11:9,21; 22:7; 1 Kgs 3:13–14; Ps 41:1–3; 91:16; Prov 10:27). The phrase occurs primarily in Deuteronomy (e.g., Deut 6:2; 25:15), not only with reference to quantity of time but with quality of time, as a blessing from God.[31] But reference to the promise of long life in the land is used in other passages such as Prov 28:16; Eccl 8:13; Isa 53:10; Jer 35:7. Most frequently the promise is connected to an admonition to keep the entire law (Deut 4:40; 5:33; 11:8–9; 30:16,20; 32:47).

In the Deuteronomy version of the fifth commandment, the promise of long life is paired with "that you may prosper," an expression absent from Exod 20:12. The phrase "that you may prosper" (twb) occurs only in Deuteronomy (Deut 4:40; 5:30[29]; 6:24; 12:25,28; 22:7).[32] This motivational language is often associated with Wisdom literature.[33]

Because of this broader association, it is possible that this final promise of the fifth commandment is actually a conclusion to the immediately previous commandments in the Decalogue.[34] In that case a violation against the parents could be punished as a violation against God's covenant, as an offense against God.[35]

Raymond Collins believes that the promise should not be limited to the first set of commandments but that it refers to all precepts of the Decalogue.[36] On the other hand, because this is the only one of the Ten Commandments that contains this promise of life, there may be some significance for its singular occurrence. Jeffrey Tigay argues that the uniqueness of the promise with the fifth commandment suggests the promise could be read as a veiled threat: if a person does not honor his father and mother, his days will be shortened (Prov

---

[30] G. von Rad, *Deuteronomy:. A Commentary* (London: SCM, 1966), 58.

[31] Childs, *The Book of Exodus*, 419.

[32] In Deut 4:40; 5:30; 6:24; and 22:7, "good" or prosper (טוב) comes before life, the opposite of the occurrence of the phrase in the Ten Commandments of Deut 5:16. The LXX of Exod 20:12 adds the term τῆς ἀγαθῆς "good land," a characteristic expression normally found in Deuteronomy.

[33] Gamberoni, "Das Elterngebot im Alten Testament," 163–64.

[34] See Weinfeld, *Deuteronomy 1–11*, 312.

[35] Gamberoni, "Das Elterngebot im Alten Testament," 187.

[36] R. Collins, "The Commandments," *ABD* 6:385.

20:20).[37] Other than its appearance in the Decalogue, however, the promise is not connected with an individual law. The promise is lacking in all parental laws outside the Decalogue (Exod 21:15,17; Lev 19:3; 20:9; Deut 27:16).[38] The mention of the "land" God is giving[39] completes what is said in the prologue: "I am the LORD your God who brought you out of the land of Egypt" (Exod 20:2). The Israelites were brought out of the *land* of Egypt that their days may be long in the new *land*.[40] Obedience to these commandments that focus on how a person is to relate and respond to God will result in the extension of an enriched life in the land. The ability of future generations to live and inherit the promised land from their parents is directly related to honoring them.

The Fifth Commandment in the Old Testament

In Lev 19, where we find a list of the holiness laws for the Israelites, the honoring of parents is the first listed obligation a human being has toward his fellow man, just as it is in the Ten Commandments. Also as in the Ten Commandments, Lev 19:3 places the law of honoring parents side by side with the law of the Sabbath. But what is distinctive about the listing in Lev 19 is that the parental law is placed immediately before the Sabbath law. Significantly, both laws are placed before the law on gods and images (Lev 19:4).[41] In Lev 19:32, the chapter addresses the proper treatment of the elders of society, returning and

---

[37] Tigay, *Deuteronomy*, 70, 357n104,105. See Fleishman, *Parent and Child in Ancient Near East and the Bible*, 245.

[38] Kremers, "Die Stellung des Elterngebotes im Dekalog," 148. Other passages indicate that Israel's eschatological salvation takes place only if Israel remains bound to the covenant and obeys all its commandments. See ibid., 154–55.

[39] The use of the participle as the predicate is a description of a condition or state. The activity of the participle as a verb stresses repeated or continual action. Kremers, "Die Stellung des Elterngebotes im Dekalog," 150. The use of "land" as a technical term for the land of promise is found in Deut 7:13; 11:17; 12:19; 21:1,23; 26:2,10; 28:4,11,18,21,33,51,63; 29:27; 30:9; 31:20; 32:43.

[40] Hakam, *The Book of Exodus*, 287. There is no evidence that the motive clause was a later addition and secondary to the parental commandment. R. Sonsino, *Motive Clauses in Hebrew Law*, SBLDS, ed. D. Knight (Chico, CA: Scholars Press, 1980), esp. 286.

[41] Note also that the mother is placed before the father in Lev 19:3.

thus reinforcing the special treatment that is to be afforded to parents and the aged in society.[42]

The Sabbath and parental commandments are the only two positive laws in the Ten Commandments and the only two that include the phrase "as the LORD your God has commanded you" in the Deuteronomy version (Deut 5:12,16). The formula "as the LORD your God commanded you" is a reference to Exod 20 with regard to the first giving of these laws on Mount Sinai.[43]

Other Old Testament passages help to explain what is involved in "honoring" parents. It involves obedience to them (Deut 21:18–21; Prov 23:22) and adhering to their teaching (Prov 1:8–9). Parents instructed their children with regard to participating in the religious feasts (Exod 12:26–27; 13:8,14–16; Josh 4:6–7,21–24), and with regard to the home and the great deeds of God and His laws (Deut 6:6–9; 11:18–21; 32:7,46–47). They were also obligated to instruct their children in the service of God as well as inform them how they might participate in the life of the community of Yahweh (Exod 12:26–27; 13:8,14–16; Deut 12:11–14,17–19; 29:9–15; 31:10–13; Josh 4:21–24).[44]

What does it mean to honor parents? The Old Testament answers this with concrete instructions. Obviously, their children must not kill them (Exod 21:15a), curse them (Exod 21:17; Lev 20:9), steal from them (Prov 28:24), or treat them with scorn (Deut 27:16). Dishonoring parents involves striking, insulting, and behaving disrespectfully toward them (Deut 27:16; Prov 30:17).[45]

Perhaps the clearest connection of the fifth commandment to other Old Testament passages is seen in those verses that legislate in regard to violation of the commandment. Most notably is the legislation in Deut 21:18–21. Here we have a violation of the fifth commandment by a stubborn and rebellious son. This son, who violated the

---

[42] W. Schmidt, *Die Zehn Gebote im Rahmen alttestamentliche Ethik* (Darmstadt: Wissenschaftliche Buchgesellschaft, 1993), 106.

[43] Dohmen, *Exodus 19–40,* 99.

[44] Kremers, "Die Stellung des Elterngebotes im Dekalog," 160. Five so-called question-and-answer texts begin with the phrase, "When your son asks you . . . you shall say . . ." (Exod 12:26–27; 13:14–16; Deut 6:20–25; Josh 4:6–7,21–24). See C. Wright, "Family," *ABD* 2:765.

[45] Tigay, *Deuteronomy,* 69–70, 357.

commandment, was to be condemned to death by the covenant community. The offense was viewed as a covenant crime, and so the son was guilty of sinning not only against his parents but against God. Allowing this activity to go on would threaten the whole theocratic community, so it had to be purged decisively with the young man's death.[46] While the parents are in the best position to observe the violation, it is the legal community that is responsible to carry out the execution. The punishment was to be carried out by court order after an application of charges by the parents.[47] The parents could not act unilaterally to put their son to death.[48] Moreover, the nature of this sin would not be an isolated act of rebellion but a demonstration of insubordination over a long period of time.[49] The severe threat posed by violation of this commandment functioned as a deterrent for those sons who had a rebellious nature.[50]

The fifth commandment does not occupy a great deal of the content of the narrative books. This is not to say that basic understanding of the commandment was foreign to Old Testament narrative texts. The teaching of it is evident in many narrative accounts, including events that occurred earlier than the Mosaic period. For example: Jacob fears that Rebekah's cunning plan could be offensive to his father (Gen 27:12 [Prov 30:17]); Esau's foreign marriage is unpleasant to his parents (Gen 26:35); Reuben commits incest and is cursed by his father (Gen 35:22; 49:3–4); Eli's sons did not know the Lord and were disobedient to Him (1 Sam 2:12,31); Absalom steals the heart of Israel and invades his father's harem (2 Sam 15:1–6; 16:21–22).

The Ham affair also violates the deep respect one was obligated to have for a parent (Gen 9:20–27).[51] This passage, which resulted in a curse on Canaan, involved a violation of the fifth commandment. Genesis 9:22–23 contrasts Noah's three sons in their conduct toward their

---

[46] C. Wright, *An Eye for an Eye: The Place of Old Testament Ethics Today* (Downers Grove, IL: InterVarsity, 1983), 168.

[47] Westbrook, *A History of Ancient Near Eastern Law,* 50.

[48] Fleishman, *Parent and Child in Ancient Near East and the Bible,* 269.

[49] A. Jepsen, "Beiträge zur Auslegung und Geschichte des Dekalogs," *ZAW* 79 (1967): 294; Fleishman, *Parent and Child in Ancient Near East and the Bible,* 252.

[50] Fleishman, *Parent and Child in Ancient Near East and the Bible,* 281. See W. Keszler, "Die Literarische, Historische und Theologische Problematik des Dekalogs," *VT* 7 (1957): 10–11.

[51] Gamberoni, "Das Elterngebot im Alten Testament," 181.

father. Ham's sin was not in a general shamelessness or unbridled sexuality but in dishonoring his father, while Shem and Japheth conducted themselves with piety. The account addresses obligations of a son to take care of his father when the father has become heavy with wine.[52] By contrast, Jewish tradition views Joseph as a champion of fifth commandment obedience in sustaining his father in Goshen. Joseph showed respect for his father when Jacob came down to Egypt, and honored his father by bringing him before Pharaoh (Gen 46:29; 47:7).[53]

The most concentrated treatment of the fifth commandment in the Old Testament is contained in the book of Proverbs (see Prov 1:8–9; 6:20–23; 15:5,20; 17:25; 19:26; 20:20; 23:22; 28:24; 30:11,17). Proverbs reiterates the admonition to honor one's parents, extolling them as the fountains of wisdom (Prov 1:8–9; 6:20–21; 10:1).[54]

The prophet Ezekiel links the defeat of God's people, loss of the land, and destruction of the temple to the breaking of the fifth commandment (Ezek 22:7,15). The fifth commandment is cited in Mal 1:6, which teaches that the honor (*kbd*) a son gives to his father should be an illustration of the honor the covenant people are to render to God.

The destruction of the intimate bond of the family is a traditional characteristic of biblical eschatology. Mic 7:5–6 speaks of the extreme decline of the order of family relations, friendships, and the neighborhood. The low point is reached when people disregard natural restraint with regard to treatment of parents and elders (see Isa 3:4–6). In the future consummation there will be a restoration of family life (see Mal 4:5-6 [3:23–24]).

The apocryphal Sir 3 gives extended advice about the ways a son or daughter should honor a father. Of all the wisdom books, Sirach has the most detailed commentary on the law of parents from the Decalogue (3:1–16).[55]

The fifth commandment is the first one that establishes a leadership position within human civilization. This law, if not the principle of the law, is expanded to address the establishment of leadership, including in Israel the laws of the king, the Levite, and the prophet

---

[52] Westermann, *Genesis 1–11*, 485.
[53] Blidstein, *Honor Thy Father and Mother*, 62.
[54] W. Propp, *Exodus 19–40*, AB (New York: Doubleday, 2006), 178.
[55] Gamberoni, "Das Elterngebot im Alten Testament," 179.

(e.g., Deut 16:18–18:22).[56] Elders are to be respected (Lev 19:32; Isa 3:5; Sir 8:6; 25:5–6; 42:8), as well as persons with responsibility and authority (Exod 22:28[27]; 1 Kgs 21:10; Lev 24:11,14–16). Johann Gamberoni says that family and parents remain the foundation of all biblical law.[57] No other law in the Decalogue is formulated in such wholly positive terms as we find in the fifth commandment.[58]

The Fifth Commandment in the New Testament

In the New Testament, the fifth commandment was subject to being exploited by the Pharisees (Matt 15:4–6; Mark 7:10–12). Resources that were available to support one's parents may have been dedicated to God and kept from them.[59] Jesus took issue with this tradition by teaching that honoring of parents was one of the weightier commandments.[60]

In Eph 6:2–3, Paul cites this commandment as part of the responsibility children are to exercise toward their parents. Paul said this is the first commandment that is accompanied by a promise of reward.[61] In Rom 1, where Paul lists the characteristics of the rebellious human heart, disobedience to parents is among these heinous sins (Rom 1:30).

Micah 7:6 demonstrates that the violation of this commandment leads to chaos and the disintegration of society. The same theme is present in the New Testament (Matt 10:21,34–36; Mark 13:12; Luke 12:53). Disobedience to parents will characterize the world before the return of Christ (2 Tim 3:2).

Near the end of His life, Jesus demonstrated His perfect obedience by providing for the care of His mother (John 19:26–27). This not only further illustrates His complete obedience but demonstrates that the fifth commandment included caring for parents in their later years.

---

[56] See Christensen, *Deuteronomy 1–11*, 124.

[57] Gamberoni, "Das Elterngebot im Alten Testament," 184.

[58] Sarna, *Exodus*, 113.

[59] R. Collins, *Christian Morality: Biblical Foundations* (Notre Dame, IN: University of Notre Dame Press, 1986), 73.

[60] In some Jewish circles, the fifth commandment was deemed to be the most difficult one to obey. See Collins, *Christian Morality*, 76.

[61] The motivation includes the phrase "that it may be well for you," indicating that Paul was citing the commandment according to the Deuteronomy version (Deut 5:16).

Conclusion

As the well-being of every child is dependent on the parent, it is only appropriate that children are responsible to obey their parents as well as care for them in the parents' later years. This service is just, and similar to payment of a debt.[62] For every child the parent is the first person he knows, and the parent's care and support for the child is second only to God as provider. As the philosopher Philo stated centuries ago: "Parents stand by their nature on the border-line between the mortal and the immortal . . . because the act of generation assimilates them to God, the Generator of them All." The lives of parents must come to an end, but by their ability to cooperate with God in the creation of life, they are endowed with a touch of the divine.[63] Yet as observed above, the honoring of parents leads to a lengthening of one's days, the same result that ensues from fearing the Lord (Prov 10:27).

Throughout the analysis of the fifth commandment, nothing has been mentioned of the right or authority of the parent. The onus for obedience to the fifth commandment is on the child. This law is about responsibilities to be carried out faithfully and lovingly, not about one's authoritative rights. It would be incorrect to cite the fifth commandment to demand obedience in order to "lord it over" a child. The child serves his father not because his father is in power, or even because of parental authority (see Eph 6:4). It makes no difference whether the parent is worthy or unworthy of this honor—God has providentially given the child his parents. The issue is rather the responsibility of the child to the parent—how a child is to treat his parent and give glory to God.[64] The Jewish sages stated that this was to be foremost among the commandments for which man is rewarded in this world (m. Pe'ah 1:1). Rabbi Simeon ben Yohai says, "Great is the commandment of honoring father and mother because God pre-

---

[62] S. Albeck, "The Ten Commandments and the Essence of Religious Faith," 273. Duties of sons regarding their parents, by virtue of fulfillment of the fifth commandment, are enumerated in the rabbinic sources (b. Qidd. 31b; m. Pe'ah 1:1,15c; t. Qidd. 1:11; etc.); see Weinfeld, Deuteronomy 1–11, 310.

[63] See Y. Amir, "The Decalogue According to Philo," in The Ten Commandments in History and Tradition, ed. B. Segal (Jerusalem: Magnes, 1990), 156–57.

[64] Blidstein, Honor Thy Father and Mother, 50.

ferred it over the honoring of himself."[65] The extreme significance of this command may be observed in the Jewish midrash (*Exod. Rab.* 30:5), which places the fifth commandment as preeminent: "If Israel neglects God's commands, it is as though they cursed their father and mother."[66] Similarly, Flavius Josephus observed that honor to parents ranks second in importance only to the honor we owe God.[67]

The Bible never commands that obedience and loyalty be shown to the father alone. The instructions and admonitions given to children are to be followed for the mother as well.[68] The foundations laid in the fifth commandment for parental authority have been extended by the church as the basis for all authority, including that of government (see 1 Pet 2:13–17).[69] "If you can't learn to get along with your family, then you are going to have problems getting along with anybody else in society."[70] Beginning with the fifth commandment, a person forms his attitude toward authority in general.[71]

As the meaning of the fifth commandment is patently clear, a perennial question in discussions of its application is something like this: "Are children to show obedient honor in absolutely everything?" The issue may regard the pathetic situation in which a parent orders a child to do something illegal or unacceptable. Here a line must be drawn, as God would not desire that in obeying a parent, a child would engage in activity contrary to the teaching of Scripture.[72] The child is to honor his parent "in the Lord" (Eph 6:1). If a father or

---

[65] For citation, see Weinfeld, *Deuteronomy 1–11*, 312.

[66] See Blidstein, *Honor Thy Father and Mother*, 8.

[67] *Ag. Ap.*, II, 206; Blidstein, *Honor Thy Father and Mother*, 12.

[68] The mother and father are addressed together as two entities, as the Hebrew language has no word for "parents." A. Hakam, *The Book of Exodus* (Jerusalem: Mossad Harav Kook, 1991), 287 [in Hb.].

[69] T. Fretheim, *Exodus*, Interpretation: A Biblical Commentary for Teaching and Preaching (Louisville: John Knox, 1973), 232.

[70] J. Vines, *Basic Bible Sermons on the Ten Commandments* (Nashville: Broadman, 1992), 57. See W. Kaiser Jr., *Toward Old Testament Ethics* (Grand Rapids: Zondervan, 1983), 90.

[71] Collins, *Christian Morality*, 55.

[72] See Blidstein, *Honor Thy Father and Mother*, 134; Collins, *Christian Morality*, 87. A great deal of the rabbinic discussion on this issue involves the parents' choice of a mate for a child and the situations in which the child does not go along. Esau's decision to marry against his parents' wishes is the great biblical illustration of this dilemma. See Blidstein, *Honor Thy Father and Mother*.

mother should lead a child into unrighteousness, obedience to that parent is to be withheld.[73]

Another question that normally surfaces in discussions of the fifth commandment has to do with the absolute nature of the promise. Are we to expect that every obedient child will live a long life? We know that not all children who give every indication of being obedient to their parents and walk with the Lord have long lives. The answer appears to be that this law is a general rule operating out of a general principle rather than an absolute law without exceptions. Many children who honor their parents will live a long and prosperous life, in no small part because disobedience to parents often results in a life fraught with danger that may result in a shorter life than that of the obedient. The scriptural principle is that obedience to God will result in blessing while disobedience leads to sin and to misery and no blessing.[74] Moreover, if children do not honor their parents and are rebellious and disobedient, they would not learn about the covenant relationship with God that had been central to the lives of their parents.[75] "If the commandment is obeyed, life will go better for one, generally speaking. But this is not inevitably the case, nor is there some point in life at which one can say that such a word has been fulfilled."[76]

In a person's efforts to obey the fifth commandment, he acknowledges an immeasurable debt to his parents and should humbly realize that his life "lies in focus beyond his own reality. For by acknowledging parents, man admits that he is not the source of his own being, that he owes existence itself to forces beyond his own personal reality."[77]

A good part of this debt is the immeasurable value of what children learn about life from their parents. But if children persist in being incorrigible and self-centered, they do not learn from their parents

---

[73] J. Calvin, *Commentaries on the Last Books of Moses,* trans. C. Bingham (Grand Rapids: Baker, 1979), 3:8.

[74] Stuart claims that this is not a promise of long individual life spans. Rather, the promise refers to God's protection of His people as long as they keep his covenant (Stuart, *Exodus,* 462).

[75] P. Craigie, *The Book of Deuteronomy* (Grand Rapids: Eerdmans, 1976), 158.

[76] Fretheim, *Exodus,* 232.

[77] Blidstein, *Honor Thy Father and Mother,* 5.

about God's deeds of the past and His work in history. As a result, the importance of their own relationship to God would suffer. These life lessons—as well as the cohesiveness of the family unit and learning in the family to live together—prepare the child to get along with people in the world. "Unless people learn to live together in the family, they aren't likely to learn to get along with anybody anywhere."[78] This law creates stability in society as it is carried out through subsequent generations. Texts that mention faithfulness to all generations imply the succession of generations of families and the preservation of culture and society. This law is sacred as it relates to the institution of the family in the Genesis creation account. The seeds of culture and society go back to the garden of Eden as well as the fifth commandment. Philo wrote that when the right regulation of private households within a society is neglected, it is idle to expect the foundation of public law to be secure.[79] What occurs within the family affects the whole nation (Deut 4:9–10; 11:21; Ps 78:5–6).

This focus on family love, family cohesion, and solidarity from the Old Testament has allowed the Jewish people to survive the Holocaust as well as thousands of years of anti-Semitism.[80] For a culture to endure, it must be transmitted, and this can only occur between generations when there exists a keen sense of love and respect.[81] God selected the family as the primary unit of society—not the individual, not the state, not the corporation, and not even the church.[82] As Jerry Vines has said, "Show me a nation where there is disobedience to parents, and I will show you a nation whose foundations are crumbling."[83] Authoritarian structures such as totalitarian governments and religious cults all seek to remove the vital role of the family as the primary social unit. These systems all ultimately seek to reject parental authority in the interest of a higher authority represented

---

[78] M. Dunnam, *Exodus*, The Communicator's Commentary (Waco, TX: Word, 1987), 261.

[79] See Blidstein, *Honor Thy Father and Mother*, 21.

[80] M. Dunnam, *Exodus*, 261.

[81] Blidstein, *Honor Thy Father and Mother,* 23.

[82] H. Titus, "God's Revelation: Foundation for the Common Law," in *The Christian and American Law: Christianity's Impact on America's Founding Documents and Future Direction*, ed. H. Wayne House (Grand Rapids: Kregel, 1998), 34.

[83] J. Vines, *Basic Bible Sermons on the Ten Commandments* (Nashville: Broadman, 1992), 66.

by the state or the religious values in question.[84] The importance of the family is indicated through all ages of the Bible—from creation through the New Testament to future prophetic activity. Even in the end-times the centrality of family for human civilization plays a vital role. From the time of Gen 2:18, when the greatest need was to find the solution to man's solitude, human community and civilization have to do primarily with man and woman, and this has determined human existence for all time.[85]

God has assigned a special value to the fifth commandment: those who honor their parents are assured of God's blessing. This commandment and the fourth commandment occupy positions in the center of the Decalogue and could be considered of central importance to the entire list. As the fifth commandment forms a transition to the more social commandments, it indicates that no sphere of life can be considered secular. Because the fifth commandment lays out the promise of living long in the land (Exod 20:12; Deut 5:16), it harkens us back to the prologue, which reminds the reader that the Lord delivered the people by bringing them out of the land of bondage (Exod 20:2; Deut 5:6). The promise of life for obedience to this command leads naturally to the next commandment, the sixth, which protects the sanctity of life. The fifth commandment also interconnects with the seventh (adultery), where we move from the necessity and vitality of the family to its destruction. The death penalty for breaking the fifth commandment as well as the seventh served to protect the family internally from the disruption of its domestic authority and its sexual integrity.[86]

---

[84] Blidstein, *Honor Thy Father and Mother,* 19.
[85] Westermann, *Genesis 1–11,* 227, 232.
[86] See C. Wright, "Family," *ABD* 2:765.

Chapter 6

THE SIXTH COMMANDMENT

Do not murder.

Introduction

Than taking of a human life has been viewed as a serious crime in every civilization. This included the cultures of the ancient Near East, and of course the Bible.

However, the situations and circumstances that led to killings were not all viewed the same, just as in modern times. In Old Babylonian law, a fatal blow delivered in the course of a skirmish or scuffle was not viewed on the same level as, for example, a premeditated murder. If the victim did not die, the culprit had to swear under oath that he did not in any way intend for the injury to take place. In that case he was under obligation only to pay the doctor for the service rendered to the injured man. If he did die, it had to be determined whether the killing was intentional or the result of negligence.[1] In Hittite law, a man who killed his wife while she was engaged in adultery was viewed as justified and did not bring any penalty or guilt.[2]

The penalties for causing a homicide were fairly standard in the ancient Near East. Raymond Westbrook has summarized the punishments and possible payments:

(1) If the killing was premeditated: death of the murderer himself, irrespective of the status of the victim. (2) If the killing was manslaughter, i.e., unpremeditated or accidental killing: death of a subordinate member of the killer's family. (3) For manslaughter of a person without civil status (e.g., slave, daughter's foetus): replacement with a slave. This order is paralleled in terms of the type of ransom payable. (1) Ransom of the killer's life at the choice set by the avenger. (2) Ransom of the subordinate's life at the choice and level set by the avenger. (3) Probably a simple debt, with consequences of the order of distraint of property or debt-slavery for non-payment.[3]

---

[1] R. Westbrook, ed., *A History of Ancient Near Eastern Law*, 2 vols. (Leiden; Boston: Brill, 2003), 1:415–16, 644.

[2] E. Eiclar, "רצח," *EncMiqr* 7:430 [in Hb.].

[3] R. Westbrook, *Studies in Biblical and Cuneiform Law* (Paris: J. Gabalda, 1988), 70.

While this listing accurately summarizes the penalties for homicide, individual cultures may have had special application or adaptation of penalties. For example, in the Laws of Ur-Namma (southern Mesopotamia, 2100 BC), not only was the murderer put to death, but his estate and his wife and children were handed over to the sons of the victim.[4]

In ancient Near Eastern law, particularly from Mesopotamia, punishments might vary based on the social status of the victim. Crimes such as homicide, wounding, or rape of a slave would not be considered as serious because the slave was part of his owner's property.[5] In Mesopotamia, punishment by death applied to the killing of a free man and not a man of lesser status, particularly a servant.[6] Moreover, for a convicted murderer, there seem to be some options open to the family of the victim with regard to type of punishment. Middle Assyrian laws provided that if a person entered the home of a family and killed one of its members, the head of the household had the option of killing him or taking his property and inheritance or one of his children.[7] In the Hittite laws the murderer was punished by payment of a fine graded according to the subjective guilt of the murderer and the status of the one who was killed. The Code of Hammurabi called for the death of a man's son if the man had been involved in bringing about the demise of another man's son.[8] The Sumerian laws mention a woman and her son from the family of a murderer who had died and prescribed that they be enslaved to the heirs of the victim.[9]

In order to match the punishment to the sin, some of the legal traditions of the ancient Near East used a measure-for-measure principle of punishment. One feature that surfaced frequently was the punishment of a child for a parent's offense. In Hittite law, if someone pushed a person into a fire and killed him, the culprit must deliver his own son to be killed.[10] If a builder did not make a structure strong

---

[4] Westbrook, *A History of Ancient Near Eastern Law,* 1:210.

[5] Ibid., 1:79, 82.

[6] Eiclar, "רָצַח," 428.

[7] See B. Arnold and B. Beyer, eds., *Readings from the Ancient Near East* (Grand Rapids: Baker Academic, 2002), 115. See Westbrook, *A History of Ancient Near Eastern Law,* 558.

[8] Westbrook, *A History of Ancient Near Eastern Law,* 1:415.

[9] Hammurabi, § 230: in *ANET,* 176; Eiclar, "רָצַח", 430.

[10] Westbrook, *A History of Ancient Near Eastern Law,* 1:646.

enough and it collapsed and killed the owner's son, the son of the builder would be put to death.[11] This sort of law shows a fundamental difference between the Torah and the laws of other nations in the ancient Near East. The practice of putting a child to death for his parent's transgressions is at odds with biblical teaching: "Fathers are not to be put to death for their children or children for their fathers; each person will be put to death for his own sin" (Deut 24:16).

Differences between ancient Near Eastern and biblical views of murder are ultimately connected to their contrastive views of the nature of God and man. Although the literature of Mesopotamia considered murder to be a severe iniquity, which aroused the anger of the gods, man was considered as part of the creation and nothing more than an economic value. He was created to be a servant of the gods. Another contrast has to do with payment of a fine as punishment for a convicted murderer. In most of ancient Near Eastern law, the acceptance of a ransom or a fine was dependent completely on the will of the relatives of the murder victim. Biblical law prohibited acceptance of a ransom or fine for a murder that happened with malice or by accident (Num 35:31; Deut 19:12). This distinction shows that the Bible places a high premium on the life of man because man was created in the image of God (Gen 1:27).

The Meaning of the Sixth Commandment

The meanings of the sixth, seventh, and eighth commandments are largely determined by analysis of single words—the terms for murder, adultery, and stealing, respectively.[12] The meaning of the sixth commandment is determined by the meaning of the root *rṣḥ*, translated in the NIV and HCSB as "murder." This root is somewhat unusual as it has no known cognates in other ancient Near Eastern languages; it occurs exclusively in Hebrew. The root occurs about 38 times in the Old Testament, but other terms within the semantic range of "killing"

---

[11] Eiclar, "רָצַח," 431.

[12] The *Rāphè* accent over the verbs "תִּרְצָח," "תִּנְאָף," and "תִּגְנֹב" is a horizontal stroke, and the opposite of both kinds of *Dageš* and *Mappîq* (GKC, 57). In the LXX, the order of this series of short prohibitions is adultery, stealing, murder.

(e.g., *hārag* and the Hiphil of *mût*) are more frequent.[13] These more common words for "kill" are used for the killing of a political enemy in battle, for execution as a legal punishment, and for the just putting to death of someone by God.[14]

Broadly speaking, the use of the root *rṣḥ* often carries such connotations as "strike" or "slay," with an emphasis on physical force or violence.[15] More narrowly, the root has a semantic range that includes "murder" or "manslaughter."[16] In view of certain passages (e.g., 1 Kgs 21:19), it has been suggested that the verb should be rendered as "murder" (so NEB; NRSV). It can also, however, refer to unintentional killing (Deut 4:41–42) but is never used of killing in war. The indication of an intention is revealed in such passages as 1 Kgs 21:12–13 and Num 35:20–21. Any act of violence against an individual out of hatred, anger, malice, deceit, or for personal gain, in whatever circumstances and by whatever method, that might result in death (even if killing was not the intention) must be classified as murder.[17] The root *rṣḥ* is thus used to refer to premeditated killing that could be viewed as illicit. While these meanings and nuances share the basic idea of killing, the distinction in the range of meaning comes from the circumstance or intentionality of the killing. These distinctions are particularly brought out in Num 35, which contains more than 35 percent of the occurrences of *rṣḥ* in the Old Testament.

Numbers 35

The context of Num 35 has to do with the cities of refuge that were established as a way of preventing vigilante violence against someone who was suspected of murder. In Num 35 we see the distinction

---

[13] W. Domeris, "רָצַח," *NIDOTTE* 3:1188. The root הרג occurs 165 times in the Old Testament while the Hiphil of *mût* occurs 201 times. B. Childs, *The Book of Exodus: A Critical-Theological Commentary* (Louisville: Westminster John Knox, 1974), 419–21.

[14] W. Schmidt, *Die Zehn Gebote im Rahmen alttestamentliche Ethik* (Darmstadt: Wissenschaftliche Buchgesellschaft, 1993), 107; E. Nielsen, *Deuteronomium*, HAT (Tübingen: Mohr [Siebeck], 1995), 78.

[15] F. Hossfeld, "רָצַח *rāṣaḥ*," *TDOT* 13:632; C. Dohmen, *Exodus 19–40* (Freiburg: Herder, 2004), 122. The verb רָצַח also has a figurative or metaphorical sense in Prov 22:13 in reference to the lion's attack that is feared by the slacker.

[16] BDB, "רָצַח," 953–54.

[17] T. Fretheim, *Exodus*, Interpretation: A Biblical Commentary for Teaching and Preaching (Louisville: John Knox, 1973), 232–33.

in meanings of *rṣḥ* being explained by the use or nonuse of an instrument in putting someone to death. The use of a weapon relates to whether the killing was premeditated or accidental. In biblical law, premeditation generally was established by the use of a deadly instrument (Num 35:16–18) or that the attacker harbored hatred or a grudge against the victim (Num 35:20–21; Deut 19:11–13). In Num 35, *rṣḥ* refers seven times to manslaughter (not premeditated) (Num 35:6,11–12,25–28; see Deut 4:42; 19:3–6), seven times to murder (premeditated) (Num 35:16–19,21,30–31; see Deut 22:26; 1 Kgs 21:19), and once to capital punishment (Num 35:30). Clearly the meaning of murder and manslaughter cannot be distinguished based on use of the term *rṣḥ* alone; the meaning must be determined by the immediate context. Again, in the context of Num 35, we find that murder is distinguished by the perpetrator's intention (Num 35:20–21,22–24; see Exod 21:12–14). The murderer is the one who plans to carry out a killing by "lying in wait" or who has hatred or malicious intent toward the victim (see Exod 21:12–14). In contrast, manslaughter is characterized by lack of intent or design to commit murder or as an accidental act (Num 35:22–24; Deut 19:11–13).[18]

For an accidental killing, the death penalty was not applied (Exod 21:13; Num 35:11). The man who committed the manslaughter would flee to one of the six cities of refuge in order to find safe haven (Num 35:9–34; Deut 19:4–10). The nearest male relative of the victim (the blood avenger) had the task of avenging his dead relative but was forbidden from entering the city of refuge where the killer had gone. The person who committed manslaughter could remain alive in a city of refuge but had to stay there until the death of the high priest. Upon the death of the high priest, the person guilty of committing manslaughter could return home. But if he left the city of refuge before the death of the high priest, the blood avenger was free to kill him without punishment (Num 35:26–28). The community had collective responsibility to demand judgment for the killer. It was the responsibility of the blood avenger to kill his relative's killer should the killer leave the city of refuge. The statute does not condemn the avenger of blood who put to death one who had killed by accident and had not

---

[18] D. O'Mathuna, "Bodily Injuries, Murder, Manslaughter," *DOTP*, 91.

yet found refuge, although the law endeavored to prevent such deeds (Num 35:26–27; Deut 19:6).[19] If the elders of the territory where the death took place determined that the man who fled to a city of refuge was a murderer, he would be taken from the city of refuge and handed over to the avenger of blood for execution. A murderer could not enjoy the asylum of a city of refuge. For unsolved murders, the community was purified by a solemn ritual that involved the slaughter of a heifer. This ritual atoned for "the guilt of shedding innocent blood" among the people (Deut 21:1–9).

In Num 35 *rṣḥ* refers to killing that was not related to a judicial execution. Numbers 35:26–28 contains the only exception to this rule, where *rṣḥ* does refer to carrying out capital punishment. But in Num 35:26–28 the use of *rṣḥ* is a play on words indicating that the death of a murderer corresponds to his own devious deed: the avenger of blood will kill (*rṣḥ*) the murderer (*rṣḥ*), according to witnesses he will kill (*rṣḥ*) the murderer.[20]

Because the use of *rṣḥ* in reference to manslaughter must be explained or qualified when it refers to an accidental homicide, it should be clear that the independent use of the term carries the connotation of murder—the premeditated, nonjudicial taking of a life. Because *rṣḥ* is unqualified in the sixth commandment, and because it is not possible to prohibit something that is accidental (manslaughter), there is no other conclusion but that what is prohibited in the Ten Commandments is the commission of murder.[21]

Genesis 9:5–6

While Num 35 provides the lexical foundation for the meaning of the root *rṣḥ*, Genesis 9:5–6 provides the theological foundation of the sixth commandment. As this statement is addressed to survivors of the flood, it has universal application because these eight individuals

---

[19] Eiclar, "רָצַח," 427.

[20] A. Hakam, *The Book of Exodus* (Jerusalem: Mossad Harav Kook, 1991), 288 and n. 56 [in Hb.].

[21] See J. Tigay, *Deuteronomy*, JPS Torah Commentary (Philadelphia: Jewish Publication Society, 1996), 70, 357n106.

became progenitors of the human race (Gen 8:18). This law is applicable to the whole of humanity and is without restriction.[22]

Genesis 9:5–6 prohibits the taking of a human life because a human life is made in the image of God (Gen 1:27). Of all the creatures God created in Gen 1, only man is made in the image of God. Human beings have a closer relationship to God and are of more value than the other creatures God made. They have a unique value in the sight of God. Humans may eat animals (which involves killing them [Gen 9:3]) and sacrifice animals, but no one is allowed to take the life of a human being (not even beasts, Exod 21:28). Because man is created in the image of God, someone who takes a person's life should have his life taken. The act of killing is "tantamount to killing God in effigy."[23] The execution of a murderer fulfills the commands of God. God alone has the right to terminate life. Human beings are never to kill on their own authority. Society must exact satisfaction for the crime of murder since life is derived from God and is precious to Him. However, only God, who alone gives and takes life, is in the position to designate the crime for which life must be taken.[24] The sin of murder is not only against the victim and his family but against God, whose image the victim bears.[25]

The verb *rṣḥ* is never used of killing in battle or even in self-defense or suicide.[26] It is used on one occasion for the execution of the death penalty, but the choice of this root was intended to create a play on words (see Num 35:26–28 above). The death penalty is the proper punishment for one who commits murder (Gen 9:6). The execution of the death penalty for murder is thus carrying out the command of God. This is because God is sovereign over life and death, and He establishes and defends the inviolability of human life.[27] Only the one who kills with malice, with hate, or with deceit deserves death (Exod

---

[22] See C. Westermann, *Genesis 1–11*, trans. J. Scullion (Minneapolis: Fortress, 1994), 466.

[23] W. Kaiser Jr., *Toward Old Testament Ethics* (Grand Rapids: Zondervan, 1983), 91.

[24] See N. Sarna, *Exodus,* JPS Torah Commentary (Philadelphia, New York: Jewish Publication Society, 1991), 113.

[25] Eiclar, "רצח," 426–27. Every murderer confronts God and revolts against Him. See Westermann, *Genesis 1–11*, 468.

[26] See W. Keszler, "Die literarische, historische und theologische Problematik des Dekalogs," *VT* 7 (1957): 11.

[27] Westermann, *Genesis 1–11*, 469.

21:12; Num 35:17; Deut 19:12).[28] Because a murderer strikes at the image of God borne by a human being, murder is an attack on God's dominion.[29]

The Sixth Commandment in the Old Testament

In the legal material from the Pentateuch, we find several parallels to the commandment against the taking of a life. The laws convey the same prohibition against murder but are written in a slightly longer form (Exod 21:12; Lev 24:17; Deut 27:24).

Early in the narrative account of the Pentateuch, virtually on the heels of the fall in Gen 3, we find the first murder in the Bible. Cain killed his brother Abel, apparently over Abel's faithfulness in offering a better sacrifice than Cain. After Abel was slain,[30] God addressed Cain and stated that his brother's blood cried out to Him from the ground (Gen 4:10)! Blood unlawfully shed pollutes the land, and there can be no expiation of the land unless the killer's blood is shed (Num 35:33). The fact that the blood cried out to God indicated that a grievous offense had taken place and that Cain could not hide his deed. It is never possible to pull off the perfect murder.[31] Furthermore, this early narrative promises little hope of righteousness for the fallen race, as we see that the first person born into the human race (Cain) kills his only brother (Abel).[32]

In the Bible, God alone seeks the blood of the one who has been murdered and has not been atoned (Gen 9:5; Ps 9:12[13]; see Gen 4:10; 2 Kgs 9:7,26; Isa 26:21; Ezek 24:7–9; Joel 3:21[4:21]). The Lord visits the guilt on the house of the murderer and seeks the blood of

---

[28] Eiclar, "רָצַח," 427.

[29] While Gen 9:6 appears as a prohibition of murder, it could be considered the core of the so-called second table of the Decalogue; Gen 17:1 functions as the chief part of the so-called first table and is addressed to Abraham as the progenitor of Israel. See W. Schmidt, *Die Zehn Gebot im Rahmen alttestamentlicher Ethik* (Darmstadt: Wissenschaftliche Buchgesellcaft, 1993), 13n3.

[30] The root is the Hb. הרג and not רצח although it is clear from context that this is a premeditated murder.

[31] C. Westermann, *Genesis 1–11*, 305.

[32] According to Jewish tradition, the "violence" that brought about the judgment of the flood (Gen 6:13) was actually "murder" (*Gen. Rab.* 31:6), and the "wicked sinners" of Sodom were "murderers" (*Sanh.* 109a).

the murdered one from the seed of the murderer (2 Sam 3:28–29; 21:1; 1 Kgs 2:32–34; see also 2 Kgs 9:7–8,25–26; Hos 1:4).

In the historical and prophetic corpus, *rṣḥ* (like *hrg*) renders the idea of literal killing, whether accidental (Josh 20:1–6) or intentional (Jer 7:9). David's intention to have Uriah the Hittite put to death is clear throughout 2 Sam 11, and the narrator explicitly tells us in 2 Sam 12:9 that David "murdered" *(hārag)* Uriah. Intentionality is clear in the execution of Naboth which resulted in Ahab's seizure of Naboth's vineyard (1 Kgs 21:14,19).

Jeremiah accused the southern kingdom of multiple sins including murder: "Do you steal, murder *(rṣḥ)*, commit adultery, swear falsely?" (Jer 7:9). Similarly, Hosea earlier accused the northern kingdom of "cursing, lying, murder *(rṣḥ)*, stealing, and adultery" (Hos 4:2). In the prophetic and Wisdom literature, *rṣḥ* invariably carries the connotation of intentional murder and violence (Isa 1:21; Hos 6:9; Job 24:14; Ps 94:6; Prov 22:13).

In Lev 19:17–18, the scope of the command on murder is internalized to cover hating one's brother from the heart.[33] This usage is similar to Jesus' application of this law in the Sermon on the Mount.

The Sixth Commandment in the New Testament

In His Sermon on the Mount, Jesus refers to the sixth commandment and expands its application. Jesus said that if anyone became angry with his brother, he had already committed murder in his heart (Matt 5:21–22). Similarly, in Mark 7:20–21, Jesus says: "What comes out of a person—that defiles him. For from within, out of people's hearts, come evil thoughts, sexual immoralities, thefts, murders." Sin originates with the inner attitude. It begins in the human heart. In the Sermon on the Mount, Jesus extends the sixth commandment beyond physical violence to include verbal abuse and other manifestations of anger. "If you perpetrate anything by deed, if you plot anything by attempt, if you wish or plan anything contrary to the safety of a neighbor, you are considered guilty of murder."[34] In addition, Jesus

---

[33] See Childs, *The Book of Exodus*, 419.

[34] J. Calvin, *Calvin: Institutes of the Christian Religion*, ed. J. McNeill, 2 vols. (Philadelphia: Westminster, 1975), 1:405.

ranks humiliation and dehumanization along with the sin of murder (Matt 5:22). Above all, Jesus expresses the concern that reconciliation among those who have a conflict be given a high priority, above their individual religious practice (Matt 5:23–24).[35] The apostle John expresses the same truth as the Sermon on the Mount when he says, "Everyone who hates his brother is a murderer" (1 John 3:15). James mentions murder along with adultery as examples of violation of the law (Jas 2:10–11). On a different plane, the unjust execution of Jesus was a breach of the sixth commandment.

Conclusion

The rabbis taught that murder, "the shedding of blood," was the most reprehensible of offenses.[36] Because of murder, the temple was destroyed and the divine Presence parted from Israel (*Šabb.* 33a). Indeed, three of the most prominent believers of biblical history, Moses, David, and Paul—were guilty of this sin. But modern civilization is even more saturated by murder and bloodshed.

The twentieth century was the most irrationally bloody hundred years in all of history, with a nearly incalculable number of deaths in two world wars. Numerous other conflicts produced just as many casualties.[37] Many factors are responsible for this cheapening of life. At the top of the list are those philosophies that regard humans as simply more complex beings on the evolutionary ladder. This view of life is contrary to the biblical position that holds to the uniqueness of human life.

Another factor is Western entertainment. By the time an average American youth has reached the age of 18, he has witnessed more than 80,000 murders via television, movies, or video games.[38]

The Image of God

In Gen 9:6, the prohibition of murder is grounded in the idea that humans are created in the image of God, a concept that confers

---

[35] See Fretheim, *Exodus*, 234.
[36] H. Cohn and M. Elon, "Homicide," *EJ* 9:506.
[37] J. Holbert, *The Ten Commandments* (Nashville: Abingdon, 2002), 76.
[38] R. A. Mohler Jr., *Words from the Fire* (Chicago: Moody, 2009), 115.

supreme value on human life and makes depriving a person of life an offense not only against the victim and his family but against God Himself (Gen 9:6; Exod 21:12; Lev 17:11; 24:17; Num 35:30–34; Deut 19:11–13; 27:24).[39] The only way to understand the sixth commandment is to view the sanctity of life as a fundamental principle.[40] In light of Gen 9:6 and Num 35:31, human life is beyond monetary compensation. As shown in the Introduction above, other nations in the ancient Near East permitted compensation from the murderer in place of capital punishment.[41] According to Brevard Childs, this high view of life expressed in the Bible was understood from the association of life and blood (Gen 9:6).[42]

As a consequence, the lives of others should be dear and important to us, and we should consider it our responsibility to defend others and protect them from harm.

In contrast with the views of Israel's ancient neighbors, life and property were never measured against each other. Thus no property offense in Israel, unlike other ancient Near Eastern cultures, could be punishable by death. However, if a *person* was kidnapped, this was a capital offense (Exod 21:16; Deut 24:7).[43]

This high value placed on life is also evident in the laws for manslaughter, or accidental homicide. This was an act so extraordinarily serious that a person convicted of manslaughter could not leave a city of refuge until the death of the current high priest. Because life was so precious, even an accidental killing could cause the manslayer's life to be separated from his family and perhaps disrupted forever. All life belongs to God (Lev 17:11; Gen 9:6). It is up to God to determine what shall be done with life. Human beings cannot act on their own authority when it comes to human life. However, the Bible sanctions the just putting to death of a person who has committed murder.

---

[39] Tigay, *Deuteronomy*, 70–71.

[40] S. Albeck, "The Ten Commandments and the Essence of Religious Faith," in *The Ten Commandments in History and Tradition*, ed. B. Z. Segal (Jerusalem: Magnes, 1990), 282.

[41] D. Christensen, *Deuteronomy 1:1–21:9*, rev. ed., WBC, 6A (Nashville: Nelson, 2001), 124–25.

[42] Childs, *The Book of Exodus*, 419.

[43] J. Wright, *An Eye for an Eye: The Place of Old Testament Ethics Today* (Downers Grove, IL: InterVarsity, 1983), 164.

Capital Punishment

The sixth commandment forbids the willful killing of the innocent but permits capital punishment.[44] In fact, execution is the very punishment for breaking this commandment and for many other violations of the Mosaic law. The Old Testament calls for the death penalty on numerous occasions (Gen 9:5; Exod 21:12–17). Willful murder generates bloodguilt not only for the perpetrator but the whole community. In modern terms murder is a "high crime" against the state.[45]

We see from the book of Romans in the New Testament that capital punishment has not been annulled: the government "does not carry the sword for no reason" (Rom 13:4). The sword refers to the power to take life and is the designated instrument of capital punishment for those guilty of murder, according to Jewish tradition (*Sanh.* 9:1).[46] In the new covenant age, the state—as did Israel under the old covenant—takes the role of leader in administration of justice and declaration of war; the church is not involved in these national matters. "But otherwise, and from the point of view of the individual believer, the prohibition works exactly the same way: no unauthorized 'private' person or group has the right to end a human life."[47]

Many individuals in our society oppose the death penalty because the perpetrator of an offense is also a human being made in the image of God. But Gen 9:6 argues for capital punishment as a response to murder, referencing the purpose and destiny of man in the image of God, after the statements of the larger contexts of sin and wickedness in Gen 4 and Gen 6:11–13.[48] The sixth commandment does not forbid capital punishment imposed by an established court of law (Exod 21:12–17), nor the killing of an enemy in war (cf. Deut 7:2; 20:17; 1 Sam 15:3; 2 Sam 8).[49] Martin Luther similarly claimed that the sixth

---

[44] R. Collins, "The Commandments," *ABD* 6:386.

[45] M. Sulzberger, *The Ancient Hebrew Law of Homicide* (Clark, NJ: The Lawbook Exchange, 2004), 42.

[46] However, imposition of the death penalty was not common in Jewish circles during Second Temple times (*m. Mak.* 1:10). See Sarna, *Exodus*, 113.

[47] D. Stuart, *Exodus*, NAC (Nashville: B&H, 2006), 463.

[48] Schmidt, *Die Zehn Gebot im Rahmen alttestamentlicher Ethik*, 13–14n4.

[49] Nielsen, *Deuteronomium*, 78; C. Houtman, *Exodus* (Leuven: Peeters, 2000), 3:61.

commandment prohibits killing by private individuals but does not abrogate that right for governments.[50]

Unlike the fifth commandment, no reason is given for obeying the sixth commandment. Chrysostom thought this was an important distinction and that the reason no motivation was given for obedience to this commandment was that the prohibition of murder, as witnessed by the legal codes of antiquity, is an innate ethic imbedded in man's moral conscience.[51] But the sixth commandment is not unrelated to the previous commandment on the family. We see the value of the family unit in this discussion particularly in the issue of manslaughter, as the avenger has a God-given role to bring justice to his family. Once again we find a focus on the cohesion and function of the family unit; each member of the family is to be faithful and fulfill his responsibilities.

Moreover, the sixth commandment is related to the fifth in another way. In the creation account we find the creation of Adam and Eve, and then read that their eldest son commits murder. After the command to obey father and mother in the fifth commandment, we have the law prohibiting murder in the sixth commandment. The sixth commandment protects human life, while the seventh upholds the sacredness of marriage and thus the sacredness of the family, the channel of human life.

---

[50] J. Holbert, *The Ten Commandments* (Nashville: Abingdon, 2002), 78.

[51] J. Lienhard, ed., *Exodus, Leviticus, Numbers, Deuteronomy*, ACCS (Downers Grove, IL: InterVarsity, 2001), 106.

Chapter 7

THE SEVENTH COMMANDMENT

Do not commit adultery.

Introduction

The establishment of marriage is a given in ancient Near Eastern law. The institution of marriage was considered to be the glue that maintained the solidarity of civilization.

Adultery, in the ancient Near Eastern world, can be defined as the consensual sexual intercourse of a married woman with a man who was not her husband. Adultery was considered the "great sin" in a number of civilizations, including the Egyptian and Syrian cultures (see Gen 20:9). It represented such a breach of faith in a marriage that it was analogous to treason. The commission of adultery (along with homicide) was so horrendous that it was thought to pollute the culture; these sins were thought to be offenses against the gods themselves.[1] In ancient Mesopotamia, the failure to consummate a marriage or the commission of adultery were the only two grounds for a divorce.[2] In Old Babylonian law, adultery was regarded as an offense against the woman's husband,[3] who could expel his wife and keep her dowry.[4]

The death penalty was a common punishment for adultery in the ancient Near East. But given the fact that adultery was considered an offense against the husband, the husband could in some cases waive the death penalty.[5] Normally, however, the sentence was capital punishment for the adulterous wife and for her lover. If a man caught his wife in the act of adultery, he could kill both lovers on the spot, without a trial. If a man did not desire to kill his adulterous wife, he did not have the authority to kill the adulterous man.[6]

---

[1] R. Westbrook, ed., *A History of Ancient Near Eastern Law*, 2 vols. (Leiden; Boston: Brill, 2003), 1:78–79.

[2] Ibid., 204.

[3] Ibid., 417.

[4] Ibid., 388–89.

[5] Hammurabi ¶ 129: in *ANET*, 171; Middle Assyrian Laws, 14–16: in *ANET*, 181; Hittite Laws, 197–98: in *ANET*, 196.

[6] J. Finkelstein, משפט המשפט משפט במזרח הקדמון *EncMiqr* 5:605–6 [in Hb.]; Westbrook,

The rape of a married or betrothed (engaged) woman was a serious offense against the husband or fiancé. The rape of an unbetrothed maiden was an offense against her father. The rape of an unattached young lady was considered less serious but would normally lead to a compulsory marriage.[7]

If a man seduced an unbetrothed young woman, the seducer would be forced to marry her and compensate her father for the loss of her potential bride-price. If the woman was a virgin but was betrothed, the seducer would be guilty of adultery and would face the death penalty.[8]

In early Greek and Roman cultures the populace as well as the intelligentsia condemned adultery. In classical Athens a man could punish an adulterer caught in the act with his wife so long as he did not use a knife. But a Roman citizen could immediately execute his wife and her illicit lover if the adulterous couple were caught in the act in his own house. Rape was universally condemned and was a capital offense in Roman law. However, prostitution was legal in the Roman Empire, and it produced substantial tax revenues.[9]

The Meaning of the Seventh Commandment

The verb "to commit adultery" is taken from the root *n'p*, which occurs 34 times in the Old Testament. The verb refers to a sexual liaison of a man and a married woman (Lev 20:10; Ezek 16:32). As Stuart succinctly stated: "No one is allowed to have sex with any married person except his or her spouse, and no married person is allowed to have sex with anyone other than his or her spouse."[10] We see from these nuances that adultery has specifically to do with sexual violations regarding married people. Fornication, or sexual intercourse between unmarried consenting adults, was never condemned in the Old Testament as strongly as adultery.[11]

A History of Ancient Near Eastern Law, 1:80, 636.

[7] Westbrook, *A History of Ancient Near Eastern Law,* 1:80, 418, 535.

[8] Ibid., 82; B. Arnold and B. Beyer, eds., *Readings from the Ancient Near East* (Grand Rapids: Baker Academic, 2002), 105.

[9] C. Keener, "Adultery, Divorce," *DNTB,* 7–11.

[10] D. Stuart, *Exodus,* NAC (Nashville: B&H, 2006), 463.

[11] J. Holbert, *The Ten Commandments* (Nashville: Abingdon, 2002), 90. The general and

Similar to the ancient Near Eastern concept, biblical law considers the adulterous man to be committing an offense against the married woman's husband. Thus the commandment calls men to respect the marriage of another man.[12] Most of the occurrences of the root are in the prophetic literature, and one-third of them are used metaphorically in describing Israel's unfaithfulness to the Lord.

The Seventh Commandment in the Old Testament

From passages such as Lev 20:10 and Deut 22:22,[13] we see that adultery was a capital offense in the Old Testament. Execution was to be carried out by stoning (Deut 22:24) or by burning (Lev 20:14; 21:9). It is an offense against both God and man (Gen 20:6; 39:9; 2 Sam 12:9; Ps 51:4[6]; Prov 2:16–17). Biblical law provides no options for mitigating the punishment as in the laws of other nations in the ancient Near East. However, the requirement that two or three witnesses testify to an adulterous act (Deut 17:6–7) undoubtedly ruled out many executions.[14]

If a jealous husband suspected that his wife had committed adultery, the accused wife underwent a self-curse ritual at the tabernacle (Num 5:11–31). The woman would be forced to drink water mixed with dust from the vicinity of the tabernacle, and if the accusation was false, no harm would overtake her. If the accusation was true, the woman would live under a curse and the portion she drank would make her thigh shrivel and her body swell (Num 5:20–22).[15]

---

broader Hb. term for illicit sexual relations is זנה. This verb refers to all forms of illicit sexual behavior including prostitution (Gen 38:15) and sexual relations outside marriage (Num 25:1), as well as the figurative use of following after other gods (Exod 34:15–16; Lev 20:5–6; Deut 31:16). Similarly, *porneia* is the broader NT term for illicit sexual relations so that every act of adultery could be considered fornication but not every act of fornication is adultery. See Sprinkle, "Sexuality, Sexual Ethics," 749; M. Greenberg, "The Tradition Critically Examined," in *The Ten Commandments in History and Tradition*, ed. B. Z. Segal (Jerusalem: Magnes, 1990), 104–5n35.

[12] R. Collins, *Christian Morality: Biblical Foundations* (Notre Dame, IN: University of Notre Dame Press, 1986), 58–59.

[13] This text uses the root שכב "to lie with," instead of נאף but the concepts undoubtedly address the same issue of adultery.

[14] See Sprinkle, "Sexuality, Sexual Ethics," 745. If one of the adulterous partners was a betrothed slave, the death penalty did not apply to either party.

[15] See ibid., 746.

The Old Testament records several references to violation of the seventh commandment, although the primary root n'p is not present in each case. Reference is made to the sexual sin of adultery in 2 Sam 11; Prov 2:16–17 (znh); Jer 7:9 (n'p); 23:10 (n'p); Hos 4:2 (n'p),13–14 (n'p); and Mal 3:5 (n'p). Undoubtedly the best-known case is the adulterous affair of David and Bathsheba in 2 Sam 11.

Sexual sins such as fornication (Num 25:1, znh), prostitution (promiscuity) (Deut 22:21, znh), homosexuality (Lev 18:22; Judg 19:22, škb; Deut 23:17–18, qdš), premarital sex and cohabitation (Exod 22:16–17; Deut 22:13–21), incest (Lev 18:6–18; 20:17–21), and bestiality (Exod 22:19; Lev 18:23; 20:15–16; Deut 27:21) are transgressions against God's law and are rightly condemned. Adultery, however, uniquely implies unfaithfulness in marriage, the most intimate of human relationships. Because the prohibition against adultery is part of the Ten Commandments and the marriage bond has a sacral dimension, the prohibition against adultery as the seventh commandment is divinely sanctioned. Because adultery was also an offense against God, the offended spouse (normally the husband in OT law)[16] had no legal authority to pardon his unfaithful wife or her illicit lover. The fact that the death penalty was the punishment for this offense indicates the detestable nature of this sin from God's perspective (Lev 20:10; Deut 22:22; cf. Jer 29:21–23; Ezek 16:38).[17] The penalty for the seduction of an unpledged virgin, on the other hand, was the offer of marriage or money (Exod 22:16–17; Deut 22:23–29).

Because the violation of the marriage bond was a form of covenant breaking, adultery was employed to describe covenant unfaithfulness on the divine-human plane.[18] The root n'p often appears in conjunction with terminology associated with covenant violation (Ps 50:18; Jer 9:2[1]; 29:23; Hos 7:1b,4; Mal 3:5).

Other forms of sex outside marriage are violations of God's law, but sex outside marriage that involves married people is particularly

---

[16] The adultery prohibition was directed toward the man because the adultery of the woman always was a consequence of the adultery of the man. C. Dohmen, *Exodus 19–40* (Freiburg: Herder, 2004), 123.

[17] N. Sarna, *Exodus*, JPS Torah Commentary (Philadelphia, New York: Jewish Publication Society, 1991), 114.

[18] See E. Merrill, *Deuteronomy* (Nashville: B&H, 1994), 154.

alarming as it threatens the basic family unit. It is the lone serious sexual offense listed in the Ten Commandments. The occurrence of polygamy in the Old Testament does not undermine this fact. Polygamy in the Old Testament should not be viewed as part of God's design but rather as evidence of the sinfulness of man.[19] The most common form of marriage in the Old Testament was monogamous (Gen 2:23–24), as Jesus testified before the Pharisees (Matt 19:3–6).

In the Ten Commandments the law is addressed to the man, but in the history of interpretation it has been applied to the woman (Ezek 16:15–26; Hos 2:7; Prov 2:16–19; 1 Cor 7:10–16).[20] Moreover, the fact that the seventh commandment addresses a man (second masculine singular) does not exclude its application to other people. Addressing man in the singular is the customary form in which laws were written in the ancient world.[21] In addition, Jews who fled from Israel to Egypt at the time of the Babylonian conquest in 586 BC (Jer 44) indicate that in the fifth century BC a woman could instigate a divorce against her husband. This may indicate that this broader interpretation was practiced from the beginning.[22]

Adultery is the subject of many of the Proverbs (Prov 2:16–19; 5:1–20; 6:24–35; 7:5–27). The book of Proverbs repeatedly warns the reader about the seductions of the adulterous woman (Prov 2:16–19; 5:1–14; 6:24–35; 7:5–27; cf. 30:20). She is seldom found in her own home (Prov 7:11–12), and she uses smooth talking to lure the naïve to her bed (Prov 2:16; 5:3; 6:24; 7:13–21). Involvement with the adulterous woman leads to a loss of wealth (Prov 5:9–10) and even life (Prov 2:18–19; 5:5; 6:32; 7:22–23,26–27).[23] This sin is so atrocious that the offended husband whose wife has committed adultery against him cannot be appeased even with lavish gifts (Prov 6:34–35).

Because the prophets frequently described the relationship between Yahweh and His people in terms of the relationship between a

---

[19] Polygamous relationships may be found in Gen 4:19; 16:1–2; 22:20–24; 26:34; 28:9; 29:15–30; 30:1–9; 36:1–5,11–12; Judg 8:30–31; and 1 Sam 1:2.

[20] See C. Houtman, *Exodus* (Leuven: Peeters, 2000), 3:62.

[21] Stuart, *Exodus*, 468n79.

[22] These documents are known as the Elephantine Papyri. See J. Sprinkle, "Sexuality, Sexual Ethics," *DOTP*, 743.

[23] See J. Tigay, "Adultery," *EJ* 1:425.

husband and wife, it was a small step to view infidelity to the covenant as spiritual adultery. Jeremiah, Ezekiel, and Hosea accused the nation of Israel of spiritual adultery for its rebellion against the Lord God (Jer 3:8–9; see 13:27; Ezek 23:37; Hos 2:4[2]). Jeremiah 31:31–34, which contains the prophecy of the new covenant, describes the failure of the Sinaitic covenant as a marital breakdown.[24] The exclusive loyalty Israel was to render to God was analogous to the exclusive loyalty a wife owes to her husband. In other parts of the Old Testament, adulterers are associated with murderers (Job 24:14–15), treacherous men (Jer 9:2), blasphemers of God's name (Jer 29:23), and oppressors of widows (Mal 3:5).[25] The penalty for adultery in Old Testament times was capital punishment, a practice that was continued by hanging as well as burning in later Judaism (see *m. Sanh.* 7:3,9; *b. Sanh.* 52b,55b,66b).[26]

The Seventh Commandment in the New Testament

In the New Testament, warnings against adultery and other forms of sexual lewdness continued (Matt 5:27–28; 15:19; 19:18; Rom 13:9; 1 Cor 6:9–10; Gal 5:19; Eph 5:5; Jas 2:11; Rev 22:15). In harmony with the seriousness of this offense in the Old Testament, the apostle Paul said that God would bring adultery to punishment (1 Thess 4:3–8). There is little to suggest that the meaning of adultery from the Old Testament—having sexual relations with anyone besides your spouse—is any different from what we find in the New Testament. But in the Sermon on the Mount, Jesus expands our understanding of the prohibition of adultery by explaining that every one who looks upon a woman with lust has already committed adultery in his heart.[27]

Sexual harassment, rape, pornography, and certainly violence against another must not be considered on a secondary level in one's moral code just because these offenses are not explicitly mentioned in Israel's laws. Jesus' own extension of the command justifies these applications

[24] J. Motyer, *The Message of Exodus* (Downers Grove, IL: InterVarsity, 2005), 229n34.

[25] B. Childs, *The Book of Exodus: A Critical-Theological Commentary* (Louisville: Westminster John Knox, 1974), 423.

[26] Cohn, "Adultery," 426.

[27] Jesus' statement combined the seventh commandment with the tenth, which speaks of coveting a neighbor's wife. See C. Keener, "Marriage, Divorce and Adultery," *DLNT*, 715.

(Matt 5:27–28). "Respect, honor, and integrity should inform both attitude and behavior toward members of the opposite sex."[28]

In addition, the significance and seriousness of adultery may be indicated by the fact that adultery appears to be the only ground for a divorce in the New Testament.[29] In Matt 5:32 Jesus stated that whoever divorces his wife, except in the case of sexual immorality (*porneia*), causes her to commit adultery. The term for sexual immorality is a broad term possibly referring to any sexual irregularity. But in this context in which the word is applied to a married couple, the term would refer to marital unfaithfulness, that is, adultery. The same restrictive clause occurs in Matt 19:9, once again stating that sexual immorality (*porneia*) is the only ground for divorce. The most widely held evangelical position is that adultery allows the offended spouse to divorce and remarry.[30] In Matt 19, Jesus avoids the pharisaical debates on the legitimate grounds for divorce and directs the audience back to the creation account, showing that marriage is part of God's design.[31]

Conclusion

In regard to the sin of adultery, the teaching of the Bible is not greatly different from the teaching of the cultures surrounding ancient Israel. These cultures commended marital fidelity and treated violation of the sacred marriage commitment as a betrayal and violation of trust. Yet with this broad-based ancient agreement on the disruption that adultery can bring, it is amazing that the violation of marital fidelity is rampant in Western culture and particularly in the United States. What is even perhaps more surprising is the general

[28] T. Fretheim, *Exodus*, Interpretation: A Biblical Commentary for Teaching and Preaching (Louisville: John Knox, 1973), 235.

[29] First Corinthians 7:15 also appears to approve divorce and remarriage when an unbelieving spouse walks away from a marriage. See A. Köstenberger and D. Jones, *God, Marriage, and Family: Rebuilding the Biblical Foundation* (Wheaton, IL: Crossway Books, 2004), 248.

[30] Ibid., 231, 239. According to later Jewish law, a woman who committed adultery was not only forbidden to remain married to her husband but was also to be prevented from marrying her lover. See M. Drori, "Inadvertent Adultery (*Shgaga*) in Jewish Law: Mistake of Law and Mistake of Fact," in *Authority, Process and Method: Studies in Jewish Law*, eds. H. Ben-Menahem and N. Hecht (Australia: Harwood Academic, 1998), 231–67.

[31] D. A. Carson, *The Sermon on the Mount: An Evangelical Exposition of Matthew 5–7* (Grand Rapids: Baker, 1978), 46.

acceptance of this practice. As John Holbert stated: "It is astonishing how much network TV is based on flagrant adultery between consenting hot-blooded 'adults.'"[32] Adultery seems to be the theme song of the average television show and movie today. Yet, sadly, adultery is one of the leading causes for the breakup of families in America today.[33]

When adultery takes place, divorce often ensues, children's lives are profoundly affected, grandparents are left in confusion, and friends in the community are forced to alter their perceptions of each person in the family.[34] Over 2,000 years ago, the Hellenistic Jewish philosopher Philo described at length the damage adultery brings to society (*Decalogue*, 121–31).

The revulsion caused by adultery is so fierce because it brings a third party into a relationship that God had designed to be uniquely a blessed relationship between one man and one woman. "[T]he Bible is clear that God wants sex to be something that is always personal (relational), exclusive and intimate."[35] Adultery disrupts God's design, which He had planned and declared to be good. Adultery "violates God's creational intention, which links a positive role for sexuality with commitment and loyalty (Gen 2:24–25)."[36] In the overall design of God, marriage is preeminent as it is the first institution in the Bible and central to civilization. The "seventh commandment is the Creator's law which guards the chastity of marriage, the sanctity of the family, and the preservation of society."[37] God established marriage before He ordained government, corporations, and even the church.

In the creation account, when it was evident that a helper had not been made that was suitable for the man, the woman was taken out of the side of man (Gen 2:18–23). God formed the woman to be united to the man, and the mode of her creation laid the foundation for the

---

[32] Holbert, *The Ten Commandments*, 87. Adultery threatens every other commitment. See R. A. Mohler Jr., *Words from the Fire* (Moody, 2009), 133.

[33] J. Vines, *Basic Bible Sermons on the Ten Commandments* (Nashville: Broadman, 1992), 87; M. Dunnam, *Exodus*, The Communicator's Commentary (Waco, TX: Word, 1987), 264.

[34] Holbert, *The Ten Commandments*, 97–98.

[35] D. Heimbach, *Counterfeit Sexuality* (Washington, D.C.: Focus on the Family, 2002), 67.

[36] Fretheim, *Exodus*, 234.

[37] J. Vines, *Basic Bible Sermons on the Ten Commandments* (Nashville: Broadman, 1992), 81.

ordinance of marriage.[38] The woman complements the man and the man is incomplete without the woman. The woman is also incomplete without the man, and the man complements her and meets her needs.[39] "The establishment of one flesh in marriage is the establishment of an irrevocable unity by two total personalities."[40] As Karl Barth eloquently stated:

> Marriage may be defined as something which fixes and makes concrete the encounter and interrelation of man and woman in the form of a unique, unrepeatable and incomparable encounter and relationship between a particular man and a particular woman. Their encounter and relationship signifies in this context a life-partnership; this partnership is not partial but complete.[41]

As marriage was grounded in a divine ordinance (Gen 2:24), a covenant arrangement (Mal 2:14) requires faithfulness and love.

The book of Proverbs, which has much to say about the sin of adultery, also provides the antidote: "Drink water from your own cistern, water flowing from your own well" (Prov 5:15). This proverbial saying complements the focus of adultery in that the command is directed to the man to respect the marriage of another. The best illustration in the Old Testament for the resistance of adultery may be the example of Joseph in Potiphar's house (Gen 39; see *Jub.* 39:5–9). Or to put it into New Testament language: "Do to others as you would have them do to you" (Luke 6:31 NIV).

At any rate, the positive content of the commandment is respect for the marriage of another man. "Marriage, so sacred in ancient Israel because it was the means by which the blessing of Abraham was made effective, was the positive value that lay behind the [this] precept of the Decalogue."[42]

Adultery occurs when a marriage partner has sexual relations with someone other than his spouse. Both parties are guilty of adultery. It is a crime against persons and a sin against God (Gen 39:9; 2 Sam

---

[38] C. Keil and F. Delitzsch, *The Pentateuch*, 3 vols. (Grand Rapids: Eerdmans, 1973) 2:89.

[39] A. Hoekema, *Created in God's Image* (Grand Rapids: Eerdmans, 1986), 77.

[40] E. White, *Marriage and the Bible* (Nashville: Broadman, 1965), 15.

[41] Karl Barth, *Church Dogmatics*, III/1 (London: T&T Clark, 1960), 182.

[42] R. Collins, *Christian Morality: Biblical Foundations* (Notre Dame, IN: University of Notre Dame Press, 1986), 58–59.

12:9). The reason adultery is the only sexual sin mentioned in the Ten Commandments is that it has to do with unfaithfulness in a relationship of commitment. Adultery is the social equivalent of the religious crime of having other gods (Exod 20:3) since marriage is a mirror of God's covenant with His people.[43] This emphasis—that faithfulness (expressed by obedience) must permeate every sphere of life, both the religious and the secular—gives a distinctive character to the Israelite law on adultery. It was employed to show negatively the constant tendency by the people of God toward "spiritual adultery" and positively the faithfulness and love of God for His people despite their unfaithfulness (Ezek 16; Hos 1–3).[44]

The seventh commandment addresses adultery and not sexual impropriety in general, as the precise verb *n'p* makes clear. If murder is a violation of life itself, adultery is a violation of its most important and sacred human relationship—the marriage of husband and wife. In the next commandment we move from taking that which is forbidden, another man's wife, to the concept of stealing in general.[45]

---

[43] See Rabbi D. Wax, ed., *The Ten Commandments* (Lakewood, NJ: Taryag Legacy Foundation, 2005), 313.

[44] P. Craigie, *The Book of Deuteronomy* (Grand Rapids: Eerdmans, 1976), 160–61. While God is willing to forgive adultery, this sin is serious enough to disqualify a pastor from church leadership. See R. Kent Hughes and J. Armstrong, "Why Adulterous Pastors Should Not Be Restored," *CT* 39,4 (1995): 33–36.

[45] Indeed, adultery is referred to in Prov 9:17 as "stolen water." In the writings of Philo as well as in the Exodus version of the Ten Commandments in the LXX, adultery is listed before murder. This order may also be seen in the New Testament in Luke 18:20. In the LXX of Deut 5:17–18 as well as in Matt 19:18, the traditional order of murder followed by adultery is preserved.

Chapter 8
THE EIGHTH COMMANDMENT

Do not steal.

Introduction

S tealing is generally referred to as "the act of taking property from another without permission and in secret."[1] In Mesopotamia, the concept of theft or stealing also included grand larceny, misappropriation, and embezzlement. This may have included not only the seizure and removal of another's property but also the selling of the property for a personal profit.[2] Moreover, the use of inaccurate weights and balances in the marketplace was thought to be a form of theft.[3]

An indication of how widespread the issue of stealing had become in the ancient Near East is illustrated by the establishment of raiding groups or gangs in several cultures. From Egyptian literature, we discover that robbers developed into professional organizations that demanded ransom from those whose property was taken. In the prologue of Ur-Nammu, the oldest Mesopotamian law code, it was reported that the king succeeded in suppressing the actions of robbers who had seized oxen, sheep, and donkeys.[4]

The punishment for theft often was a fine. In the Code of Hammurabi, a citizen who stole an ox or sheep from a government official was fined 30 times the value of the animal. If he stole the same kind of animal from another citizen, he would be fined 10 times its value. However, if the thief failed to pay the fine, he could be put to death.[5] The fining of thieves a multiple of the value of what was stolen was

---

[1] S. Lowenstein, "גֶּנֶב," *EncMiqr* 2:536 (in Hb.; author's translation).

[2] R. Westbrook, ed., *A History of Ancient Near Eastern Law*, 2 vols. (Leiden; Boston: Brill, 2003), 2:962.

[3] K. Van Der Toorn, *Sin and Sanction in Israel and Mesopotamia: A Comparative Study* (Assen, The Netherlands: Van Gorcum, 1985), 19.

[4] B. Jackson, *Theft in Early Jewish Law* (Oxford: Clarendon, 1972), 15.

[5] See V. Matthews and D. Benjamin, *Old Testament Parallels: Laws and Stories from the Ancient Near East* (New York: Paulist, 1991), 63. A person who stole an object from the temple could be fined up to 30 times its value. Westbrook, *A History of Ancient Near Eastern Law*, 2:962.

the practice in Hittite law as well as in the Twelve Tables (Roman law).[6] Fines could be as high as 30 times the value of goods stolen.[7] Alternatively, the punishment might be confinement of the thief to a time of servitude.[8] In both Assyrian and Babylonian law some property crimes resulted in the death penalty.[9]

The stealing of a human being (kidnapping) was classified as a crime against property and could be punished by death. In Middle Assyrian laws a woman who had stolen from a neighbor could be ransomed by her husband when her husband returned the stolen goods, but her ears or her nose still might be cut off. Similarly, in Hittite law, if a slave burglarized a house, the owner could disfigure the slave's nose and ears and return him to his owner.[10] Ancient Near Eastern laws differed notably from biblical law in that no crime against property was penalized by capital punishment under biblical law.

Private ownership of land existed throughout the history of the ancient Near East. An estate passed directly and immediately to the legitimate heirs.[11] Abundant material has been uncovered concerning the many problems that arose in settling inheritances.[12] Moreover, evidence is lacking to support the sometimes-popular notion that communal ownership of land by clans or villages evolved into individual ownership.[13]

The Meaning of the Eighth Commandment

The meaning of the eighth commandment is directly related to the verb *gnb*, "to steal." This root occurs in almost all Semitic languages, and in several occurrences it is ethically neutral; that is, it has no

---

[6] R. Westbrook, "The Laws of Biblical Israel," in *The Hebrew Bible: New Insights and Scholarship*, ed. F. Greenspahn (New York: New York University Press, 2008), 101.

[7] J. Finkelstein, מִשְׁפָּט הַמִּשְׁפָּט בִּמְזֹרַח הַקַּדְמוֹן *EncMiqr*, 5:613.

[8] Westbrook, *A History of Ancient Near Eastern Law*, 1:220.

[9] M. Greenberg, "Some Postulates of Biblical Criminal Law," in *Yehezkel Kaufmann Jubilee Volume: Studies in Bible and Jewish Religion Dedicated to Yehezkel Kaufmann on the Occasion of His Seventieth Birthday*, ed. M. Haran (Jerusalem: Magnes, 1960), 17.

[10] B. Arnold and B. Beyer, eds., *Readings from the Ancient Near East* (Grand Rapids: Baker Academic, 2002), 114–15.

[11] Westbrook, *A History of Ancient Near Eastern Law*, 1:56.

[12] Westbrook, "The Laws of Biblical Israel," 112–13.

[13] Westbrook, *A History of Ancient Near Eastern Law*, 1:55–56.

connection to illicit seizure or stealing (Job 21:18; 27:20; cf. 2 Sam 19:3[4],41[42]; 21:12; 2 Kgs 11:2).[14]

In order to understand the technical meaning of *gnb* and the eighth commandment, it is helpful to distinguish between this root and its synonym, *gzl*. The synonymous nature of these two verbs is illustrated by the fact that they occur in parallel in Gen 31:27–31. Laban accused Jacob of stealing (*gnb*) the household gods, and Jacob responded by saying that Laban intended to rob (*gzl*) him of his two wives. Thus, both of these verbs occur in the Bible and refer to the misappropriation of property. In rabbinic literature the difference between the two words had to do with the fact that *gnb* referred to theft in secret while *gzl* referred to robbery characterized by open force.[15] The verb *gzl* always involves the taking away of property (see 2 Sam 23:21; *gnb* is more often neutral) and is linked to armed robbery.[16]

The second major feature in the meaning of this verb has to do with the range of the prohibition. It has been a major position in Jewish tradition to limit the use of *gnb*, "stealing," in the Ten Commandments to that of stealing a life, i.e., kidnapping. A second position does not view the verb so narrowly and understands that it has a broader meaning and refers to stealing in general.

In defense of the first position, that the eighth commandment is a prohibition of kidnapping, it is often pointed out that in the immediate context of the Ten Commandments this prohibition follows commandments on murder and adultery, which deal with human relationships. So it would seem more natural to continue that theme and conclude that stealing refers to the taking of persons (see *b. Sanh.* 86a). From the fifth commandment the Decalogue addresses relationships within the covenant community rather than property. After all, the stealing of property is addressed in Lev 19:11. In addition, because the commandments on murder and adultery are punishable by death, the commandment not to steal must also be considered to be punishable by death—which would be true only if what is being referred to is

---

[14] See V. Hamp, "גָּנַב *gānab*," *TDOT* 3:41.

[15] B. Childs, *The Book of Exodus: A Critical-Theological Commentary* (Louisville: Westminster John Knox, 1974), 423; R. Westbrook, *Studies in Biblical and Cuneiform Law* (Paris: J. Gabalda, 1988), 15; C. Houtman, *Exodus* (Leuven: Peeters, 2000), 3:63.

[16] Westbrook, *Studies in Biblical and Cuneiform Law*, 36.

kidnapping (see Gen 40:15). Furthermore, in the next chapter, Exod 21, this root is used with a person as the direct object: "Whoever kidnaps *(gnb)* a person must be put to death" (Exod 21:16). Peter Craigie believes kidnapping is the subject of the eighth commandment. He maintains that the commandment is concerned with relationships between people in the covenant community and should not be thought of as referring to personal belongings. Craigie thinks this commandment is more serious than mere stealing and what is being addressed is the act where one person assumes control over the life and fate of another by kidnapping him. That person must be punished because he is assuming a role that belongs only to God.[17]

The case for restricting application to that of kidnapping is defensible and has strong support in Jewish tradition. Yet it is more reasonable to take *gnb* in its usual sense as theft of property.[18] While the Hebrew verb *gnb* occurs with persons as a direct object with the meaning of kidnapping (Exod 21:16), the verb alone does not convey the sense of kidnapping without qualification. When the verb stands alone as here in the Ten Commandments, it is best to take the broader understanding of the term as theft of property.[19] Nothing about the etymology of the root or its usage in the Old Testament suggests that its inherent meaning is "to steal persons."[20] Christoph Dohmen states that limitation of the verb to kidnapping presumes a specialized application that is unusual and unsuitable for the Decalogue. Consequently, because of the kinds of prohibitions we find in the context of the Ten Commandments, it is more natural to follow the general meaning of the taking of property.[21] The shortened form of the eighth commandment without an explicit object has the effect of broadening the scope of the prohibition.[22]

The restriction of the law to kidnapping is too narrow. This is not to say that the verb in certain situations might also refer to

---

[17] P. Craigie, *The Book of Deuteronomy* (Grand Rapids: Eerdmans, 1976), 161.

[18] M. Greenberg, "The Tradition Critically Examined," in *The Ten Commandments in History and Tradition,* ed. B. Z. Segal (Jerusalem: Magnes, 1990), 105–6.

[19] B. Jackson, *Essays in Jewish and Comparative Legal History* (Leiden: Brill, 1975), 207–8.

[20] Hamp, *TDOT* 3:42.

[21] C. Dohmen, *Exodus 19–40* (Freiburg: Herder, 2004), 124; N. Sarna, *Exodus,* JPS Torah Commentary (Philadelphia, New York: Jewish Publication Society, 1991), 114.

[22] Childs, *The Book of Exodus: A Critical-Theological Commentary,* 424.

persons.[23] But as Moshe Weinfeld states: "the fact that 'you shall not steal' is attached to two injunctions that deal with capital crimes (murder and adultery) does not mean that all three transgressions are to be punished similarly. Besides, punishment is irrelevant in the Decalogue."[24] Because the Decalogue does not specify penalties, there is no reason to read and interpret this commandment in light of its penalty.[25]

The Eighth Commandment in the Old Testament

The act of stealing is the secret taking of another's property without the owner's knowledge or permission.[26] When stealing takes place, it is often accompanied by other duplicities, including deception, trickery, and oppression (see Pss 35:10; 50:18; 62:10[11]; Jer 7:9; Ezek 18:7,12,16,18; Hos 4:2; Mic 2:1–2). Examples of this deception include the secret moving of boundary markers (Deut 19:14; 27:17; Job 24:2; cf. Prov 22:28; 23:10; Hos 5:10), the use of false measures and balances (Deut 25:13–16: Prov 11:1), the selling of goods of inferior quality (Amos 8:4–6), and the charging of interest (Exod 22:25[24]).[27]

Punishment for theft in the Old Testament demanded that the thief return double the amount he had stolen (Exod 22:7[6]). In effect, the criminal loses the sum he had hoped to gain. Theft of property in Israel was considered a tort; that is, the injured party was restored so far as possible to the pretheft position. As an apparent deterrent, overcompensation was called for in certain cases (Exod 22:1[21:37],7[6],9[8]). This command is extended to include any form of dishonesty in Deut 25:16.[28]

---

[23] W. Keszler, "Die literarische, historische und theologische Problematik des Dekalogs," VT 7 (1957): 12; W. Schmidt, Die Zehn Gebot im Rahmen alttestamentlicher Ethik (Darmstadt: Wissenschaftliche Buchgesellschaft, 1993), 123.

[24] M. Weinfeld, Deuteronomy 1–11, AB 5 (New York: Doubleday, 1991), 314.

[25] See J. Tigay, Deuteronomy, JPS Torah Commentary (Philadelphia: Jewish Publication Society, 1996), 71, 357–58.

[26] C. Houtman, Exodus (Leuven: Peeters, 2000), 3:63–64.

[27] Ibid., 64.

[28] T. Fretheim, Exodus, Interpretation: A Biblical Commentary for Teaching and Preaching (Louisville: John Knox, 1973), 236.

We find examples of stealing in the narrative sections of the Bible. Rachel stole her father's teraphim (Gen 31:19,30,32). Joseph's brothers were concerned that they would be accused of stealing Joseph's silver cup (Gen 44:1–12), while Achan stole items that were devoted to God (Josh 7:1). In the book of Judges, Micah stole 1,100 pieces of silver from his own mother.[29] Also, the parable of stealing the poor family's pet sheep in 2 Sam 12:1–4 illustrates the meaning of stealing. David's call for the fourfold punishment for this offense is a reference to Exod 22:1 (21:37), which requires a person convicted of stealing a sheep to pay back four sheep.[30] "The very choice of a lamb by Nathan in the parable together with the fact that the stolen lamb is slaughtered, and that the judgment is for fourfold, make it almost undeniable that, despite the fact that the verb *ganav* is not used, the analogy with Exod 21:37 is intended."[31] Perhaps the best-known biblical example of stealing as well as kidnapping in the narrative texts is the selling of Joseph to Egypt (*gnb*, 2x; Gen 40:15).[32]

Many times the prophets of Israel reprove the people over the issue of stealing (Isa 1:23; Jer 7:9; Hos 4:2; Zech 5:3–4). The prophets rage particularly against the affluent of Israel at this point (see Isa 3:13–15; Amos 8:4–6; Mic 3:1–3; Jas 5:1–6). The Bible includes proverbs and expressions and other descriptions taken from the realm of stealing. The locust, for example, is compared to a thief (Joel 2:9). It is said of men who were driven from their habitation: "People shouted at them as if they were thieves" (Job 30:5). The sudden invasion of enemies is compared to thieves who come in the night (Jer 49:9; Obad 5; cf. 1 Thess 5:2). The shame of a thief who is caught (Jer 2:26) is used as a metaphor for a man who is seized in shame (cf. Jer 48:27). Wisdom literature, however, recognizes another side to stealing. Poor people may be forced to steal just to stay alive (Prov 6:30; cf. Prov 30:9).

The Old Testament contains a threefold differentiation for the punishment of theft: (1) the death penalty is for kidnapping (Exod 21:16; Deut 24:7) and stealing of God's property (Josh 7); (2) the punishment for the theft of livestock and valued goods is usually double

[29] Hamp, *TDOT* 3:44.
[30] Lowenstein, גְּנֵבָה, 537.
[31] Jackson, *Theft in Early Jewish Law*, 148.
[32] See Schmidt, *Die Zehn Gebot im Rahmen alttestamentlicher Ethik*, 122.

the value (Exod 22:4[3],7[6],9[8]); (3) fourfold or fivefold replacement is demanded if cattle or sheep were slaughtered or sold (Exod 22:1[21:37]).[33]

The Eighth Commandment in the New Testament

We find in the New Testament that stealing is still regarded as a serious transgression. Paul declares that no thief will have a portion in the kingdom of God (1 Cor 6:9–10). On the positive side, however, Paul also states that those who had been thieves should steal no longer but do honest work to help those in need (Eph 4:28). Peter places stealing in the context of sins such as murder and evildoing (1 Pet 4:15), while Paul juxtaposes this sin with adultery (Rom 2:21–22). The principle of the eighth commandment lies behind the outrage of not paying workers their earned wages (Jas 5:4). The word for stealing frequently occurs in a list of a select portion of the Ten Commandments as in Matt 19:18 = Mark 10:19 and Rom 13:9.[34] Moreover, Judas, who betrayed Christ, is perceived to be a thief who would steal from the apostles' moneybag (John 12:6). Jesus speaks about his second coming as being like a thief entering in the night (Matt 24:42–44; cf. Rev 3:3) in a use reminiscent of the prophetic literature. It is not without significance that the moral transformation within the earliest Christian community reflected virtually the opposite of the attitude that characterizes stealing, as these devoted followers of Christ were willing to give up their possessions to minister to those in need (Acts 4:32–37). This attitude reflects the way believers should look at their possessions, as Paul stated: "For we brought nothing into the world, and we can take nothing out" (1 Tim 6:7).

Jesus does not attack the right to ownership of private property. He accepts the generosity of the wealthy (Luke 7:36; 8:3), although He mentions that wealth and the desire for wealth may lead to corruption (Matt 19:23–26). Even in the Ananias and Sapphira affair, Peter did not challenge their ownership of property (Acts 5:4) but their

---

[33] Ibid., 124.

[34] The order in Matt 19:18 and Mark 10:19 is murder, adultery, stealing, false witness, and honoring of father and mother, while the order in Rom 13:9 is adultery, murder, stealing, and coveting.

deception. Repentance from sin may involve repayment of what you have stolen, as it was in the case of Zacchaeus (Luke 19:1–10).

Believers are to owe nothing but rather to love one another (Rom 13:8). The antidote for stealing is found in Phil 4:19: "And my God shall supply all your needs according to His riches in glory in Christ Jesus"—a truth finally realized by a man who was apparently a thief and was crucified with Jesus (Luke 23:40–43).

Conclusion

The understanding of what is meant by stealing, taking something that does not belong to you, has not changed over the centuries. Part of the reason may be that the issue of theft and stealing has never abated. Stealing has been a perennial problem for all civilizations in all history. Modern culture is not in any way immune. In the United States today, property theft occurs in some form every three seconds.[35]

The taking of something that does not belong to you assumes that the possession belongs to someone. The issue of stealing would not exist unless there was an assumed right of private property ownership. At the philosophical and foundational base of the eighth commandment is the right to own property.[36] All kinds of theft, including fraud and kidnapping, fall under the purview of this commandment. On the other hand, even when stealing takes place, it should not be forgotten that what we possess is a gift from God, who owns everything (Exod 19:5; Deut 8:18; Jas 1:17).

Part of that gift from God is in the tasks He gives each person to do. T. Freitheim stated:

> God dignifies human beings by giving them work to do, from which they can expect to receive some of the fruits of their labor. This is central to God's creational intentions for humankind (Gen 2:15–16). Moreover, human beings make use of God-given gifts in and through their work. For the thief not to consider these gifts and the blessings they bring is to treat with disdain what God has given.[37]

---

[35] J. Holbert, *The Ten Commandments* (Nashville: Abingdon, 2002), 8.

[36] This affirmation is in conflict with the communistic philosophy, which calls for the abolition of private property. See D. Ryanzanoff, *The Communist Manifesto of Karl Marx and Friedrich Engels* (New York: Russell & Russell, 1963), 43–44.

[37] Fretheim, *Exodus*, 236.

This gift is undermined when a man cannot enjoy the fruit of his toil because someone has stolen what he has produced. Theft then is an attack on the dignity of human beings and their work. As Walter Eichrodt has stated: "This commandment does far more than protect property. It warns against taking advantage of a brother (or sister) in need. It stands against all exploitation of the weak, and is a guide for all social and economic action and restraint."[38]

The principle behind the eighth commandment has broader implications. A worker who is not compensated for his labor or who receives inadequate wages and benefits is virtually the victim of theft. Any action that involves the manipulation of another human being for personal gain violates the spirit of this prohibition. Perhaps the temptation to manipulate other people may never have been stronger than in contemporary American culture where personal progress and success are often accompanied by a cutthroat mentality.[39] This applies as well to those gifts that belong to God. The withholding of tithes and offerings is said to be robbing of God (Mal 3:8–10). Everything belongs to the Lord, and we are His stewards during our brief pilgrimage on this earth (Pss 24:1; 115:16). We will take nothing from this world when we die (1 Tim 6:7).

Just as adultery (the seventh commandment) is the violation of one's family, so theft (the eighth commandment) is the violation of one's property. Just as ownership of property places a certain dignity on the right to work, the fourth commandment (Sabbath) regulates how one approaches his job in the workweek. The eighth commandment prepares us for the tenth commandment on coveting because the tenth commandment brings to the foreground the issue of the property of others.[40] Like the subject of the tenth commandment, theft betrays an essential dissatisfaction with one's lot in life and the desire to obtain more than the Lord has granted.[41]

---

[38] W. Eichrodt, "The Law and the Gospel," *Int* 11 (1957): 38.
[39] Craigie, *Deuteronomy*, 161.
[40] Dohmen, *Exodus 19–40*, 124–25.
[41] See E. Merrill, *Deuteronomy*, NAC (Nashville: B&H, 1994), 155.

Chapter 9

THE NINTH COMMANDMENT

Do not give false testimony against your neighbor.

Introduction

The various laws of the ancient Near East are unanimous in their denunciation of perjury and false witness in court. All these cultures and civilizations recognized that the reliability of the witness and the validity of the accusation were paramount to reaching a fair and objective verdict. To prevent false testimony, every witness in the Tomb Robbery Papyri from New Kingdom Egypt was admonished to take the following oath: "If I speak falsehood, may I be mutilated and sent to Kush."[1] The oath to provide accurate testimony would be imposed by the court and directed to the parties involved as well as the witnesses. The oath would involve the promise of giving accurate testimony, invoking the name of a god. The oath would be taken in front of a representation of the god or at a temple. The possibility or likelihood (in their minds) that a false statement would invoke the fury of a god was meant to be a sufficient threat to constrain the oath taker to speak the truth.[2]

Accurate testimony was so valued in ancient Mesopotamia that the substantiation of a witness's allegation could result in a reward. Incorrect allegations, however, could lead to punishment.[3] In the Code of Hammurabi, false testimony in a capital case would result in death for the false witness.[4] In the Neo-Sumerian period, a son who falsely accused his father of embezzling from the temple was subject to the death penalty. In Egypt the standard penalty for false testimony was 100 blows. There is also documentation for the view that false testimony might bring disfigurement, including the cutting off of the nose

---

[1] R. Westbrook, ed., *A History of Ancient Near Eastern Law*, 2 vols. (Leiden; Boston: Brill, 2003), 1:315.

[2] Ibid., 34.

[3] K. Van Der Toorn, *Sin and Sanction in Israel and Mesopotamia: A Comparative Study* (Assen, The Netherlands: Van Gorcum, 1985), 19.

[4] B. Childs, *The Book of Exodus: A Critical-Theological Commentary* (Louisville: Westminster John Knox, 1974), 425.

and ears. In the Old Babylonian period, false accusation and perjury resulted in the same penalty the accused would have suffered had the false testimony been accepted.[5]

False testimony could occur outside the legal realm as well and could bring harsh punishment. In the Code of Hammurabi as well as Middle Assyrian law, slanderous remarks about sexual acts could lead to penalties including flogging. A perennial slanderer could be punished by 40 lashes with a rod, a month of servitude, a monetary fine, or the loss of an ox.[6]

The assurance of truthful testimony is a social condition that is essential for human survival, sociologists tell us. Communal living is not possible without minimal trust in the veracity of one's words. The obligation of courts to adjudicate conflicting claims cannot be met unless it is assumed that truthfulness will prevail.[7] "As embodiments of society's commitment to justice, legal procedures set the moral tone for society."[8]

The Meaning of the Ninth Commandment

The verb of the ninth commandment translated "give" is the Hebrew 'nh. This root occurs 316 times in the Old Testament and is understood to have the basic meaning of "react, respond, or answer."[9] In this construction with the preposition bě, the verb carries the sense of "witness against,"[10] and the formula would carry this nuance in any legal situation. When 'nh is followed by the preposition bě, "against," the evidence is assumed to be damning (1 Sam 12:3; 2 Sam 1:16;

---

[5] Westbrook, *A History of Ancient Near Eastern Law*, 1:81, 346, 423; 2:965 (see Deut 19:15–21).

[6] Ibid., 1:556.

[7] C. Swezey, "Exodus 20:16—'Thou Shalt Not Bear False Witness against Thy Neighbor,'" *Int* 34 (1980): 407.

[8] Ibid.

[9] F. Stendebach, "עָנָה 'ānâ I," *TDOT* 11:217; C. Labushagne, "ענה 'ānâ," *TLOT* 2:927. The identification of the root in the *TDOT* lexicon as 'ānâ, root I, indicates that some scholars are convinced this root is a homonym. A homonym has an identical spelling with another word that has a different meaning.

[10] The phrase "witness against" (בְּ עֵיד) occurs in Deut 31:28 and 1 Sam 8:9. The use of the preposition as adversative is parallel to its use in the phrase עָנָה בְּ. This is the normal nuance of עָנָה when the verb is followed by the בְּ preposition.

Hos 5:5; Mic 6:3).[11] When *'nh* is followed by the *lĕ* preposition, it is expected to bring exculpatory testimony.[12]

The noun *šeqer* conveys the idea of "falsehood or untruth" in the phrase "false testimony."[13] This root has the notion of "act deceptively" and often represents a breach of faith or trust. The meaning "to commit a breach of contract or faith" for this root is apparent in Gen 21:23. There the verb is used in the negated phrase: "You will not break an agreement with me." In Lev 19:11b, the verb of this root is used in the phrase "*lie* to one another."

This root has a significant role in Israelite legal terminology because the effectiveness of the Old Testament legal system is interwoven with the presuppositions of fidelity and trust.[14] The noun is used in the Exodus version of the Ten Commandments with reference to the "false" witness. A lying or false witness represents a severe threat to the entire legal system (*'ēd šĕqār[îm]*; Ps 27:12; Prov 6:19; 12:17; 14:5).[15] However, Christoph Dohmen believes that in the ninth commandment the focus is not on telling the truth but on lying—about the potential damage to a person caused by a lying witness. It is about the person, not the matter of telling the truth versus lying.[16] Exodus 20:16 is not directed to the problem of truth versus lying. It has much rather to do with the person's relationship with his neighbor. It addresses the question: what happens through a lying witness? The ninth commandment has to do with caring for the neighbor. The neighbor may be diminished in his authority by a false testimony; he could lose his material possessions or his integrity could be compromised.[17]

---

[11] This formula occurs 15 times in the Old Testament, six in the Pentateuch. The verb is translated in Greek most often as ἀποκρίνομαι, which carries essentially the same nuance.

[12] W. Propp, *Exodus 19–40*, AB (New York: Doubleday, 2006), 180.

[13] The phrase שֶׁקֶר עֵד is a construct phrase with the noun שֶׁקֶר indicating an attributive usage, functioning as a modifier in the phrase "false testimony."

[14] H. Seebass, "שֶׁקֶר *šeqer*," *TDOT* 15:471; A. Hakam, *The Book of Exodus* (Jerusalem: Mossad Harav Kook, 1991), 299 [in Hb.].

[15] Seebass, *TDOT* 15:473.

[16] This is not to deny that the reliability of the spoken word was of tremendous importance not only in Israel but also in regions of Mesopotamia. Van Der Toorn, *Sin and Sanction in Israel and Mesopotamia*, 20.

[17] C. Dohmen, *Exodus 19–40* (Freiburg: Herder, 2004), 125. The idea of neighbor in these kinds of contexts would refer to anyone with whom one may come into contact in everyday situations. See Kimchi in M. Carasik, "מקראות גדולות." *The Commentators' Bible: The JPS Miqra'ot Gedolot. Exodus* (Philadelphia: Jewish Publication Society, 2005), 163; M. Noth, *Exodus*, OTL

The use of the noun *šeqer* in relation to false witness before the court should, however, be considered its basic meaning.[18] Thus the original focus of this commandment pertained to the giving of false testimony in legal proceedings (see Exod 23:2). The concern would not have been limited to the detriment of an individual and his reputation but undermining the legal system.[19]

In the Deuteronomy version of the ninth commandment, the word *šāw'* occurs in the place of *šeqer*. This term was used in the third commandment, prohibiting the taking of God's name in vain. Because of this connection, Cornelis Houtman maintains it is more plausible that *'ēd šeqer* takes priority and that *'ēd šāw'* was chosen so as to establish an explicit link, by means of *šāw'*, between the third and ninth commandments.[20] *Šāw'* may not be as specific as *šeqer*; *šāw'* often conveys the idea of evil or worthlessness, not just falsehood. Thus Moshe Weinfeld argues that the use of *šāw'* in the Deuteronomy version is meant to prohibit not only false witness but "testimony of circumvention that comes to evade true evidence."[21] Yet the terms are close in meaning since they are parallel in Ps 144:8. Hossfeld concludes that in the juridical context the terms are to be regarded as synonyms.[22]

The Ninth Commandment in the Old Testament

Evidence of legal activity is apparent in various sections of the Old Testament (Deut 25:5–10; Ruth 4; 2 Sam 15:2; 1 Kgs 21; Amos 5:12,15). The trials of the accused were conducted at the gates of the towns. The elders of the villages served as judges. From a modern Western perspective these law courts appear rather informal.[23]

(Philadelphia: Westminster, 1962), 166; U. Cassuto, *A Commentary on the Book of Exodus*, trans. I. Abrahams (Jerusalem: Magnes, 1974), 248.

[18] M. Klopfenstein, "שׁקר *šeqer*," *TLOT* 3: 1401; P. Craigie, *The Book of Deuteronomy* (Grand Rapids: Eerdmans, 1976), 162n26.

[19] T. Fretheim, *Exodus*, Interpretation: A Biblical Commentary for Teaching and Preaching (Louisville: John Knox, 1973), 236–37. The word also is used to refer to a false oath that may have been sworn to Yahweh (Lev 19:12; Zech 5:4) or to a false god (Jer 5:7).

[20] C. Houtman, *Exodus* (Leuven: Peeters, 2000), 3:67.

[21] M. Weinfeld, *Deuteronomy 1–11*, AB 5 (New York: Doubleday, 1991), 315.

[22] Houtman, *Exodus*, 67; F. Reiterer, "שׁוא *šāw'*," *TDOT* 14:452. Some Masoretic manuscripts of Deuteronomy read שׁקר rather than שׁוא. Moreover, in Deut 19:18 we find further support for the Exodus reading עֵד שֶׁקֶר.

[23] J. Holbert, *The Ten Commandments* (Nashville: Abingdon, 2002), 112, 114.

This is not to say that the legal system was not characterized by due process. The court system presented in the Old Testament is characterized by complete fairness and equity. The translation of the ninth commandment into regulations, as in Exod 23:1–3 and 23:6–8, deals with the crucial question of a fair judicial system. In the court of law, there can be no partiality toward the poor (Exod 23:3), just as there should surely be no partiality for the rich (Exod 23:6). Here we see that the poor were protected and their justice was guaranteed. But a legal setting was established to render legal decisions, not to address the ills of society.

The Role of the Witness

The administration of justice was a community affair for the people of God in the Old Testament. Apparently any male Israelite who witnessed a crime could be called on to give testimony, while a curse could be publicly uttered against a person who refused to give testimony. The person who refused to give testimony could expect the judgment of God (Lev 5:1; cf. Prov 29:24). Every indication is that the sentence for the convicted party was immediately executed; apparently there were no appeals, even in capital cases. It appears that the accused was presumed guilty upon the testimony of two witnesses, a role that was vital to the legal system.[24] Thus the burden of proof was placed to a large extent on the accused, who was under obligation to prove his innocence in the face of the accusation from the witnesses.[25]

In the Israelite legal system there was no clear dividing line between the role of witness and accuser. The witness was under communal and religious obligation to report what he knew. In this way the witness contributed to the fight against evil and injustice and so contributed to the preservation of stability in society, assuming his words were true (Prov 14:25).[26] Because of the fear of punishment and retribution for false testimony, there was all the more need to find good witnesses (Deut 19:16–21).[27] The concern for honest judicial testimony also

---

[24] R. Collins, *Christian Morality: Biblical Foundations* (Notre Dame, IN: University of Notre Dame Press, 1986), 60.

[25] G. von Rad, *Deuteronomy: A Commentary* (London: SCM, 1966), 59.

[26] Houtman, *Exodus*, 65.

[27] S. Lowenstein, "עֵד," *EncMiqr* 6:81–83 [in Hb.].

motivated the requirement for two witnesses in capital cases (Num 35:30; Deut 17:6; 19:15). Deuteronomy 19:16–21 elaborates on the consequences of false testimony (see also Exod 23:1; Lev 19:16; Deut 5:20).[28] False witnesses were punished on the basis of just punishment or talion. For untrue and damaging testimony, the false witness would receive the same punishment that would have been rendered to the person he falsely accused if he had been convicted. As a further incentive to speak the truth, the witnesses themselves had to initiate the procedure for capital punishment (Deut 13:9; 17:7; 19:16–21).[29]

False Testimony in Narrative Texts

In the narrative portions of the Old Testament, we find numerous examples of false testimony and accusation, although not in a judicial setting. For example, Potiphar's wife falsely accused Joseph of attempted rape and planted evidence against him (Gen 39). The first time Abram speaks in the Bible, he tells Sarai, his wife, to tell a lie (Gen 12:10–13). The Hebrew midwives lie in order to save the lives of the Hebrew infants (Exod 1:19). Rahab lies in order to protect the Hebrew spies (Josh 2:2–6). Jonathan lies to his father about David to determine whether Saul desired to kill David (1 Sam 20:27–29). While not all these practices are necessarily condoned in the Old Testament, they appear to differ from the offense of false testimony that the ninth commandment prohibits.

False Testimony in Legal Texts

From the legal material in the Pentateuch, we find that the penalties for a false witness were severe (Deut 19:16–19). Deuteronomy 19:19 specifies that if a witness is proven false, "you must do to him as he intended to do to his brother." Because false accusations could result in serious punishment, it is unlikely there were many frivolous lawsuits in those days.[30]

---

[28] Propp, *Exodus*, 180.

[29] N. Sarna, *Exodus*, JPS Torah Commentary (Philadelphia, New York: Jewish Publication Society, 1991), 114. A similar law from Mesopotamia was in effect during the Old Babylonian period. See Westbrook, *A History of Ancient Near Eastern Law*, 1:423.

[30] See also *Jos. Ant.* 4:219; Code of Hammurabi, 1–4, in *ANET*, 166.

False Testimony in Wisdom Literature

Deuteronomy 19 shows the inherent problems of having a single witness and why a single witness would never convict any defendant; the possibilities of error, confusion, outright lies, monetary gain, or revenge make single-witness testimony inherently unreliable.[31] False testimony could be a matter of life or death (1 Kgs 21). Wisdom literature is replete with admonitions against a false witness (Ps 27:12; Prov 6:19; 12:17; 14:5,25; 19:5,9; 21:28; 24:28; see Exod 23:1; Ps 35:11). According to Prov 6:19, a lying witness is one of six things the Lord hates. Lying lips are an abomination to the Lord (Prov 12:22). The prayers of the psalmists that deceitful plaintiffs meet their punishment depend on the conviction that a liar in court sins not only against the innocent but before God (Pss 27:12; 35:11–28; cf. 1 Kgs 21).[32] The frequent complaint of the psalmists (e.g., Ps 27:12) against deceitful witnesses confirms how widespread the abuse had become (see Pss 35:19; 69:4[5]).

Many of the complaints in the Psalms may be in response to unjust or false accusations. Many other psalms echo the complaints of those who were adversely affected by lying speech (Pss 31:18[19]; 63:11[12]; 101:7; 109:2; 119:69; 120:2).[33] Biblical proverbs also dwell on the theme of false and reliable witnesses, calling the former an abomination to the Lord (Prov 6:16–19) and the latter a redeemer of lives (Prov 14:25). The wicked speak lies from the womb (Ps 58:3).

At the heart of the matter in the ninth commandment is that false testimony and false accusation are not only a threat to an individual's reputation and well-being but a threat to the whole structure of the justice system. The people's faith in judicial proceedings had to be wedded to their conviction that all such proceedings are based on truthfulness and fairness. At stake was the whole notion of justice in the judicial system.[34]

---

[31] Holbert, *The Ten Commandments*, 117.
[32] Van Der Toorn, *Sin and Sanction in Israel and Mesopotamia*, 19, 163n113.
[33] Seebass, *TDOT* 15:474.
[34] Fretheim, *Exodus*, 236–37.

Exhibiting Truthfulness

Although the primary focus of the ninth commandment would appear to be its use in the legal context, a false statement of a more general kind might also be within the purview of this commandment.[35] Indeed, the word "neighbor" can refer to an adversary (1 Sam 15:28; 2 Sam 12:11) rather than a person on trial. Thus the context supports the argument that the commandment prohibits any false statement that may bring harm to any neighbor. The law would ensure that a member of a community would be protected against the threat of a false accusation. The requirement that witnesses had to be produced to convict a person was a safeguard for this principle (see Num 35:30; Deut 17:6; 19:15; Prov 25:18).[36]

Dishonesty in general, not merely in court cases, is also forbidden.[37] This statute generally protects a person's name and forbids harming and defaming one's neighbor through slander and unbridled defamation. Gossip, slander, and obsequious flattery are to be shunned. "Flattery goes wrong when it sacrifices truth and dignity in order to obtain some material advantage—be it objects, money, affection, relationship, or favors. Flattery actually becomes an act of stealing, for which, instead of stealth and weapons, false words of approval are the tools of the theft."[38] Or as Sir Walter Raleigh stated: "Flatterers are the worst kind of traitors for they will strengthen thy imperfections, encourage thee in all evils, correct thee in nothing."[39] This is evident in the biblical text already in Lev 19:16, which extends the ninth commandment to the prohibition of slander.

In addition to the admonition in the ninth commandment not to bear false witness, honesty in judicial procedures could be expected when the mandates to be honest in all situations were honored (Exod 23:1–3,6–9; Lev 19:11–19) and when two witnesses testified at a criminal trial (Deut 17:6; 19:15). The extension of the commandment to lying more generally (see Lev 19:16; Deut 5:20; Hos 4:2) is

---

[35] A. Hartom and M. Cassuto, "Exodus" and "Leviticus" in *Torah, Prophets, Writings* (Tel Aviv: Yavneh 1977), 72 [in Hb.].

[36] Childs, *The Book of Exodus*, 424.

[37] D. Stuart, *Exodus*, NAC (Nashville: B&H, 2006), 466.

[38] L. Schlessinger, *The Ten Commandments* (New York: HarperCollins, 1998), 291–92.

[39] Ibid., 292.

evident in other biblical texts and included any deceptive, slanderous, or empty talk about other persons that would undermine their reputation.[40] Lies and falsehood are abhorred by the Lord and are in conflict with the values of righteous and holy living (Pss 5:6; 31:18[19]; 40:4; 58:3; 62:4; 109:2; Prov 6:16–19; 10:18; 12:19,22; 17:7; 19:5,22; 21:6; 26:28).

The Ninth Commandment in the New Testament

In the New Testament narrative the most salient examples of false testimony take place in conjunction with the trial of Jesus. The chief priests and the Sanhedrin actively looked for false testimony to accuse Jesus and put Him to death (Matt 26:59–61; see Mark 14:55–59). Perhaps Peter's repeated denial of Jesus under oath (Matt 26:69–75) provides the most memorable example of false testimony. Ananias and Sapphira lied about the price they received for their property when they claimed to be giving all of it to the church (Acts 5). At the trial of Stephen, false witnesses accused him of blasphemy (Acts 6:13). When believers say they are in fellowship with God and walk in darkness, they lie and do not practice the truth (1 John 1:6). The fate for liars is the lake of fire, which is the second death (Rev 21:8).

On the positive side, this commandment calls for a commitment to the truth in one's dealings. To the extent that the New Testament places a premium on truth telling, it is intolerant of false testimony. The false prophets who disbursed falsehood in the New Testament (Matt 7:15; 24:11,24–27) were viewed alongside their Old Testament precursors (Luke 6:26). The letter of James is particularly pointed regarding truthfulness and control of the tongue (Jas 1:26; 3:1–18). Satan has not stood in the truth from the beginning (John 8:44).

In the imitation of "God who cannot lie" (Titus 1:2), God's people should be truthful to their word. They should speak the truth with their neighbors and speak the truth in love (Eph 4:25,15). It is still a serious offense to be considered a false witness (1 Cor 15:15). "A witness who testifies falsely against his fellow, who bears the image of

---

[40] T. Fretheim, *Exodus*, 237.

God, is considered as one who testified against God Himself" (*Zohar, Vayikra* 12a).[41] God desires truth in the inner man (Ps 51:6).

Conclusion

Justice in the courtroom must be carried out with fairness and equity. Americans are reminded that the law must prevail and that Lady Justice is blindfolded in order to ignore appearances and circumstances, ruling only according to legal statute. These principles are firmly embedded in the legal traditions of the Old Testament. Injustices do often prevail in society; but the courts, in the process of adjudicating our laws, should not attempt to correct injustices on their own.[42]

The ninth commandment covers both false accusation and false testimony in court. The placement of this commandment between stealing and coveting may show that false accusation is a means of depriving someone of what belongs to him (cf. Lev 19:11). This can happen when a person claims ownership of something in another's possession. The most notable example of false accusation leading to acquisition of someone's property has to be Jezebel's attainment of Naboth's vineyard for Ahab by having false witnesses accuse Naboth of blasphemy. Her desire was for Naboth's property to be awarded to the crown (1 Kgs 21:1–16).[43] The incident of Naboth's vineyard illustrates the serious nature of false testimony as well as its potentially tragic results. The placement of this command, after murder, adultery, and theft, may indicate that all these offenses call for a legal trial.[44]

The ninth commandment forbids false testimony against another. False testimony is tantamount to character assassination and so constitutes another form of killing.[45] It steals a man's reputation and then kills it in the public eye.

The basis of biblical truth is God's character, which cannot be false; not being a man but God, he cannot deal falsely (1 Sam 15:29; cf. Num

---

[41] Rabbi D. Wax, ed., *The Ten Commandments* (Lakewood, NJ: Taryag Legacy Foundation, 2005), 357.

[42] Holbert, *The Ten Commandments*, 116.

[43] J. Tigay, *Deuteronomy*, JPS Torah Commentary (Philadelphia: Jewish Publication Society, 1996), 71.

[44] Propp, *Exodus 19–40*, 179–80.

[45] E. Merrill, *Deuteronomy*, NAC (Nashville: B&H, 1994), 155.

23:19). First Samuel 15:29 says: "The Eternal One of Israel does not lie or change His mind." "God is not a man who lies" (Num 23:19). God destroys "those who tell lies" (Ps 5:6[7]). Yet Satan has lied from the beginning as he deceived the woman and lied about God's judgment in the garden of Eden (Gen 3:4–5).

A God of faithfulness, who does not deal deceitfully with His people, requires of His people the same transparency and honesty in personal relationships.[46] Ephesians 4:25 states, "Speak the truth, each one to his neighbor, because we are members of one another." As Augustine stated, "In the Decalogue itself it is written, 'You shall not bear false witness,' in which classification every lie is embraced."[47]

The ninth commandment preserves with its few words one of the bedrock ideas of our Western civilization, although it predates the Magna Carta by 3,000 years. "Bearing false witness" has become a well-known phrase in our secular vocabulary about the importance of telling the truth in all legal contexts. It is eloquent proof that the ninth commandment has through the centuries borne the primary force of addressing false testimony in legal contexts.[48]

---

[46] Craigie, *The Book of Deuteronomy*, 163; W. Kaiser Jr., *Toward Old Testament Ethics* (Grand Rapids: Zondervan, 1983), 95.

[47] J. Lienhard, ed., *Exodus, Leviticus, Numbers, Deuteronomy*, ACCS (Downers Grove, IL: InterVarsity, 2001), 107.

[48] Holbert, *The Ten Commandments*, 113–14.

Chapter 10

THE TENTH COMMANDMENT

*Do not covet your neighbor's house. Do not covet your
neighbor's wife, his male or female slave, his ox or donkey, or anything that belongs to your neighbor.*

Introduction

The tenth commandment is unique on a number of levels.
Examination of comparable laws from other cultures does
not appear to show any culture with a law that approaches
the law of coveting.[1] Moreover, the tenth commandment is distinct
from the others of the Ten Commandments in that it does not address an overt action but one's intention. The apostle Paul appeared
to distinguish this commandment from the rest when he said it was
the tenth commandment that uniquely revealed to him the nature of
his own sinfulness.

The Meaning of the Tenth Commandment

Critical to understanding the tenth commandment is the meaning of the verb "covet" (*ḥmd*). The tenth commandment begins with
a prohibition against coveting a neighbor's house. "Covet" occurs
21 times in the Old Testament, in the Qal (16x), Niphal (4x), and
Piel (1x) stems. Of critical importance for the meaning of this root is
whether it includes some sort of overt action. The view that the root
means more than desire, and includes the physical attempt to acquire
what is desired, is widespread, particularly among Jewish interpreters. An ancient halakhic midrash, *Mekilta de Rabbi Ishmael*, states
that the tenth commandment needed to be read in light of Deut 7:25,
where coveting and taking of silver and gold is prohibited. Because
the person is culpable only if he follows through and takes the silver
and gold, so should one understand the tenth commandment—the

---

[1] In the Egyptian *The Book of the Dead*, there is a denial by a worshipper that he had ever
coveted, but this is not based apparently on any legal text. G. Wallis, "חָמַד *ḥāmad*," *TDOT*
4:459; see *ANET*, 35.

commandment is violated only when a person follows through and takes what he desires. Thus, Jewish tradition argues that coveting involves action. Maimonides is one who holds this position.[2]

The view that the tenth commandment includes commission of an act has recently gained cohorts from non-Jewish scholars as well for three reasons: (1) the rest of the Ten Commandments refer to deeds, so a commandment that only forbids thoughts seems out of place; (2) the root *ḥmd* denotes a feeling that inevitably leads to an action (Deut 7:25; Josh 6:18; 7:21); and (3) the Phoenician cognate of *ḥmd* involves not only desiring but also seizing.[3]

The second alternative position on *ḥmd* limits the meaning of the verb to desire or yearning without the commission of any illicit act to obtain the desired object. Nevertheless, *ḥmd* has as its goal the possession of what is coveted. Thus the commandment is not just to prohibit the yearning because the yearning may contribute to overt criminal acts, but the commandment addresses the desire itself because it too is a transgression.[4] Otherwise, the commandments against such overt acts as murder, adultery, and stealing would be superfluous. The idea that the desire itself is being addressed is in harmony with such passages as Gen 6:5, where intention or imagination alone was enough to justify the judgment of the flood. The intention to carry out a wrong was wrong itself. Thus mere wishes without actions constitute coveting and are a violation of the tenth commandment.[5] Just because verbs such as *lāqaḥ* "take" (Deut 7:25; Josh 6:18; 7:21) occur in the same context as *ḥmd* does not mean *ḥmd* carries the same connotations as these active verbs. Rather, this more likely implies that *ḥmd* does not carry the same connotations, and a word must be added to convey the idea of taking or appropriating.[6] These words are thus

---

[2] See A. Rofé, "The Tenth Commandment in the Light of Four Deuteronomic Laws," in *The Ten Commandments in History and Tradition*, ed. B. Z. Segal (Jerusalem: Magnes, 1990), 45–46.

[3] Ibid., 47–48. Wallis also maintains that the root חמד includes the act of possession as expressed in Josh 7:21. Wallis, *TDOT* 4:454.

[4] See U. Cassuto, *A Commentary on the Book of Exodus*, trans. I. Abrahams (Jerusalem: Magnes, 1974), 240; Wallis, *TDOT* 4:454.

[5] B. Jackson, *Essays in Jewish and Comparative Legal History* (Leiden: Brill, 1975), 213; W. Propp, *Exodus 19–40*, AB (New York: Doubleday, 2006), 180.

[6] M. Weinfeld, *Deuteronomy 1–11*, AB 5 (New York: Doubleday, 1991), 316. The same observation could be made for Mic 2:2.

not parallel to *ḥmd,* which describes the thought processes prior to the action. Jewish medieval scholar Ibn Ezra argued for the restrictive meaning of *ḥmd* as he observed that coveting is about one's heart or thoughts and does not entail taking action. It refers to a state of mind.[7] Coveting means having thoughts of taking or acquiring someone else's possessions.[8] The meaning of the root is illustrated by the Qal passive participle, which refers to something desirable (Job 20:20; Ps 39:11[12]; Isa 44:9). The root is used in reference to the outward appearance of something that appears to be valuable or pleasing, and therefore desirable to own or possess.[9]

In the Deuteronomy version of the tenth commandment (Deut 5:21), the verb *ḥmd* does not occur twice as in Exod 20:17 but only once and is replaced by *ʾwh* in the second occurrence.[10] This root occurs 27 times in the Old Testament. It often refers to an "evil desire" that is contrary to God's will.[11] The overwhelming focus is on the emotion or feeling of craving without any accompanying action (Deut 12:20; 14:26; 2 Sam 23:15; Ps 10:17; Prov 13:12; Amos 5:18; Mic 7:1).[12] The use of the root expresses itself as rebellion against God and leads to disobedience, guilt, and punishment. The most memorable and perhaps most significant use of this root with this meaning comes from Gen 3:6, where Eve yields to the delight (*taʾăwâ*) of her eyes and becomes disobedient (see Num 11:4; Pss 78:29–30; 106:14). The term stresses desire and may be distinguished from *ḥmd,* which focuses on something that is material, visible to the eye.[13] Or as Moshe Weinfeld observed, *ʾwh* denotes a desire that stems from an inner need,

---

[7] This law may not preclude a desire to have something like someone else has.

[8] M. Greenberg, "The Tradition Critically Examined," in Segal, *The Ten Commandments in History and Tradition,* 107.

[9] Wallis, *TDOT* 4:454.

[10] Texts such as the SP, the mss of Deuteronomy from Qumran Cave IV, and the two phylacteries from Qumran that contain the text of Deut 5 repeat the verb חָמַד twice when rendering Deut 5:18. The LXX uses the same verb to translate both חָמַד and אָוָה. The Nash papyrus has a peculiar variant that attempts to alter תחמד to bring it in line with the reading תתאוה. Many of these texts tried to bring the Decalogue in Deuteronomy in line with its primary formulation in Exod 20. This is evident in other passages in the Qumran Cave IV document and in the Nash papyrus. Rofe, "The Tenth Commandment in the Light of Four Deuteronomic Laws," 51.

[11] Ps 45:12 may be an exception.

[12] B. Childs, *The Book of Exodus: A Critical-Theological Commentary* (Louisville: Westminster John Knox, 1974), 426–27; Wallis, *TDOT* 4:453.

[13] W. Williams, "אוה," *NIDOTTE* 1:305.

while *ḥmd* refers to a desire that is stimulated by sight.[14] The focus on *ḥmd* has to do with the desire to acquire something or someone visible.[15] As Wallis states: "The occasion for *ḥmd* is inspection, for *ʾwh* imagination."[16]

The roots are clearly to be distinguished, yet it is possible that *ʾwh* merely qualifies *ḥmd* since the two terms occur in parallel. The addition of the root *ʾwh* may be no more than a stylistic variation.[17] The two roots seem to be interchangeable in their usage.

In Exod 20:17, the first clause mentions only the neighbor's house as the object of coveting. The second clause expands this by explaining that the prohibition includes the neighbor's wife, servants, and livestock. In Exodus, "house" carries the idea of "household" (see Gen 7:1; 35:2; Lev 16:6; Num 16:32; Deut 11:6). It would refer to any part of the household with economic value. That would include more than the structure of the house.[18] The wife is mentioned after the house because her value in Exod 20 is with regard to her position in the household (cf. Prov 31) and possibly the assets she represents.[19] The Exodus version reflects descriptions of life in patriarchal and wilderness times when the Israelites lived as nomadic herders without owning property (see Gen 12:5; 26:14; Num 16:30,32; Deut 11:6).

Deuteronomy catalogs the neighbor's property with more discrimination. It separates family from property and possessions by placing the wife in the first clause by herself.[20] Ibn Ezra argued that the wife was placed at the beginning of the list of coveted items in Deut 5:21 because a young woman would be what a young man would desire the most.[21]

---

[14] M. Weinfeld, *Deuteronomy 1–11*, 318.

[15] Rofé, "The Tenth Commandment in the Light of Four Deuteronomic Laws," 54n31; D. Talley, "חמד," *NIDOTTE* 2:167–68.

[16] Wallis, *TDOT* 4:455.

[17] A. Phillips, *Ancient Israel's Criminal Law: A New Approach to the Decalogue* (Oxford: Basil Blackwell, 1970), 152; G. Mayer, "אָוָה *ʾāwâ*," *TDOT* 1:135.

[18] Propp, *Exodus 19–40*, 181.

[19] C. Houtman, *Exodus* (Leuven: Peeters, 2000), 3:71.

[20] Some, including Weinfeld and Merrill, believe the placement in Deuteronomy of women at the top of the list indicates a special attention to women's rights. Weinfeld, *Deuteronomy 1–11*, 318; E. Merrill, *Deuteronomy*, NAC (Nashville: B&H, 1994), 156–57.

[21] *Miqráot Gedolot*, 5 vols. (Jerusalem: Eshkol, 1976), 1:87 [in Hb.]; M. Carasik, "גדולות מקראות," *The Commentators' Bible: The JPS Miqráot Gedolot. Exodus* (Philadelphia: Jewish Publication Society, 2005), 163.

The second clause adds "fields," which is absent from Exod 20. This shows that in Deuteronomy, in contrast with Exodus, "house" has the narrower sense of a dwelling or structure. By including actual houses and fields, the Deuteronomy version of the list refers to the type of life that people would have in Canaan. The goal of the book of Deuteronomy was to prepare the Israelites for life in the promised land.[22]

The listing of people first, then servants, and then animals is based on order of importance. The ox may have been listed before the donkey because the ox was regarded as a clean animal while the donkey was unclean. In the ancient world one was considered wealthy by the abundance of slaves and animals he possessed.[23]

The Tenth Commandment in the Old Testament

The verb *ḥmd* first occurs in the narrative literature of the Bible in Gen 2:9, in the description of the trees God caused to grow. The trees were "pleasing" *(neḥmād)* in appearance and good for food (Gen 2:9). In the next chapter the root occurs again in describing the trees of the garden as "desirable" *(neḥmād)* for obtaining wisdom (Gen 3:6).

The verb is also used in Josh 7 in reference to the defeat at Ai and Achan's confession regarding his stealing of spoils set aside for destruction. Achan confessed that when he saw the beautiful cloak from Babylon, 200 silver shekels, and a bar of gold weighing 50 shekels, he coveted them *(wā'eḥmĕdēm)* and took them (Josh 7:21).

Yet the concept of coveting is evident in the Old Testament even though the technical term *ḥmd* is not used. Narrative examples include the desire, planning, and then confiscation of Naboth's field by Ahab in 1 Kgs 21 and David's desire and then action to have Bathsheba in 2 Sam 11. Both of these examples as well as the actions of Pharaoh in Gen 12:10–16 reveal the actions of covetousness by those in positions of power. However, coveting is not limited to the powerful. Gehazi,

---

[22] The pairing of a field with a house is a typical formulaic expression for immovable property in the ancient Near East (see Gen 39:5; 2 Kgs 8:3,5; Isa 5:8; Mic 2:2). Weinfeld, *Deuteronomy 1–11*, 319. The SP adds several words to the end of the verse, similar to phrases in Deut 7:1; 11:29–30; 27:2–8, to legitimate the Samaritans' claim that Shechem, not Jerusalem, was God's favored sanctuary. Propp, *Exodus 19–40*, 114.

[23] A. Hakam, *The Book of Exodus* (Jerusalem: Mossad Harav Kook, 1991), 290 and 290n59 [in Hb.].

servant of Elisha, coveted the property of Naaman to the extent that he lied to get access to the property and was as a consequence struck with leprosy (2 Kgs 5:19–27). The law applies to everyone. No one should endeavor to deprive by legal means or by wheeling and dealing the necessities of life of a fellow human being.[24] Covetousness is condemned throughout the Bible, particularly in the book of Proverbs (e.g., 3:31).[25] A person characterized by covetousness will eventually bring trouble to his family (Prov 15:27).

In the legal texts we find another use of *ḥmd*, in reference to God's promise in Exod 34:24. The Lord promises that when the Israelite males go up to Jerusalem three times a year to worship Him, the foreign nations around them will not covet (*yaḥmōd*) the Israelites' land. This commandment is unique among the Ten Commandments in that, apart from its occurrence there, it is not repeated in the Pentateuch.[26]

From the Prophetic texts we find that Micah excoriates the wicked who covet (*wĕḥāmdû*) fields and seize them and deprive people of their homes and inheritance (Mic 2:2). This shows that greed and covetousness are at the root of all social injustice. Since covetousness may be defined as a state of mind that wishes to change the way things are, there is an inherent relationship between the condemnation of covetousness and the maintenance of time-honored social and economic justice (see Hab 2:9).[27]

The Tenth Commandment in the New Testament

In the Sermon on the Mount, Jesus understood *ḥmd* within the framework of pure intention. Jesus applied this principle in a broad sense to the interpretation of the commandments against murder and adultery in Matt 5:21–30. We see this in Matt 5:28 where Jesus states that whoever looks at a woman with lust in his heart has already

---

[24] C. Dohmen, *Exodus 19–40* (Freiburg: Herder, 2004), 127. Weinfeld maintains that the focus of the tenth commandment is on addressing those who would legally appropriate a man's wife or household, in contrast with the commandments against adultery and stealing where "the culprit commits the crime stealthily." *Deuteronomy 1–11*, 316.

[25] S. Schwarzschild, "Covetousness," *EJ* 5:254.

[26] M. Weinfeld, "The Uniqueness of the Decalogue and Its Place in Jewish Tradition," in Segal, *The Ten Commandments in History and Tradition*, 1.

[27] Schwarzschild, "Covetousness," 254.

committed adultery with her in his heart. Jesus interprets lust or coveting with the same meaning that it had in the Old Testament. "Each person is tempted when he is drawn away and enticed by his own evil desires" (Jas 1:14). Lust and coveting are pure intention, not action, but they do begin with vision. Not only the act but the desire is condemned, partly because of what the unmet desire might lead to and partly because the desire, whether or not it leads to an action, betrays the wrong attitude, characterized by coveting.[28] The spirit of the tenth commandment may be viewed as permeating the Sermon on the Mount. Jesus' frequent saying, "You have heard that it was said," may be viewed as a drawing out of the Ten Command-ments "in terms of the coveting roots of all disobedience."[29] As D. A. Carson stated with reference to the seventh commandment: "In ef-fect, by labeling lust adultery, Jesus has deepened the seventh com-mandment in terms of the tenth, the prohibition of covetousness."[30] It is the function of the tenth commandment to make explicit the internalization of the whole law and reveal the sin of the heart.[31] A person may not overtly commit the sins of murder, adultery, or stealing; but this does not exhaust his duty. He must endeavor to rid his mind of the evil desires of coveting.

In effect, in the Sermon on the Mount, Jesus is correctly inter-preting the law and arguing as the law should be.[32] Because greed and covetousness may lead to all types of sins, Jesus warned His fol-lowers to be on guard against all their forms (Luke 12:15). Greed, covetousness, and inordinate desire are frequently addressed in the New Testament (Mark 7:21–22; Luke 12:15; Rom 1:24; 2 Cor 9:5; Eph 5:3; Col 3:5; 1 Tim 6:9–10; 2 Pet 2:3).[33] These sins cannot be seen because they arise in the heart. Jesus said, "For from the heart come evil thoughts, murders, adulteries, sexual immoralities, thefts,

---

[28] "Concupiscence is never without desire, although the will may not altogether yield." J. Calvin, *Commentaries on the Last Books of Moses,* trans. C. Bingham (Grand Rapids: Baker, 1979), 3:189.

[29] T. Fretheim, *Exodus.* Interpretation: A Biblical Commentary for Teaching and Preaching (Louisville: John Knox, 1973), 238.

[30] D. A. Carson, *The Sermon on the Mount* (Grand Rapids: Baker, 1978), 43–44.

[31] J. Motyer, *The Message of Exodus* (Downers Grove, IL: InterVarsity, 2005), 230.

[32] B. Jackson, *Essays in Jewish and Comparative Legal History* (Leiden: Brill, 1975), 213–14.

[33] W. Kaiser Jr., *Toward Old Testament Ethics* (Grand Rapids: Zondervan, 1983), 95.

false testimonies, blasphemies" (Matt 15:19). The rich young ruler appears to have missed his opportunity for the kingdom because he was a covetous man (Matt 19:16–22). "The love of money is a root of all kinds of evil" (1 Tim 6:10).

Another important passage that reveals the uniqueness of the tenth commandment is Rom 7:9–10. Here the apostle Paul alludes to the perfection of the law and imperfection in himself. Apart from the tenth commandment, all the other commandments can be obeyed ostensively, outwardly.[34] But the tenth commandment applies to the heart, a matter of attitude. This commandment thoroughly convinced Paul that he was a sinner. The New Testament views covetousness as a great sin, on the same level as idolatry (Eph 5:5; Col 3:5). It is also named in the comprehensive list of the sins of man's total depravity in Rom 1:29. It is equated with immorality and impurity and so must be put away (Eph 5:3).

Conclusion

The tenth commandment forms an inclusio with the introduction to the Ten Commandments in Exod 20:2: "I am the LORD your God, who brought you out of the land of Egypt, out of the place of slavery." We find in this prologue as well as in the tenth commandment a repetition of the Hebrew term *bayit* ("house"; Exod 20:2b,17a) as well as *'ebed* ("slave[s]"; 20:2b,17b). Moreover, the tenth commandment ends with the word "neighbor," which forms a parallel to the opening statement, "I am the LORD your God" (Exod 20:2).[35] Also, whereas the first commandment prohibits the worship of other gods, the tenth commandment prohibits the coveting of others' goods.[36] Only God is to occupy the thoughts of those who desire to walk with Him and please Him. Thoughts and actions must be directed by and toward the Lord who is our deliverer.[37]

---

[34] One could conclude from this that an individual has lived a faultless or obedient life. See Phil 3:4–6.

[35] U. Cassuto, *A Commentary on the Book of Exodus*, trans. I. Abrahams (Jerusalem: Magnes, 1974), 249.

[36] D. Christensen, *Deuteronomy 1:1–21:9*, rev. ed., WBC 6A (Nashville: Thomas Nelson, 2001), 129.

[37] J. Holbert, *The Ten Commandments* (Nashville: Abingdon, 2002), 130.

The tenth commandment is also unique in other ways. For example, it is the only commandment that is repeated, with the use of *ḥmd* twice in Exod 20:17 and *ḥmd* and *'āwâ* in Deut 5:21. This repetition may demonstrate that this, the last of the Ten Commandments, is of extraordinary importance.[38] One aspect of its importance is evident from the fact that, in contrast with the other commandments that address outward acts, the tenth commandment uniquely addresses a person's thoughts and desires. It thus addresses attitudes that are less overtly violent and injurious, yet it is the commandment most at the root of covenant disobedience in that it logically precedes the rest.[39] It is to be a restraint upon evil desires before they prevail.[40]

The desires of the heart always precede overt behaviors (Mark 7:20–23). Desire is the root from which every sin springs. Before someone murders, or commits adultery, or steals, or bears false witness (e.g., 1 Kgs 21), he first covets or longs for a different sort of circumstance. People who covet desire a situation that either involves removal of another person from the world, or else allows them to have sexual relations with someone else's wife, or possess the property of a neighbor.[41] Sin is more than the outward act; it includes a person's attitude, thoughts, and desires. Merely the intention to do wrong is a transgression in itself (see *m. 'Abot* 4:21). Sin must be addressed at this prior stage of covetousness so as not to lead to the actual act. As Augustine stated, "The law said, 'Thou shalt not covet,' in order that, when we find ourselves lying in this diseased state, we might seek the medicine of grace."[42]

True obedience involves avoiding not only certain actions but also intentions or attitudes toward others in relationship. These actions and intentions are perhaps best captured in such words as "envy" or "greed" or "lust." But as this sin is not always visible, it cannot be policed. It can be observed only by God, who alone knows the level

---

[38] A. Heschel, *The Earth Is the Lord's and the Sabbath* (New York: Harper & Row, 1966), 90.

[39] Merrill, *Deuteronomy*, 157.

[40] Calvin, *Commentaries on the Last Books of Moses*, 3:188.

[41] Like the eighth commandment, the tenth assumes the right to own private property as well as the protection of property rights. See W. Keszler, "Die literarische, historische und theologische Problematik des Dekalogs," *VT* 7 (1957): 13.

[42] J. Lienhard, ed., *Exodus, Leviticus, Numbers, Deuteronomy*, ACCS (Downers Grove, IL: InterVarsity, 2001), 108.

of obedience or disobedience within the human spirit. The degree of compliance to the tenth commandment is a defining gauge of the level of maturity of one's personal relationship with God. The believer should be satisfied with what God sovereignly has given to him (see 1 Tim 6:7). This last commandment could therefore be viewed as the interpreting clause of the whole Decalogue (Rom 7:7).[43]

Some early church fathers believed the essence of original sin was related to coveting and that all the Ten Commandments in one way or another prohibit envy.[44] Illicit desire not only offends ethical norms toward fellow human beings but also violates God's sovereign decrees. This was not only what happened in the fall but the story of humanity ever since. Some church fathers more specifically connected the fall not merely to the act of eating the forbidden fruit but to the heart's craving for the fruit.

Another feature of the uniqueness of the tenth commandment is the comprehensive nature of this law. This law forms a suitable conclusion to commandments six through nine, but it may be viewed as encapsulating all ten of them. It is the most scrupulous of the commandments in that it aims to prevent the evil acts enumerated in the previous commandments by mastering those impulses that drive people to commit them.[45] As Janzen has stated:

> In reaction to a tradition that suspected and repressed desire, we as a society have arrived at a point where desire increasingly becomes its own justification, no matter what the nature of that desire or the identity of the objects on which it seeks to satisfy itself.[46]

Although covetousness is by nature covert and thus undetected, it is a catchall to prevent overt crimes. Covetousness is a basic source of social disorder and trouble in interpersonal relationships.

At the heart of the sin of coveting is the disregard and detriment that may accrue to others as a result of covetousness and envy. A neighbor's world should not be coveted. One should seek the highest good for one's neighbor, who is to be loved as a fellow member of

---

[43] Motyer, *The Message of Exodus*, 230.
[44] D. Stuart, *Exodus*, NAC (B&H, 2006), 467–68.
[45] Greenberg, "The Tradition Critically Examined," 108–9.
[46] J. Gerald Janzen, *Exodus* (Louisville: Westminster John Knox, 1997), 157.

the family of God.[47] You should love your neighbor as yourself (Lev 19:18; Matt 5:43; 19:19; 22:39; Mark 12:31; Luke 10:27; Rom 13:9). If you are loving your neighbor, you do not have an agenda against him and covet what he has. Whether the desire leads to the prohibited act, the desire for that which belongs to your neighbor betrays the wrong attitude toward your fellow man. Yes, the desire is prohibited because it may lead to the illicit action. But not just the material possessions in the narrow sense of the word should be so protected. What is valuable to the neighbor and means something to him should be respected. From the Old Testament standpoint, it was a matter of protecting and ensuring the communal life of the nation that Yahweh delivered from Egypt.[48] The main objects of coveting mentioned in the tenth commandment are house and wife—in other words, property and family—the core of man's existence.[49]

As Martin Luther remarked in his shorter catechism: "We should fear and love God, that we may not estrange, force, or entice away from our neighbor his wife, servants, or cattle. We should fear and love God, that we may not desire by craftiness to gain possession of our neighbor's inheritance or home, or to obtain it under pretext of a legal right."[50] Similarly, Augustine challenges the believer to reflect on his relationship to God: "What haven't you acquired, if you have got hold of God? So don't covet your neighbor's property."[51] The cure for covetousness and greed may be found in an attitude of humbleness and contentment with what God has provided for you. Man should be content with what God provides. As noted in the rabbinic tradition: "Who is rich? He who delights in his share" (*m. ʾAbot* 4:1).

---

[47] P. Craigie, *The Book of Deuteronomy* (Grand Rapids: Eerdmans, 1976), 164.

[48] Dohmen, *Exodus 19–40*, 127–28.

[49] See Prov 19:14; Jer 6:11–12; 29:5–6. Weinfeld, *Deuteronomy 1–11*, 317.

[50] Quoted from Wallis, *TDOT* 4:458.

[51] Lienhard, *Exodus, Leviticus, Numbers, Deuteronomy*, 108.

CONCLUSION

Interrelationship of the Ten Commandments

Broadly speaking, the Ten Commandments are to be divided into two groups. The first four commandments are concerned with man's vertical relationship to God while the last five deal with man's horizontal relationship to his fellow man. Without a proper relationship to God, a proper relationship to a fellow human being is not possible, and fellowship with God can take place only when a person treats his neighbor as he would like to be treated.[1] "Apart from the fear of God men do not preserve equity and love among themselves."[2] The fifth commandment dealing with the honoring of parents falls between these two broad categories as it specifically and more directly addresses human relationships beginning with the foremost human relationship, the family. Only two commandments, the Sabbath and parental laws, are in the form of positive imperatives. This is not surprising because law is essentially restrictive. It functions as a deterrent.

The first two commandments are so closely related that with good reason many have seen them as constituting one commandment—the proper way to worship God. And yet there is a distinction. The first commandment addresses the inward worship of God, while the second speaks to the issue of external idolatry.[3] The third commandment, addressing the misuse of God's name, is similar to the ninth, regarding false testimony. They are to be distinguished by the fact that the third commandment is in the first portion of the Decalogue, which focuses on one's relationship to God, while the ninth occurs in the second portion, where the focus is on one's relationship to man. While the ninth commandment would focus on legal issues within the community, the third commandment, which focuses directly on

---

[1] See Luke 6:31; 1 John 4:20.

[2] J. Calvin, *Institutes of the Christian Religion*, ed. J. McNeill, 2 vols. (Philadelphia: Westminster, 1975), 1:377.

[3] See J. Calvin, *Commentaries on the Last Books of Moses*, trans. C. Bingham (Grand Rapids: Baker, 1979), 2:419.

how one relates to God (as in the first two commandments), is outside the legal realm. The third commandment is concerned with the proper use of the name of the true God.

The central commandment in terms of elaboration and detail is the fourth, the Sabbath law. The Sabbath is not only the focus of the Ten Commandments; it is also the climax of the creation account (Gen 1:1–2:3) and suggests that creation and the giving of the Ten Commandments are related. The creation of the nation of Israel is placed on a par with the creation of the universe! The concern of God for the creatures He has made begins to be developed in the fourth commandment, where people are directed not to make life too difficult for others. They must give others a weekly day of rest. This concern begins the transition to the section concerned with interpersonal relationships, commandments six through ten.

The fifth commandment, the parental law, completes the transition from the commandments related to how a person responds to God to the more social commandments.[4] The promise of long life for obedience to this command prepares for the protection of life in the sixth commandment. Since the fifth commandment refers to family, it is also related to the seventh commandment, which has to do with the faithfulness of a spouse in the marriage relationship. The eighth commandment moves from taking that which is forbidden—another man's wife—to the concept of stealing in general, the violation of one's property and possessions. This commandment is thus related to the fourth commandment, as it addresses the theft of what man has worked six days a week to obtain. The eighth commandment also prepares us for the tenth commandment on coveting because it brings the issue of the property of another to the foreground.

The ninth commandment covers false accusation and/or false testimony and frequently involves depriving someone of what belongs to him. The placement of this command after ones concerning murder, adultery, and theft may indicate that all these offenses may call for a decision based on a legal trial. As the ninth commandment forbids false testimony against another, which may be tantamount

---

[4] The fourth and fifth commandments are related by serving as transitional commandments, as well as being the only two stated positively.

to character assassination, it is related to the sixth commandment, against murder.

In contrast with commandments that address outward acts, the tenth commandment uniquely addresses thoughts and desires. It may be at the root of all the other commandments.

Medieval Jewish commentator Nahmanides argued that the commandments are listed in decreasing order of severity: idolatry, murder, adultery, stealing, bearing false witness, and coveting, for one who merely covets does not harm his fellow.[5] The Ten Commandments are introduced by the phrase "I am the Lord your God" and ends with the word "neighbor." Jesus summarized this twofold focus in reference to the two great commandments, to love the Lord your God (Deut 6:5=Matt 22:37) and to love your neighbor as yourself (Lev 19:18=Mark 12:31).[6]

Mosaic Covenant and the Plan of God

The Ten Commandments are part of the Mosaic or Sinaitic covenant. This covenant established by God through the instrumentality of Moses was inaugurated on Mount Sinai and was based on the foundational covenant established earlier with Abraham.[7] The dependence of the Mosaic covenant on the Abrahamic covenant can be illustrated by comparing their respective blessings. The blessings of the Mosaic covenant (see Lev 26; Deut 6–11;28) restate the earlier promises made to the patriarchs, but now to the whole nation. Compare the blessings first given to Abraham with the later promises made to the nation of Israel:

1. God will bless them (Lev 26:4–12; Deut 7:13–15; 28:3–12; see Gen 12:2b).
2. God will multiply them (Lev 26:9; Deut 6:3; 28:11; see Gen 12:2a; 17:2,6).

---

[5] M. Carasik, מקראות גדולות. *The Commentators' Bible: The JPS Miqráot Gedolot. Exodus* (Philadelphia: Jewish Publication Society, 2005), 163.

[6] See M. Klopfenstein, *Die Lüge nach dem Alten Testament* (Zürich Frankfurt: Gotthelf-Verlag, 1964), 322.

[7] The theophany on Mount Sinai resembled the ratification of the Abrahamic covenant in Gen 15 as the smoke from Mount Sinai (Exod 19:18; 20:18) recalls Gen 15:17.

3. God will give them the land (Deut 6:3; 8:1; 9:4; 28:11; see Gen 12:1; 17:8).
4. God will make them a great nation (Deut 7:14; 28:1; see Gen 12:2a).
5. God will be their God, and they will be His people (Lev 26:11–12; Deut 7:6–10; 28:9–10; see Gen 17:1,7).

The Abrahamic covenant is the fundamental relationship. The Mosaic covenant came later and was dependent on the Abrahamic covenant as its foundation.

As the Abrahamic covenant was established with the patriarchs Abraham, Isaac, and Jacob as individuals, the Mosaic covenant was established with their descendants as a nation, distinguishing Israel from all the other nations. In addition, the Mosaic covenant offered a more extensive revelation of the will of God in the giving of the law and in doing so provided the means for blessing an entire nation. Through this nation that had graciously been entrusted with God's law, all the peoples on the earth would also be blessed.[8] Israel's task as a chosen and holy nation was to be a light to the Gentiles. The Ten Commandments were a means toward that end.

While the purpose of a covenant was to create new relationships, the purpose of law was to regulate a newly established relationship. Exodus 19 presents the historical context for the inauguration of the Mosaic covenant. In Exod 20 and following the laws of the Mosaic covenant are presented. Obedience to the law was not to be the means to a relationship with God but was the desired response to that relationship. It was the great deliverance of the exodus that served as the foundation for the Lord's right to expect obedience to His commands. Similarly, in the New Testament, the responsibilities of Christians are based on redemption provided by Christ's atonement (1 Cor 6:20).

While the Mosaic law was not explicitly addressed to the Gentiles, that does not mean it is irrelevant to them. Rather, the law was given to Israel to enable Israel to live as a model, as a light and a witness to the nations. So within the Old Testament itself, there is awareness that the law given to the children of Israel as God's unique people has

---

[8] C. Blaising and D. Bock, *Progressive Dispensationalism* (Wheaton, IL: Victor Books, 1993), 151.

a wider relevance for the rest of humanity (Deut 4:5–8). This realization attests to the universal validity of the biblical laws.[9] The laws of the Mosaic covenant assume and amplify the Abrahamic covenant (Exod 2:23–25; 3:6–8; Deut 7:7–8; Rom 4; Gal 3), which declares God's intention not only to bless Israel but to bless the whole world through her mediatory role. Further insight into the role of the law in the life of Israel may be found in the fact that in the future work of God on Israel's behalf, the prophets saw the vital role the law would play in her spiritual life and her blessing from God (Isa 2:3; Jer 31:31–37; Ezek 36:26–32).

Israel and the Law

God chose the nation of Israel as His special people not only to have a relationship with Him but, as noted above, to mediate blessing for the world (Gen 12:3). Yet in order to have a relationship with the holy God and in order for this holy God to reside in their midst, it was absolutely necessary that the nation of Israel must exhibit holiness; they must be a separate and distinct people. This essential need for purity and holiness was the rationale for the sacrificial system, instituted to make it possible for the Israelites to receive forgiveness of sins and thereby exhibit holiness. The precepts and meanings of sacrifices were part of the instruction of the law. The law legislated the means for atonement as well as the admonitions and prohibitions Israel had to obey to live a life pleasing to God. In a word the revealed law was at the heart of what it meant for Israel to be holy. The laws provided the instruction defining what living a holy life before a holy God entailed (Lev 11:44–47; 20:22–26; Exod 22:31[30]; Deut 14:21). By obeying this written instruction, Israel was ensured of living a holy life (Lev 19:2–37; 20:7–27; Num 15:39–41). The law of Moses was the will of God for those whom God had graciously redeemed. It was the practical guide for the man who was grateful for God's deliverance and who had as his highest ambition adherence to the wishes and plans of God. The "Law was given as the means of binding Israel to

---

[9] C. Wright, *Old Testament Ethics for the People of God* (Downers Grove, IL: InterVarsity, 2004), 320–21.

its God."[10] The holiness of the law may also be seen from the fact that the Ten Commandments were placed in the ark, the most holy place in the tabernacle. In short, the law was not a burden or yoke for the people of God in the Old Testament but was rather one of the greatest blessings that God had given to them (Deut 4:7–8; Ps 147:19–20; Rom 9:4–5).[11]

Consequently this law that God had graciously revealed to Moses was not the means whereby the Israelites were declared righteous before God. On the contrary, the historical context of these laws is the redemption from Egypt and God's election of Israel as His people. The law was given in the context of grace. "In Israel's faith, the good news of what God has done precedes the exposition of what the people must do."[12] Thus salvation by grace through faith is the message of the Bible from Genesis to Revelation. It is grounded in the Old Testament (Gen 15:6; Neh 9:8; Ps 106:12–31; Isa 45:25; 54:17; Mic 6:6–8; Hab 2:4) and is affirmed and reiterated in rabbinic Judaism.[13] The rabbis encouraged the people to obey the commandments because they loved God.[14] Works have never been the instrument of salvation; they are the evidence of salvation. Obedience to the laws should be placed in the domain of sanctification rather than justification wherein by adherence to these laws a social distinction was maintained between the Israelites and the rest of the world.

---

[10] G. Ladd, *A Theology of the New Testament*, rev. ed. (Grand Rapids: Eerdmans, 1993), 540. Or put differently, the law was the means whereby man was joined to God by holiness of life. Calvin, *Institutes of the Christian Religion*, 1:415.

[11] G. Vos, *Biblical Theology* (Grand Rapids: Eerdmans, 1948), 128.

[12] B. W. Anderson, *Understanding the Old Testament*, 4th ed. (Englewood Cliffs: Prentice-Hall, 1986), 535.

[13] This has been the major contribution of E. P. Sanders in his monumental book, *Paul and Palestinian Judaism* (Minneapolis: Fortress, 1977). See also, G. Moore, *Judaism*, 2 vols. (Peabody: Hendrickson, 1997) 2:94–95.

[14] Sanders, *Paul and Palestinian Judaism*, 122. This response of faith would be true of all those believing Israelites in the Old Testament as well as individuals such as Simeon and Anna in the New Testament (Luke 2:25–38). In correcting the long-held view that the Old Testament and rabbinic Judaism was a works-based system, however, Sanders may have overstated his case since there is New Testament evidence of legalistic views among Jews (see D. Carson, *Divine Sovereignty & Human Responsibility* [Atlanta: John Knox, 1981], 86–95; T. Schreiner, *The Law and Its Fulfillment*, [Grand Rapids: Baker, 1993], 93; and J. Meyer, *The End of the Law*, NACBT [Nashville: B&H, 2009], 5).

The Church and the Law

In recent years many articles and books have appeared addressing the use and application of the law of Moses for the Christian life.[15] These treatments discuss the degree to which the particular laws have any relevance for the Christian in the modern world, especially in Western society. More to the point, should a Christian be motivated to read the law to find truth and guidance for his personal life today? The following discussion will address the meaning of the law for the Christian believer today and will proceed with the vitally important question regarding the unity of the Mosaic law.

Is the Law a Monolithic Unity?

For many the most important issue regarding the relevance of the Mosaic law for the contemporary Christian is the issue of the unity of the law.[16] Those under the old covenant viewed the Mosaic law as a complete unity. Or as Jason Meyer has recently stated, "No one living under the law of Moses seriously thought they could pick which parts were binding and which were optional."[17] If the law is a monolithic unity and the Christian is not under the law in any sense (Rom 3:19; 6:14–15; Gal 3:23; 4:5,21; 5:18), there is no need for further discussion. The law as a whole has no authority or relevance for the Christian life. If, on the other hand, we determine that there are distinctions in the law, then the statements made in the New Testament seeming to indicate the law is not binding for the Christian may pertain to certain categories or types of law but not all laws. Thus the law may still have jurisdiction and relevance for the Christian's life.

Scholars who tend to argue that the law has no relevance for the Christian life are prone to suggest that the Mosaic law be viewed as a unified entity and that it has been nullified entirely through the work of Christ. Conversely, scholars who see more of a continuity in God's

[15] For evangelical treatments, see W. Strickland, ed., *Five Views on Law and Gospel* (Grand Rapids: Zondervan, 1993); Schreiner, *The Law and Its Fulfillment*; F. Thielman, *Paul & The Law* (Downers Grove, IL: InterVarsity, 1994), and C. Kruse, *Paul, the Law, and Justification* (Peabody: Hendrickson, 1996).

[16] W. Kaiser Jr., "The Weightier and Lighter Matters of the Law: Moses, Jesus and Paul," in *Current Issues in Biblical and Patristic Interpretation* (Grand Rapids: Eerdmans, 1975), 180.

[17] Meyer, *The End of the Law*, 282.

plan between the Testaments are more apt to see divisions in the law and argue for a greater role of the law in the life of the New Testament Christian. The latter frequently follow the view promoted and popularized by John Calvin dividing the law into the moral, ceremonial, and civil categories.

The Law Is Unified. Proponents of the unity of the law often argue that the Jews regarded the Mosaic law as a unified corpus. Support for this view may be found in the New Testament itself (e.g., Gal 5:3). The fact that the law could be summarized by "Love the Lord your God with all your heart, mind, and strength" (Deut 6:5) and "Love your neighbor as yourself" (Lev 19:18) suggests that there is a certain unity to the entire legal corpus of Mosaic laws. Moreover, the purpose of all the laws was the making of a holy nation (Exod 19:6; Lev 19:2), suggesting a unity of purpose as well. An argument for the unity of the law is perceived in the sense that the whole of the law foreshadowed Christ as it was fulfilled in Him (Luke 24:27).

Distinctions in the Law. And yet, although it is not ostensibly possible to pinpoint specific terminology for neatly dividing the law, it does seem valid to see a diversity within this basic unity. A distinction can be made between what is universal and what uniquely applied to Israel's special circumstance. The same statement by Jesus in Matt 22:37–40 (quoting Deut 6:5 and Lev 19:18), claimed to support the unity of the law, could also suggest that there are distinctions. These summary statement laws, like the Ten Commandments, should be viewed as a special category of moral laws. Jesus did not single out these laws as merely illustrative; nor did He ever claim that all the laws are the same.

Matthew 23 records Jesus' last major controversy with Jewish leaders. In v. 23 Jesus Himself seems to make a distinction about the Old Testament law when He accuses the Pharisees of ignoring the "weightier matters of the law." Gustaf Dalman provided the proper context for understanding this phrase:

> The Rabbis did not differentiate between the smallest and the greatest commandments but rather between "light" (Hb. *kallīn*) and "heavy" (Hb. *ḥamārin*). This distinction between commandments is made only in connexion with "the words of the (Mosaic) law," but not with "the words of the scribes." Moreover, "light" and "heavy" commandments are not those which are in themselves easy

or difficult to keep, but such that cause the keeping of other commandments to be either light (*ḳōl*) or heavy (*ḥōmer*). . . . Among such commandments the freeing of the mother bird (Deut 22:6) is considered to be the "lightest" of all; the "heaviest" of all—the honouring of father and mother (Exod 20:12); in the law the same great reward is promised for each of these. . . . Our Lord's "least" is of the category of these "lightest" commandments of the Rabbis.[18]

Thus, Jesus was in harmony with the Jewish rabbis of His time in distinguishing the weightier and lighter laws. In Matt 23:23 the weightier law is one of the Ten Commandments: the honoring of parents. The Old Testament itself seems to make distinctions between different types of laws, as illustrated by prophetic discussions of sacrifice. The prophets argued that the offering of sacrifices, as important as they were to maintain Israel's spiritual and national life, were not as important as personal obedience and a commitment to keep the law. The prescriptions of sacrifice, given in the law, were ineffective if the worshipper did not bring with his offering a heartfelt love for God (Deut 6:5) and a desire to live a life dedicated to obedience (1 Sam 13:15). Walter Kaiser has listed the passages that require a distinction between various categories of the law and give priority for obedience to the moral laws:

> Assigning priority to the moral aspect of the law over both its civil and ceremonial aspects can be observed in a plethora of passages found in the prophets. One need only consult such texts as 1 Samuel 15:22–23; Isaiah 1:11–17; Jeremiah 7:21–23; Micah 6:8; as well as texts in the Psalter such as Psalms 51:16–17. The moral law of God took precedence over the civil and ceremonial laws in that it was based on the character of God. The civil and ceremonial laws functioned only as further illustrations of the moral law. That is why holiness and love could serve as veritable summaries of all that the law demanded.[19]

[18] G. Dalman, *Jesus—Jeshua: Studies in the Gospels*, trans. by P. Levertoff (London: SPCK, 1929), 64–65. The command to honor parents because it was a weightier commandment can also be found in rabbinic literature (Moore, *Judaism* 2:5–6, 9, 131). The rabbis used other expressions as well to indicate what appears to be a hierarchy in the law. They employed in addition to qualifications such as "grave" and "light" such qualified statements like the "essentials of the law" (Moore, *Judaism*, 2:84nn3,93). In this vein, Rabbi Akiba (d. AD 135) labeled Lev 19:18, "You shall love your neighbor as yourself" as the most comprehensive law (Moore, *Judaism*, 2:85).

[19] "The Law as God's Guidance for the Promotion of Holiness," in Strickland, *Five Views on Law and Gospel*, 189–90. As E. Lucas concluded in analyzing the prophetic teaching of Amos 5:25 and Jer 7:21–23, "God also gave the moral law. Failure to obey the moral law breaks the covenant and renders the offering of material sacrifices null and void as an act of worship of Yahweh" ("Sacrifice in the Prophets," in *Sacrifice in the Bible* (ed. R. T. Beckwith and M. J. Selman [Grand Rapids: Eerdmans, 1995], 63).

But it was not just the prophets who were making this distinction. The Jewish rabbis were in complete agreement. As esteemed Jewish scholar C. G. Montefiore stated:

> The Rabbis, we may say, were familiar with the distinction between ceremonial and moral commands, and on the whole they regarded the "moral" as more important and more fundamental than the "ceremonial." In this respect they would, to a considerable extent, have agreed with Jesus. . . . Again, there was some tendency to distinguish "heavy" and "light" commands according to certain punishments or threats which happen to be attached to their infractions in the Codes. Nevertheless, on the whole, the "heavy" commands are the moral commands. The "heaviest" (apart from circumcision) are commands such as the prohibition of unchastity, idolatry or murder, the honouring of parents, the Sanctification of the Name. The distinction between "light" and "heavy" commands was well known, and is constantly mentioned and discussed.[20]

Moreover, those who may be prone to argue that the entire law has no relevance for the Christian life should be reminded that in the Law (Pentateuch) we find the promises made to the patriarchs. Paul in fact appealed to the example of Abraham from the book of Genesis, the first book of the Law, to support the doctrine of justification by faith (Rom 4; Gal 3).[21] But whether we concede and affirm that the Jews viewed the law as unified (a difficult proposition in light of the discussion above) or we continue to believe that the Old Testament laws may be categorized, all must agree that a shift has occurred in salvation history that touches on the relevance of the application of the law.

Indeed, while it may not be clear to everyone that divisions are to be made in the law, it is equally unclear from the Old Testament perspective that the ministry of the Messiah was to be accomplished in two separate advents—and separated by at least 2,000 years! The function of the law has changed with the inauguration of the Messianic age (1 Cor 10:11) in ways that might not have been completely

---

[20] C. G. Montefiore, *Rabbinic Literature and Gospel Teachings* (New York: KTAV, 1970), 316–17.

[21] The reader will note the interchange between referring to the law as legal statutes and commands as opposed to the law as a body of literature, the Torah or Pentateuch. The interchange is not meant to cause confusion, but it illustrates this lack of distinction in discussions about the unity of the law/Law. Those who argue for the unity of the law may have confused the unity of the Pentateuch as a body of literature with the various collections of laws in the Pentateuch. This lack of clarification appears to also exist in J. Sailhamer's new work, *The Meaning of the Pentateuch* (Downers Grove, IL: InterVarsity, 2009).

clear from the Jewish perspective developed from the Old Testament.[22] This change is represented in the words of Christ wherein He claimed that in His coming the law had been fulfilled (Matt 5:17).

The moral law frequently is associated with the Ten Commandments as well as other ethical principles that are not fulfilled in Christ. For example, nine of the Ten Commandments are repeated in the New Testament, strongly suggesting the ongoing applicability of the Old Testament law in the church age.[23] Moral laws are understood to have permanent validity. The ceremonial law includes various regulations for the Israelites such as sacrifices, feast days, dietary laws, the priesthood, and temple worship. The ceremonial laws symbolize and foreshadow the nature of Christ's redemptive work on the cross. They were a shadow of things to come (Rom 3:25; Col 2:17; 1 Pet 2:5; Heb 4:14–16; 9:14). The civil laws pertain to those laws given to Israel by which they are to be governed as a nation.[24]

Followers of John Calvin often promote a threefold use of the Mosaic law. This includes first of all the political (or civil) use of the law. According to this purpose of the law, the law functions as a restraint on sin in society. The second use of the law is the pedagogical use, where the law has the function of bringing human beings under the conviction of sin. The law serves to show a person his need for Christ as the only basis for salvation. Finally, the third use of the law is called the normative use of the law, where the law serves as a standard or

---

[22] And as the coming of the Messiah in two advents is not made clear until the revelation of the New Testament, the same may be said for the division of the law into different categories.

[23] Only the fourth commandment regarding the observance of the Sabbath is not repeated in the New Testament. This should not surprise us given the special and distinctive role the Sabbath played in the Old Testament period as a covenant sign for the nation of Israel (Exod 31:12–17). The covenant sign lasted only as long as the covenant. It is representative of ceremonial law and was part of the shadow of things to come (Rom 14:5–6; Gal 4:10–11; Col 2:14–17). It does have a function for the church as it typifies a believer's salvation (Heb 4:9) and serves as a principle of setting aside a day a week for rest (Matt 12:8; Mark 12:27) (see H. Dressler, "The Sabbath in the Old Testament," in *From Sabbath to Lord's Day*, ed. D. Carson [Grand Rapids: Zondervan, 1982], 34). The church fathers were practically unanimous in rejecting the literal observance of the Sabbath for the Christian church (S. Bacciocchi, *From Sabbath to Sunday: A Historical Investigation of the Rise of Sunday Observance in Early Christianity* [Rome: The Pontifical Gregorian University Press, 1977], 213–14).

[24] See, e.g., R. L. Harris, *Man—God's Eternal Creation* (Chicago: Moody, 1971), 144–45, and V. Poythress, *The Shadow of Christ in the Law of Moses* (Brentwood, TN: Wolgemuth & Hyatt, 1991), 99.

rule of conduct for the Christian believer, revealing to him his Christian duties and responsibilities.[25]

Civil Laws and the Christian

Virtually all Christians would agree that the ceremonial laws of the Old Testament have been fulfilled in Christ and consequently have a different application in the church age. No one comes to church with an unblemished sacrificial animal as an offering to God. We are not under this ceremonial law, and the book of Hebrews goes to great lengths to prove the point that the sacrificial system has been fulfilled in Christ in His sacrifice once for all (Heb 9:26).

Among those who find justification for a threefold division of the law, there is some debate, however, about the role and function of the civil laws for the Christian today. The civil Mosaic laws, it is argued, are not fulfilled in the New Testament like the ceremonial laws. And since their is nothing about these laws being superseded or suspended in the New Testament, we should assume that they have continuing validity in matters of state.

The view that the Old Testament civil laws are somehow normative has several difficulties, although faithful believers including the Puritans have maintained a similar position about the role of the Bible in governing the state. Vern Poythress insightfully points out one particular difficulty in the application of Old Testament civil laws in contemporary society, which suggests that the laws were restricted to Israel's unique experience before the coming of Christ:

> Consider now some alternatives for modern society. We could specify the death penalty for all adultery. But how do we account for the fact that intercourse between a married man and a prostitute received no penalty in Mosaic law or in the Old Testament as a whole, and that intercourse between a married man and a virgin had a different solution?[26]

Having said all this, however, a case could still be made in principle for the application of the civil laws without bringing them over wholesale as authoritatively definitive for the governing of the contemporary state. For example, principles regarding the penal code in

---

[25] See L. Berkhof, *Systematic Theology* (Grand Rapids: Eerdmans, 1939), 614–15.

[26] Poythress, *The Shadow of the Cross*, 220.

the Old Testament, such as quick punishment for offenses, appear to be valid for application (Eccl 8:11). As Gordon Wenham has astutely observed:

> Instead of distinguishing between moral and civil laws, it would be better to say that some injunctions are broad and generally applicable to most societies, while others are more specific and directed at the particular social problems of ancient Israel. . . . The principles underlying the OT are valid and authoritative for the Christian, but the particular applications found in the OT may not be. The moral principles are the same today, but insofar as our situation often differs from the OT setting, the application of the principles in our society may well be different too.[27]

The division of law as well as the specific application of laws to Israel should thus not be overplayed, or else we miss the meaning the ceremonial and civil laws do have for the Christian. These laws are part of the Mosaic law within the Christian canon of Scripture. There is a moral dimension to all laws at least at the level of principle, which requires a teaching and reading of laws no longer directly binding on the Christian.[28] The status of the law has changed in that it pointed to Christ and has been fulfilled in him. It has been superseded or transformed but has not been abrogated.[29]

The New Testament and the Law

Introduction

The New Testament writers consistently chose the Greek term *nomos* to translate the Hebrew *tôrâ*, "law." *Nomos* occurs 195 times in the New Testament, with 121 of these usages occurring in Paul's letters. By the time of the postexilic period and extending into rabbinic writings and the New Testament, the term was normally used to refer to the Pentateuch, the Hebrew *tôrâ*.[30] And yet *nomos* has a range of meaning in the New Testament as it did in Classical Greek. While it

[27] G. Wenham, *The Book of Leviticus*, NICOT (Grand Rapids: Eerdmans, 1979), 35.

[28] C. Wright, "Ethics," *NIDOTTE* 4:586; Similarly, Sailhamer suggests that Old Testament laws should be read in the same way that we find biblical principles in Wisdom literature (*The Meaning of the Pentateuch*, 526).

[29] Poythress, *The Shadow of the Cross*, 285.

[30] W. Gutbrod, "νόμος," *TDNT* 4:1046, 1054, 1059.

most often refers to the Pentateuch, both John and the apostle Paul use the term to refer to the complete revelation of God in the Old Testament (John 10:34; 12:34; 15:25; 1 Cor 14:21). This use of the term was probably due to the pride of place the Mosaic law occupied in the Old Testament and is evident in Palestinian Judaism of the first century AD.[31] *Nomos* might also be used to refer to human law (Rom 7:2–4) or to a principle, whether of faith (Rom 3:27), sin (Rom 7:25), or the spirit of life (Rom 8:2).

Jesus and the Law

The influence of the Mosaic law permeated the Jewish culture of the first century, when God became man and took on flesh. Paul in fact encapsulated an unavoidable aspect of Jesus' life even at his birth— He was "born under the law" (Gal 4:4).

The law played a crucial role in the life and ministry of Christ, as we see Jesus being frequently challenged on issues of law by Jewish religious leaders. He declared that He did not come to abolish the law or the prophets; rather, He came to fulfill them (Matt 5:17). In those passages where Jesus appears to be at odds with the law, His statements are not challenges to the law at all but rather His responses to the oral law of the Pharisees, the tradition of men (Mark 7:8). On those occasions when Jesus seems critical of the law, it is not the law He critiques but the incorrect interpretation or application of the laws by Jewish leaders (Matt 9:13; 12:7; 23:23). [32] He stands with the Old Testament prophets in condemning illicit practices without criticizing the law itself (Isa 1:11–18; Jer 7:21–24; Hos 6:6; Amos 5:21–24; Mic 6:6–8).[33]

Jesus gave the true interpretation of the law of God in the Sermon on the Mount. For example, Jesus stated *explicitly* what was contained *implicitly* in the seventh commandment.[34] Jesus said: "You have heard it said, Do not commit adultery. But I tell you, everyone who looks

---

[31] See S. Sandmel, *The Genius of Paul: A Study in History* (Philadelphia: Fortress, 1979), 47; Moore, *Judaism*, 1:263.

[32] See Calvin, *Institutes* 1:374.

[33] D. Peterson, *Engaging with God* (Grand Rapids: Eerdmans, 1992), 113.

[34] R. Barcellos, *In Defense of the Decalogue: A Critique of New Covenant Theology* (Enumclaw, WA: WinePress, 2001), 74.

at a woman to lust for her has already committed adultery with her in his heart" (Matt 5:27–28). Jesus' explanation of adultery included not just the physical act but also the desire to have illicit sexual relations. Jesus interpreted the seventh commandment in light of the tenth. Jesus respected the law, while occasionally expanding upon it or sharpening its intention.

Jesus did not detract, devalue, or deny the Mosaic law.[35] In the most severe terms, He sternly warned anyone who would dare to do so (Matt 5:19). Jesus regarded the Decalogue as the revealed will of God and in this respect did not differ from the Judaism of His age. For Jesus the Messiah, the law of Sinai was still unquestionably the will of God for Israel and for His disciples.[36] He taught that the whole Old Testament is authoritative between the two advents of Christ, that is, until heaven and earth pass away (Matt 5:17–20).[37] The Old Testament law pointed toward Jesus Christ (Rom 8:3; 10:4; Gal 3:24) and was only properly revealed in Him.[38]

Paul and the Law

In the various discussions about the law in the New Testament, invariably the writings of Paul come to the forefront. However, Paul's writings are cited to support what appear to be various, even contradictory, positions. Passages such as Rom 6:14; 7:4; 2 Cor 3:11; Gal 3:19–26; 4:1–5; Eph 2:15; Col 2:14 have been cited to suggest Paul viewed the law as obsolete for the Christian. On the other hand, Rom 3:31; 7:12–14; Eph 6:2 have been used to teach the ongoing relevance of the law for the Christian today.

Paul's sometimes apparently negative criticisms of the law should be understood in the same way the railings of Jesus and the prophets were viewed: Paul was condemning a misuse of the law and not the law itself, which he calls holy, just, and good (Rom 7:12).[39] With the

---

[35] W. Kaiser Jr., "Response to Douglas Moo," in Strickland, *Five Views on Law and Gospel*, 399.

[36] B. Childs, *The Book of Exodus: A Critical-Theological Commentary* (Louisville: Westminster John Knox, 1974), 429–30.

[37] Barcellos, *In Defense of the Decalogue*, 62–63.

[38] G. von Rad, *Old Testament Theology*, 2 vols., trans. D. Stalker (New York: Harper & Row, 1962, 1965), 2:408.

[39] See J. Dunn, *Parting of the Ways: Between Christianity and Judaism and Their Significance for*

coming of Christ and the creation of the new man, there has been a shift in the working of God's kingdom program. This shift is most notable in the shift from the Mosaic covenant to the inauguration of the new covenant ratified by the blood of the sacrificial victim, Jesus Christ.

Paul declared that the Mosaic covenant and the Mosaic law belonged to the old age that is to be contrasted with the newly inaugurated eschatological age. In the old covenant God demanded obedience to the covenantal laws but did not provide Israel with the means or ability to carry out these commands, to receive the law in their hearts. The primary difference between the old covenant and the new is that in the new covenant God will deal with people in a completely new way, turning them to Himself. This is accomplished by the presence and working of the Holy Spirit (Ezek 36:27). Under the new covenant the Spirit of God removes the heart of stone and provides His people with a new heart that is predisposed to obedience (Jer 31:33–34). The law as "script" or letter lacked the power to effect the obedience it demanded. It could not affect the heart change the law called for.[40]

The new man of the new covenant consisted of both Jew and Gentile, one in Christ (Eph 2:15). Thus with the coming of Christ, those Old Testament laws that had earlier served as a badge for the nation of Israel and as a boundary to keep her distinct and separate from the world, were no longer in force (Eph 2:14–15). These laws, particularly Sabbath, circumcision, and food laws (see Mark 7:19), had served their purpose and were completed or fulfilled in Christ (Eph 2:15; Col 2:16–17).[41] A change in the administration of God's redemptive plan has taken place, and believers are no longer under the law; they are no longer under the religious system determined by the law but under the better promises of the new covenant (Gal 5:18; Rom 14:14).[42] But,

---

the Character of Christianity (London: SCM, 1991), 137–38.

[40] See Meyer, The End of the Law, 6, 37–38, 48, 58, 60, 74, 84, 110, 154, 195, 228, 268, 277; Sailhamer, The Meaning of the Pentateuch, 562.

[41] See especially J. Dunn, Jesus, Paul, and the Law (Westminster: John Knox, 1990), 200, 250.

[42] G. Bahnsen, "The Theonomic Reformed Approach to Law and Gospel," in Strickland, Five Views on Law and Gospel, 108.

as part of Holy Scripture, the law still has a function in the Christian life.

In 1 Tim 1:8–11, Paul referred to the Ten Commandments as the God-given ethical norm for the behavior of all men. Ephesians 6:2 is especially telling as Paul admonishes the Ephesian church not on his apostolic authority but on the authority of the Mosaic law.[43] Concerning Eph 6:2, B. B. Warfield wrote, "The acknowledged authority of the fifth commandment as such in the Christian Church is simply taken for granted."[44]

Romans 7:7 and 13:9 also speak of the continuing role of the Ten Commandments in the Christian life. As Barcellos has stated: "The Law of Moses no longer functions *as it once used to*; but this is not to say that it no longer functions. . . . The New Testament views the Old Covenant as a permanent revelation of binding moral principle" (see Matt 5:17–18; Rom 3:19–20,31; 7:12,14; 13:8–10; 1 Cor 9:9–10, and the all-inclusive 2 Tim 3:16).[45]

The New Testament and the Ten Commandments

In discussing the Old Testament law or any other portion of the Old Testament, it is critical to begin by recalling Paul's crucial claim that all Scripture is inspired (lit., "God-breathed"; 2 Tim 3:16). Since not all the books of the New Testament had been written when Paul made this claim, this declaration would appear to be clearly directed to the contents of the Old Testament. Added to this statement on the rightful application of the Old Testament to the Christian life is the unqualified recognized authority of the Old Testament by the New Testament writers. The New Testament writers did not refer to "the Old Testament" but to "Scripture." With regard to the special relevance of the Ten Commandments to the early church, Israeli scholar David Flusser stated, "Included in the legacy of Christianity from Judaism is a high regard for the Ten Commandments. Indeed, from the

---

[43] See Poythress, *The Shadow of Christ in the Law of Moses*, 323. For non-Pauline passages that indicate the law is still authoritative, see Jas 1:25; 2:8,12.

[44] B. B. Warfield, *Selected Shorter Writings of Benjamin B. Warfield* (Nutley, NJ: P&R, 1970), 1:322.

[45] Barcellos, *In Defense of the Decalogue*, 68 (italics his).

time of the earliest Fathers of the Church, Christians assigned an even more exalted position to the Decalogue than Judaism did."[46]

Indeed, the individual precepts of the Ten Commandments are more frequently cited in the New Testament than they are in the Old Testament even though the Old Testament is four times as long. The Ten Commandments are featured in Jesus' Sermon on the Mount (Matt 5:21–37) and highlighted in the call of the rich young man (Matt 19:16–30; Mark 10:17–31; Luke 18:18–30). Individual commandments are also cited in the epistolary literature (Rom 8:7–13; 13:8–10; Eph 6:1–4; Jas 2:8–13).[47]

The Ten Commandments and Moral Law

The Ten Commandments are frequently associated with the moral law. The repetition of the Ten Commandments in the New Testament strongly suggests the contemporary relevance of these laws in the church age.[48] Moral laws like the Ten Commandments are understood to have permanent validity. The ceremonial law is distinct from the moral law in that it includes regulations for the maintenance of Israel's unique system of worship. The ceremonial laws foreshadow Christ's redemptive work on the cross. The civil laws regulate the social life of Israel as a nationally governed body. But the moral law is distinctive in the New Testament. As an indication of the superior nature of the moral law, Jesus accuses the Pharisees of ignoring "the more important matters of the law" (Matt 23:23). In this particular case the weightier or more important law is one of the Ten Commandments, the honoring of parents.[49]

---

[46] D. Flusser, "The Ten Commandments and the New Testament," in *The Ten Commandments in History and Tradition*, ed. B. Z. Segal (Jerusalem: Magnes, 1990), 219. Moreover, when the New Testament speaks of the sins of murder and adultery, it assumes the reader knows exactly what the nature of these offenses are. They are actually defined in the Old Testament, and the New Testament writers assume we know their basic meanings, and so they are not given any further definition or qualification.

[47] R. Collins, "Ten Commandments," *ABD* 6:386.

[48] Only the Sabbath law is not repeated in the New Testament. The Sabbath law is unique among the Ten Commandments as it uniquely served as the sign of the Mosaic covenant (Exod 31:12–17).

[49] The command to honor parents because it was a weightier commandment can be found in rabbinic literature. See Moore, *Judaism*, 2:5–6, 9, 131.

Justin Martyr (ca. 100–165) and Origen (ca. 185–254) recognized the distinctions between the moral and ceremonial laws.[50] Saint Augustine also recognized this distinction and considered the Decalogue to be a divine expression of the moral law, valid for Jews and Christians alike.[51] Thomas Aquinas distinguished moral, ceremonial, and judicial precepts of the law. Aquinas argued that the moral precepts were dictated by the natural law, the ceremonial precepts were determinations of the divine worship, and the judicial precepts were determinations of the justice to be maintained among men.[52] John Calvin followed Aquinas in dividing the Mosaic legislation into moral, ceremonial, and judicial laws. He believed this moral law was summarized in the Ten Commandments.[53] The entire law applies to the church but in various ways and differently than it applied to Israel. The status of the law has changed in that it pointed to Christ and has been fulfilled in Him.

Moral Law and the Christian

While the law reveals God's character, it also demands conformity to that character. The believers' response to obey the law and demonstrate holiness is a response of love that is in no way foreign to the demands of the law. Jesus said this was the essence of the law, and the New Testament focus on love as a summation of the law is in harmony with the moral theme of the Old Testament: to love God with one's entire being (Deut 6:5). For us, who like Abraham are not under the law (Rom 4; Gal 3), the natural outcome of faith should be obedience to the law (Gen 26:5; Rom 8:4).

Beginning in the second century AD, the Ten Commandments were seen to be critical for the ethical stance of the Christian church.

---

[50] H. Cunningham, "God's Law, 'General Equity' and the Westminster Confession of Faith," *TB* 58,2 (2007): 292.

[51] See M. Butler, "Must We Teach Morality According to the Decalogue?" *Worship* 37,5 (1963): 297–98.

[52] Cunningham, "God's Law, 'General Equity' and the Westminster Confession of Faith," 292.

[53] See Calvin, *Institutes of the Christian Religion,* ed. J. McNeill, 2 vols. (Philadelphia: Westminster, 1960), 1:368 [*Institutes* 2.8.1]; L. Walker, "The Abiding Value of Biblical Law," in *The Christian and American Law: Christianity's Impact on America's Founding Documents and Future Direction* (Grand Rapids: Kregel, 1998), 213.

This is evident in such works as *De Doctrina Apostolorum*, the *Didache* (2:2–3), and *The Shepherd of Hermas*. It is also evident in the writings of Chrysostom, Augustine, Aquinas, and the Reformers, particularly Luther and Calvin.[54] Calvin understood the most important role of the law as instruction for the Christian life.[55] Similarly, Luther said, "Apart from these Ten Commandments no deed, no conduct can be good or pleasing to God."[56]

The Moral Law and the Natural Law

According to John Van Engen, natural law is "a moral order divinely implanted in humankind and accessible to all persons through human reason."[57] From this definition we discover that natural law is a product of God's creation that was given to every human being. Being aware of natural law is a derivative of being human. Because natural law is part of a moral order recognized by humans, it is related to being in the image of God (Gen 1:26–27). Human beings, who bear God's image more than all creation, are most like the Creator, who is a moral being. Human beings *are* the image of God (1 Cor 11:7; Jas 3:9). Scripture's teaching that sinful human beings continue to be image bearers indicates not only that there is still a natural law in the fallen world but that human beings still have some knowledge of it.[58] Or as stated by D. VanDrunen:

> The image of God carried along with it a natural law, a law inherent to human nature and directing human beings to fulfill their royal commission in righteousness and holiness. . . . Natural law cannot be understood properly apart from the reality of God's creating this world in the way he did and in particular his creating man in his own image. Natural law reflects who God is and how he has related to the world.[59]

---

[54] See Childs, *The Book of Exodus*, 432–33; Walker, "The Abiding Value of Biblical Law," 211; J. Lienhard, ed., *Exodus, Leviticus, Numbers, Deuteronomy*, ACCS (Downers Grove, IL: InterVarsity, 2001), 106.

[55] See Wright, *Old Testament Ethics for the People of God*, 393.

[56] D. Wright, "The Ethical Use of the Old Testament in Luther and Calvin: A Comparison," *SJT* 36 (1983): 472.

[57] J. Van Engen, "Natural Law," *EDT* (2001), 814.

[58] That knowledge, or alternatively their consciences, can be distorted by sin (1 Cor 8:7,10; 10:29; 1 Tim 4:2; Titus 1:15).

[59] D. VanDrunen, *A Biblical Case for Natural Law* (Grand Rapids: Acton Institute, n.d.), 14.

According to Rom 1:18–32, "God can judge all people and not just those with access to biblical revelation, because God's general revelation in nature confronts every person."[60]

Thus natural law is not grounded in redemption but in the reality of creation in God's image. Evidence of the universal nature of natural law stamped on human nature can be seen from the fact that many of the moral laws of the Bible are attested in the pagan law codes of the ancient Near East. Even in the Bible itself we find a moral code or a natural law assumed prior to the giving of the pertinent revelation (Gen 12:19; 20:3–7; 26:8–11). Humans created in the image of God along with this common concomitant moral standard are evidence of God's creation and His common grace over all creation.

Many have found scriptural evidence of the existence of natural law in Rom 2:14–15:

> So, when Gentiles, who do not have the law, instinctively do what the law demands, they are a law to themselves even though they do not have the law. They show that the work of the law is written on their hearts. Their consciences testify in support of this, and their competing thoughts either accuse or excuse them.

This natural law of the conscience is in some way comparable to the Mosaic law, as those without law instinctively do what the law demands. As a confirmation of the existence of this moral law, we need not look further than the book of Genesis, which records the biblical history prior to the giving of the Ten Commandments on Mount Sinai. In the pre-Sinai record of biblical events, all Ten Commandments are recognized as reflecting appropriate ethical positions.[61] Thus it is no surprise that Abraham can be presented as one who is obedient to the law (Gen 26:5). The law was "in principle available to and observed by Abraham."[62]

Many have concluded that what the Gentiles possess in natural law is a basic understanding of the Ten Commandments, although maybe

---

[60] Ibid., 17. See also R. A. Mohler Jr., *Words from the Fire* (Chicago: Moody, 2009), 35.

[61] See W. Kaiser Jr., *Toward Old Testament Ethics* (Grand Rapids: Zondervan, 1983), 82. This is also the thrust of Harvard University Law professor Alan Durchowitz's book, *The Genesis of Justice* (New York: Warner Books, 2000).

[62] Wright, *Old Testament Ethics for the People of God*, 283n2.

not in the identical form in which they appear in the Decalogue.[63] Yet passages such as Rom 1 indicate that those without the law still have a rather comprehensive knowledge of moral sins from general revelation and that these sins will result in God's judgment. They are accountable to God even without the written communication of the Mosaic laws. "People are 'laws unto themselves' because their own nature declares it."[64]

Many of the church fathers such as Justin, Irenaeus, Tertullian, and Aquinas took the position that moral concepts in the Bible reflect and are dictated by natural law.[65] Aquinas taught that "'eternal law' by which God established all things became when impressed upon humans and their nature a 'natural law.'"[66] Reformers such as Calvin,[67] Vermigli, Zanchi, Althusius, and Turretin, and later scholars such as John Locke and Charles Hodge all argued for understanding natural law as the preferred system of ethics.[68]

Although Luther generally took the approach that the Old Testament law was for Israel and not the church, his understanding of natural law allowed him to develop a system of ethics based on the Ten Commandments. The Ten Commandments as natural law were not the laws of Moses but divine laws given by God. They ceased to be Moses' law but go back to the creation itself. As such they were not limited to Israel or the Jewish people but had universal application.[69]

The understanding of the moral law of the Ten Commandments as natural law renders the Ten Commandments universally applicable as an ethical guide for all generations. This would include the

---

[63] See Barcellos, *In Defense of the Decalogue*, 81.

[64] VanDrunen, *A Biblical Case for Natural Law*, 19.

[65] See Childs, *The Book of Exodus*, 432–33; Cunningham, "God's Law, 'General Equity' and the Westminster Confession of Faith," 292.

[66] Van Engen, "Natural Law," 815.

[67] Calvin said, however, that the written law was given to make clear what might be obscure in natural law. See Calvin, *Institutes*, 1:368.

[68] See S. Grabill, *Rediscovering the Natural Law in Reformed Theological Ethics* (Grand Rapids: Eerdmans, 2006), 53, 185; Walker, "The Abiding Value of Biblical Law," 214. C. Wright does not believe that the continuity of ethical standards between the Testaments should be sought in a universal moral law, but rather it stems from the continuity of the relationship between God and Israel and God and His church (*Old Testament Ethics for the People of God*, 317).

[69] See D. Wright, "The Ethical Use of the Old Testament in Luther and Calvin: A Comparison," 470. See also Childs, *The Book of Exodus*, 433.

Sabbath law, the only commandment not repeated in the New Testament. While the ceremonial aspects of the Sabbath were typologically fulfilled in Christ, the setting aside of one day a week for public worship and physical rest should be considered universal and in effect for all periods and all times. Calvin believed the fourth commandment's provision of a day of public worship and physical rest from normal labor applies to every age.[70]

The Ten Commandments are the ethical guidelines of the human conscience. As Jerry Vines has succinctly stated, "Down inside, mankind has an understanding that the Ten Commandments are not obsolete, but rather are absolute."[71]

Ceremonial and civil laws are not without meaning for the Christian. These are part of the Mosaic law within the Christian canon of Scripture. There is still a moral dimension to them that makes them relevant to the modern Christian.[72] "To the degree that the civil and ceremonial laws illustrate the principles of the moral law, as they generally do, they contain normative teaching for evangelicals."[73]

A Final Word

Neglect of the law has resulted in a lack of reverence for the God who is the author of the law. The laws of the Old Testament are not arbitrary but reflect God's character. Through the law we come to better understand his holiness or moral perfection.[74] "The laws He gives flow out of who He is."[75] As Millard Erickson eloquently states:

> The law . . . should be seen as the expression of God's person and will. The law is something of a transcript of the nature of God. . . . Disobeying the law is serious, not because the law has some inherent value or dignity which must be preserved, but because disobeying it is actually an attack upon the very nature of God himself. . . . But if we hold that God is an objective reality,

---

[70] R. Barcellos, *In Defense of the Decalogue*, 96.

[71] J. Vines, *Basic Bible Sermons on the Ten Commandments* (Nashville: Broadman, 1992), 13.

[72] C. Wright, "Ethics," *NIDOTTE* 4:586.

[73] W. Kaiser Jr., "Law and Good Works in Evangelical Christianity," in *A Time to Speak*, ed. A. Rudin and M. Wilson (Grand Rapids: Eerdmans, 1987), 123–24.

[74] The logical connection between law and God's wisdom may be seen in Deut 4:6 and Prov 8:22–31. Wisdom and law were frequently juxtaposed in rabbinic works. See Moore, *Judaism* 1:263–65, 269.

[75] J. McDowell and B. Hostetler, *Right from Wrong* (Dallas: Word, 1994), 91.

and that he has revealed rational, objective truth about himself, surely there is also room for the law as an objective representation of his will and, even more, of his nature.[76]

The law, holiness, and the character of God are intricately and indissolubly combined.[77] God has revealed in biblical law the standards that reflect His holy nature and are beneficial for individuals and society.

According to the rabbinic tradition, the Decalogue was offered by God to all the peoples of the earth. The fact that the law was proclaimed in the wilderness, outside national boundaries, highlights its universality. The commandments would have been understood, even perhaps within ancient Israel, as valid for all peoples in all times and places.[78]

Although the Christian is no longer "under the law" (Rom 3:19; 6:14), he is nevertheless not "without the law" (1 Cor 9:21), as though it has nothing to say to him.[79] It could be said that the law illuminates sanctification. It provides a guide for the believer to what is pleasing in God's sight.[80] Because the Ten Commandments are expressive of the character of God—and for that reason alone—they are timeless and universally applicable.

The Ten Commandments should not be viewed as a restriction on life; on the contrary, they lead to fullness of life. As R. Albert Mohler has stated: "So, the law itself is written as a gift, given to us that we would know how to live, not only to maximize *our* happiness but to demonstrate God's holiness."[81] The Ten Commandments demand a response of love, because the grace of God, experienced already in the liberation from Egypt and in the divine initiative in the covenant

[76] M. Erickson, *Christian Theology* (Grand Rapids: Baker, 1985), 802–3. See also Childs, *The Book of Exodus,* 397.

[77] See B. Childs, *Introduction to the Old Testament as Scripture* (Philadelphia: Fortress, 1979), 185.

[78] See N. Sarna, *Exodus,* JPS Torah Commentary (Philadelphia, New York: Jewish Publication Society, 1991), 108, and D. Christensen, *Deuteronomy 1:1–21:9,* rev. ed., WBC 6A (Nashville: Thomas Nelson, 2001), 115.

[79] C. Wright, *An Eye for an Eye: The Place of Old Testament Ethics Today* (Downers Grove, IL: InterVarsity, 1983), 160; id., *Old Testament Ethics for the People of God,* 318.

[80] See Walker, "The Abiding Value of Biblical Law," and Vines, *Basic Bible Sermons on the Ten Commandments,* viii.

[81] Mohler, *Words from the Fire,* 135 (italics his).

promise, elicited such a response from man in gratitude.[82] The law is not understood as a means of salvation but as instruction regarding the shape a redeemed life is to take in everyday affairs.[83] It is perhaps for reasons such as these that Israel's law evoked admiration and envy from other nations (Deut 4:6–8).

In conclusion, the Ten Commandments are absolute and ultimate. We do not observe them for social stability, for happiness, or for security and prosperity. The Ten Commandments manifest the attributes of God. Thus we should delight in carrying out His commands (Ps 112:1).

When the teachings of God's law are rejected by a nation, that nation will experience the wrath of God as indicated by the progressive breakdown of social order and moral decency (Rom 1). The examples of this degeneration now permeate all aspects of Western culture. Thus the relevancy of the Ten Commandments for today's Christian is not a matter of interest or continuity with tradition but rather one of critical urgency.[84]

---

[82] See P. Craigie, *The Book of Deuteronomy* (Grand Rapids: Eerdmans, 1976), 150.

[83] See Fretheim, *Exodus*, 224.

[84] See Walker, "The Abiding Value of Biblical Law," 212, and R. Collins, *Christian Morality: Biblical Foundations* (Notre Dame, IN: University of Notre Dame Press, 1986), 51.

SELECT BIBLIOGRAPHY

Albright, William F. *Yahweh and the Gods of Canaan.* Winona Lake, IN: Eisenbrauns, 1968.

André, Gunnel. *Determining the Destiny: PQD in the Old Testament.* Lund, Sweden: CWK Gleerup, 1980.

Andreasen, Niels-Erek. *The Old Testament Sabbath: A Tradition-Historical Investigation.* Missoula, MT: The Society of Biblical Literature, 1971.

Arnold, Bill T., and Bryan E. Beyer, eds. *Readings from the Ancient Near East.* Grand Rapids: Baker Academic, 2002.

Arnold, Bill T., and J. Choi, *A Guide to Biblical Hebrew Syntax.* New York: Cambridge, 2003.

Barcellos, R. *In Defense of the Decalogue: A Critique of New Covenant Theology.* Enumclaw, WA: WinePress, 2001

Barth, Karl. *Church Dogmatics*, III/1. London: T&T Clark, 1960.

Basser, H. *Studies in Exegesis: Christian Critiques of Jewish Law and Rabbinic Responses 70–300 C.E.* Leiden: Brill, 2000.

Bauckham, Richard. *God Crucified: Monotheism and Christology in the New Testament.* Grand Rapids: Eerdmans, 1998.

Betz, Hans D. *The Sermon on the Mount.* Minneapolis: Fortress, 1995.

Blidstein, Gerald. *Honor Thy Father and Mother: Filial Responsibility in Jewish Law and Ethics.* New York: KTAV, 1975.

Block, Daniel Isaac. *The Gods of the Nations: Studies in Ancient Near Eastern National Theology.* Jackson, MI: Evangelical Theological Society, 1988.

Broadus, John A. *Commentary on the Gospel of Matthew.* Philadelphia: American Baptist Publication Society, 1886.

Calvin, John. *Commentary on a Harmony of the Evangelists, Matthew, Mark, and Luke.* Translated by Rev. W. Pringle. Grand Rapids: Baker, 1979.

———. *Commentaries on the Last Books of Moses*, Vol. 3. Translated by C. Bingham. Grand Rapids: Baker, 1979.

Carasik, M. מקראות גדולות. *The Commentators' Bible: The JPS Miqra'ot Gedolot. Exodus.* Philadelphia: Jewish Publication Society, 2005.

Carmichael, Calum M. *The Origins of Biblical Law: The Decalogues and the Book of the Covenant.* Ithaca and London: Cornell University Press, 1992.

Carson, D. A. *The Sermon on the Mount: An Evangelical Exposition of Matthew 5–7.* Grand Rapids: Baker, 1978.

———. *Jesus' Sermon on the Mount: An Exposition of Matthew 5–10.* Toronto: Global Christian Publishers, 1987.

———. *The Gagging of God.* Grand Rapids: Zondervan, 1996.

Cassuto, Umberto. *A Commentary on the Book of Exodus.* Translated by I. Abrahams. Jerusalem: Magnes, 1974.

———. *A Commentary on the Book of Genesis. Part 1: Adam to Noah.* Jerusalem: Magnes, 1978.

Childs, Brevard S. *The Book of Exodus: A Critical-Theological Commentary.* Louisville: Westminster John Knox, 1974.

Christensen, Duane. *Deuteronomy 1:1–21:9.* Rev. ed. Word Biblical Commentary 6A. Nashville: Thomas Nelson, 2001.

Collins, Raymond F. *Christian Morality: Biblical Foundations*, Notre Dame, IN: University of Notre Dame Press, 1986.

Craigie, Peter. *The Book of Deuteronomy.* Grand Rapids: Eerdmans, 1976.

Dershowitz, Alan M. *The Genesis of Justice.* New York: Warner Books, 2000.

Dohmen, C. *Das Bilderverbot: Seine Entstehung und Entwicklung.* Bonn: Peter Hanstein, 1985.

———. *Exodus 19–40.* Freiburg: Herder, 2004.

Doorly, William J. *The Laws of Yahweh: A Handbook of Biblical Law.* New York, Mahwah, NJ: Paulist Press, 2002.

Dunnam, Maxie. *Exodus.* The Communicator's Commentary. Waco, TX: Word, 1987.

Ehrlich, A. *Miqrâ kî-Peshutô.* New York: KTAV, 1968 [in Hb.].

Eichrodt, Walter. *Theology of the Old Testament.* 2 vols. Translated by J. A. Baker Old Testament Library. Philadelphia: Westminster, 1961, 1967.

Elssner, Thomas R. "Das dekalogische Namensmissbrauch-Verbot (Ex 20,7/ Dtn 5,11)." *BN* 114/115 (2002): 61–70.

Enns, Peter. *Exodus.* The NIV Application Commentary. Grand Rapids: Zondervan, 2000.

Evans, Craig, and J. A. Sanders, eds. *The Function of Scripture in Early Jewish and Christian Tradition.* Journal for the Study of the New Testament: Supplemental Series 154. Sheffield: Sheffield Academic Press, 1988.

Fitzpatrick-McKinley, Anne. *The Transformation of Torah from Scribal Advice to Law,* Journal for the Study of the Old Testament: Supplemental Series 287. Sheffield: Sheffield Academic Press, 1999.

Fleishman, Joseph. *Parent and Child in Ancient Near East and the Bible.* Jerusalem: Magnes, the Hebrew University, 1999 [in Hb.].

Frankfort, Henri, H. A. Frankfort, John A. Wilson, Thorkild Jacobsen, and William A. Irwin. *The Intellectual Adventure of Ancient Man.* Chicago: The University of Chicago Press, 1946.

Fretheim, Terence E. *Exodus.* Interpretation: A Biblical Commentary for Teaching and Preaching. Louisville: John Knox, 1973.

Freund, Richard A. *Understanding Jewish Ethics,* vol. 1. San Francisco: EMText, 1990.

Gamberoni, Johann. "Das Elterngebot im Alten Testament." *BZ* 8 (1964): 161–90.

Gingrich, N. *Rediscovering God in America.* Nashville: Thomas Nelson, 2006.

Grabill, Stephen J. *Rediscovering the Natural Law in Reformed Theological Ethics.* Grand Rapids: Eerdmans Publishing, 2006.

Greenberg, Moshe. "Some Postulates of Biblical Criminal Law." Pages 5–28 in *Yehezkel Kaufmann Jubilee Volume: Studies in Bible and Jewish Religion Dedicated to Yehezkel Kaufmann on the Occasion of His Seventieth Birthday.* Jerusalem: Magnes, 1960.

Grudem, Wayne. *Systematic Theology*. Leicester, England: InterVarsity, and Grand Rapids: Zondervan, 1994.

Gundry, Robert H. *Matthew: A Commentary on His Literary and Theological Art*. Grand Rapids: Eerdmans, 1982.

Gutmann, Joseph. "The 'Second Commandment' and the Image in Judaism." *HUCA* 32 (1961): 161–74.

Hakam, A. *The Book of Exodus*. Jerusalem: Mossad Harav Kook, 1991 [in Hb.].

Halbertal, Moshe, and Avishai Margalit. *Idolatry*. Translated by Naomi Goldblum. Cambridge, MA: Harvard University Press, 1992.

Hartom, A. S., and M. D. Cassuto, "Exodus" and "Leviticus" in *Torah, Prophets, Writings*. Tel Aviv: Yavneh, 1977 [in Hb.].

Hasel, Gerhard F. "The Sabbath in the Pentateuch." Pages 21–43 in *The Sabbath in Scripture and History*. Edited by Kenneth A. Strand. Washington, D.C.: Review and Herald, 1982.

——— , and W. G. C. Murdoch. "The Sabbath in the Prophetic and Historical Literature of the Old Testament." Pages 44–56 in *The Sabbath in Scripture and History*. Edited by Kenneth A. Strand. Washington, D.C.: Review and Herald, 1982.

Heimbach, Daniel. *Counterfeit Sexuality*. Washington, D.C.: Focus on the Family, 2002.

Hendriksen, William. *Exposition of the Gospel of Matthew*. Grand Rapids: Baker, 1973.

Heschel, Abraham Joshua. *The Earth Is the Lord's and the Sabbath*. New York: Harper & Row, 1966.

Hinneman, I. "אַחְדוּת הָאֱלֹהִים." *EncMiqr* 1:201–5 [in Hb.].

Hoekema, Anthony A. *Created in God's Image*. Grand Rapids: Eerdmans, 1986.

Hoffner, Harry A. *The Laws of the Hittites: A Critical Edition*. Leiden; New York: Brill, 1997.

Holbert, John C. *The Ten Commandments*. Nashville: Abingdon, 2002.

Horrell, D. "Idol-Food, Idolatry and Ethics in Paul." Pages 120–40 in *Idolatry: False Worship in the Bible, Early Judaism and Christianity*. Edited by S. Barton. London: T&T Clark, 2007.

House, Wayne, ed. *The Christian and American Law: Christianity's Impact on America's Founding Documents and Future Direction*. Grand Rapids: Kregel, 1998.

Houtman, C. *Exodus*. Vol. 3. Leuven: Peeters, 2000.

Jackson, Bernard S. *Essays in Jewish and Comparative Legal History*. Leiden: Brill, 1975.

———. *Theft in Early Jewish Law*. Oxford: Clarendon, 1972.

Jacobsen, Thorkild. *The Treasures of Darkness*. New Haven: Yale University Press, 1976.

Janzen, J. Gerald. *Exodus*. Louisville: Westminster John Knox, 1997.

Jepsen, Alfred. "Beiträge zur Auslegung und Geschichte des Dekalogs." *Zeitschrift für die alttestamentliche Wissenschaft* 79 (1967): 275–304.

Kaiser, Walter C. Jr. "Exodus." In *The Expositor's Bible Commentary*. Vol. 2. Edited by F. Gaebelein. Grand Rapids: Zondervan, 1990.

———. *Toward Old Testament Ethics*. Grand Rapids: Zondervan, 1983.

Kaufmann, Yehezekel. *The Religion of Israel: From Its Beginnings to the Babylonian Exile*. Translated and abridged by Moshe Greenberg. New York: Schocken, 1960.

———. "דָּת יִשְׂרָאֵל," *EncMiqr* 2:724–72 [in Hb.].

Keil, C. F., and F. Delitzsch. *The Pentateuch*. 3 vols. Grand Rapids: Eerdmans, 1973.

Keszler, W. "Die literarische, historische und theologische Problematik des Dekalogs." *VT* 7 (1957): 1–16.

Klopfenstein, M. *Die Lüge nach dem Alten Testament*. Zürich und Frankfurt: Gotthelf-Verlag, 1964.

Köstenberger, Andreas, and David Jones. *God, Marriage, and Family: Rebuilding the Biblical Foundation*. Wheaton, IL: Crossway, 2004.

Kremers, Heinz. "Die Stellung des Elterngebotes im Dekalog." *Evangelische Theologie* 21 (1961): 145–61.

Lenski, R. C. H. *The Interpretation of St. Matthew's Gospel.* Minneapolis: Augsburg, 1961.

Lessing, R. Reed. *Jonah.* Saint Louis: Concordia, 2007.

Levin, C. "Der Dekalog Am Sinai." *VT* 35,2 (1985): 165–91.

Lewis, Joseph. *The Ten Commandments.* New York: Freethought Press Association, 1946.

Licht, J. "מִקְרָא קֹדֶשׁ." *EncMiq* 5:437–39 [in Hb.].

Lienhard, J. T., ed. *Exodus, Leviticus, Numbers, Deuteronomy.* ACCS. Downers Grove, IL: InterVarsity, 2001.

Luz, Ulrich. *Matthew 1–7.* A Continental Commentary. Translated by Wilhelm C. Linss. Minneapolis: Fortress, 1989.

Matthews, Victor H., and Don C. Benjamin. *Old Testament Parallels: Laws and Stories from the Ancient Near East.* New York: Paulist Press, 1991.

McDowell, Josh, and B. Hostetler. *Right from Wrong.* Dallas: Word, 1994.

McKay, Heather A. *Sabbath and Synagogue: The Question of Sabbath Worship in Ancient Judaism.* Leiden, New York: Brill, 1994.

McKinion, Steven A., ed. *Life and Practice in the Early Church: A Documentary Reader.* New York: New York University Press, 2001.

McNeile, A. H. *The Book of Exodus.* 3rd ed. London: Methuen, 1931.

Merrill, Eugene. *Deuteronomy*, New American Commentary. Nashville: B&H, 1994.

Meyer, Jason C. *The End of the Law.* NACBT. Nashville: B&H, 2009.

Mohler, R. Albert Jr. *Words from the Fire.* Chicago: Moody, 2009.

Motyer, J. Alec. *The Message of Exodus.* Downers Grove, IL: InterVarsity, 2005.

———. *The Revelation of the Divine Name.* London: Tyndale, 1949.

Nielsen, Eduard. *Deuteronomium* Handbuch zum Alten Testament. Tübingen: Mohr (Siebeck), 1995.

Noth, Martin. *Exodus*. Old Testament Library. Philadelphia: Westminster, 1962.

Oppenheim, A. Leo. *Ancient Mesopotamia: Portrait of a Dead Civilization*. 2nd ed. Revised by Erica Reiner. Chicago: University of Chicago Press, 1977.

Paul, Shalom M. *Studies in the Book of the Covenant in the Light of Cuneiform and Biblical Law*. Leiden: Brill, 1970.

Phillips, Anthony. *Ancient Israel's Criminal Law: A New Approach to the Decalogue*. Oxford: Basil Blackwell, 1970.

Poythress, Vern S. *The Shadow of Christ in the Law of Moses*. Brentwood, TN: Wolgemuth & Hyatt, 1991.

Procksch, Otto. *Theologie Des Alten Testament*. Gütersloh: C. Bertelsmann Verlag, 1950.

Propp, W. *Exodus 19–40*, Anchor Bible. New York: Doubleday, 2006.

Rosner, Brian. *Greed As Idolatry: The Origin and Meaning of a Pauline Metaphor*. Grand Rapids: Eerdmans, 2007.

Roth, Martha T. *Law Collections from Mesopotamia and Asia Minor*. Atlanta: Scholars Press, 1995.

Rushdoony, Rousas. *The Institutes of Biblical Law*. Nutley, NJ: The Craig Press, 1973.

Sarna, Nahum. *Exodus*. JPS Torah Commentary. Philadelphia, New York: Jewish Publication Society, 1991.

———. *Exploring Exodus: The Origins of Biblical Israel*. New York: Schocken, 1996.

Schaeffer, Francis. *How Should We Then Live?* Old Tappan, NJ: Revell, 1976.

Schlessinger, L. *The Ten Commandments*. New York: HarperCollins, 1998.

Schmidt, W. *Die Zehn Gebote im Rahmen alttestamentliche Ethik*. Darmstadt: Wissenschaftliche Buchgesellschaft, 1993.

———. *The Faith of the Old Testament*. Translated by J. Sturdy. Philadelphia: Westminster, 1983.

Segal, Ben-Zion, ed. *The Ten Commandments in History and Tradition*. Jerusalem: Magnes, 1990.

Strickland, Wayne G., ed. *Five Views on Law and Gospel.* Grand
    Rapids: Zondervan, 1993.

Stuart, Douglas. *Exodus.* New American Commentary. Nashville:
    B&H, 2006.

Sulzberger, Mayer. *The Ancient Hebrew Law of Homicide.* Clark, NJ:
    The Lawbook Exchange, 2004.

Tigay, Jeffrey H. *Deuteronomy, JPS Torah Commentary.* Philadelphia:
    Jewish Publication Society, 1996.

———. "שַׁבָּת." *EncMiqr* 7:504–17.

Tomasino, Anthony J. *Written upon the Heart: The Ten
    Commandments for Today's Christian.* Grand Rapids: Kregel,
    2001.

Turner, David L. *Matthew.* Baker Exegetical Commentary on the
    New Testament. Grand Rapids: Baker Academic, 2008.

Urbach, Ephraim E. *The Sages: Their Concepts and Beliefs.* Translated
    by I. Abrahams. Jerusalem: Magnes, 1975.

Van Der Toorn, K. *Sin and Sanction in Israel and Mesopotamia: A
    Comparative Study.* Assen, The Netherlands: Van Gorcum,
    1985.

VanDrunen, D. *A Biblical Case for Natural Law.* Grand Rapids: Acton
    Institute, n.d.

Vines, Jerry. *Basic Bible Sermons on the Ten Commandments.*
    Nashville: Broadman, 1992.

Von Rad, Gerhard. *Deuteronomy. A Commentary.* London: SCM,
    1966.

———. *Old Testament Theology.* 2 vols. Translated by D. M. G.
    Stalker. New York: Harper & Row, 1962, 1965.

Walton, John H. *Ancient Israelite Literature in Its Cultural Context.*
    Grand Rapids: Zondervan, 1989.

———. *Ancient Near Eastern Thought and the Old Testament.* Grand
    Rapids: Baker Academic, 2006.

Wax, Rabbi D., ed. *The Ten Commandments.* Lakewood, NJ: Taryag
    Legacy Foundation, 2005.

Weinfeld, Moshe. *Deuteronomy 1–11.* Anchor Bible. 5. New York:
    Doubleday, 1991.

———. "The Uniqueness of the Decalogue and its Place in Jewish Tradition." In *The Ten Commandments in History and Tradition.* Edited by B. Z. Segal. Jerusalem: Magnes, 1990.

Westbrook, Raymond, ed. *A History of Ancient Near Eastern Law.* Leiden. Vol 1–2. Leiden; Boston: Brill, 2003.

———. *Studies in Biblical and Cuneiform Law.* Paris: J. Gabalda, 1988.

Westermann, Claus. *Genesis 1–11.* Translated by John J. Scullion. Minneapolis: Fortress, 1994.

Wiseman, D. J. "Law and Order in Old Testament Times." *Vox Evangelica* 8 (1973): 5–21.

Wright, Christopher J. H. *An Eye for an Eye: The Place of Old Testament Ethics Today.* Downers Grove, IL: InterVarsity, 1983.

———. *The Mission of God.* Downers Grove, IL: InterVarsity, 2006.

———. *Old Testament Ethics for the People of God.* Downers Grove, IL: InterVarsity, 2004.

Wright, David. "The Ethical Use of the Old Testament in Luther and Calvin: A Comparison." *Scottish Journal of Theology* 36 (1983): 463–85.

Zimmerli, Walther. "Das Gesetz im Alten Testament." *Theologische Literaturzeitung* 85 (1960): 481–98.

———. "Das zweit Gebot." Pages 550–63 in *Festshrift für Alfred Bertholet.* Tübingen: Verlag Mohr (Seibeck), 1950.

———. *Gottes Offenbarung: Gesammelte Aufsätze zum Alten Testament.* Munich: Chr. Kaiser Verlag, 1969.

———. "Sinaibund und Abrahambund: Ein Beitrag zum Verständnis der Priestershrift." *Theologische Zeitschrift* 16 (1960): 268–80.

NAME INDEX

SUBJECT INDEX

SCRIPTURE INDEX

Leviticus